STRATEGY FORMULATION IN ENTREPRENEURIAL FIRMS

To my family

Strategy Formulation in Entrepreneurial Firms

AZHDAR KARAMI
Bangor Business School
University of Wales Bangor, UK
and
University of Tabriz, Iran

Routledge
Taylor & Francis Group
LONDON AND NEW YORK

First published in paperback 2024

First published 2007 by Ashgate Publishing

Published 2016 by Routledge
4 Park Square, Milton Park, Abingdon, Oxon OX14 4RN

and by Routledge
605 Third Avenue, New York, NY 10158

Routledge is an imprint of the Taylor & Francis Group, an informa business

Publisher's Note
The publisher has gone to great lengths to ensure the quality of this reprint but points out that some imperfections in the original copies may be apparent.

British Library Cataloguing in Publication Data
Karami, Azhdar
Strategy formulation in entrepreneurial firms
1. Strategic planning 2. Entrepreneurship
I. Title
658.4'012

Library of Congress Cataloging-in-Publication Data
Karami, Azhdar.
Strategy formulation in entrepreneurial firms / by Azhdar Karami.
p. cm.
Includes bibliographical references and index.
ISBN 978-0-7546-4792-8
1. Small business--Management. 2. New business enterprises--Management. 3. Strategic planning. 4. Business planning. 5. Entrepreneurship. I. Title.
HD2341.K287 2007
658.4'012--dc22

2007011098

ISBN: 978-0-7546-4792-8 (hbk)
ISBN: 978-1-03-283785-7 (pbk)
ISBN: 978-1-315-61100-6 (ebk)

DOI: 10.4324/9781315611006

Contents

List of Figures

List of Tables

Preface

The past decade of organizational research has moved from an investigation of organizational static to an investigation of organizational dynamics, much of it focused on strategy and its formulation and implementation. While the volume of research on strategic management in large firms is extensive, the research on strategic management in small and medium-sized enterprises in general and entrepreneurial firms in particular is more limited. In short, research into strategic management, to date, has come a long way since 1960s. Many of the earlier theories are still valid and are reflected in the assumptions of the contemporary writers on the subject. The recent theories including the present work, have shifted the focus on strategy processes in entrepreneurial small and medium enterprises. As shown above there has been an over emphasis on the leaders and strategists at corporate level and international organizations. This preoccupation with big organizations on the part of the writers and theorists has created a vacuum for scholars and practitioners alike who work or deal with small and medium sized firms in the industry. The present work is a direct response to this perceived need. It raises questions such as, what is the strategic role of entrepreneurship in small businesses. How top management of the small firms perceives the processes associated with strategy formulation? How business strategies are formatted and implemented in entrepreneurial SMEs? And more importantly, are there lessons that can be learnt by giant corporations from the smaller ones? These and other concerns form the focus of this novel study. This study focuses on top management of the small and medium-sized enterprises in the UK. The sample covers a wide range of the entrepreneurial firms in terms of their activities within the industries, operating in *SME* sector. By and large this book highlights the issue of lack of strategic thinking in managing small firms. This book reports that, the firms which employ strategic management techniques, whether formal or informal, exhibit enhanced levels of success in formulation and implementation of business strategies than those firms which do not employ such procedures. It has been concluded that there is a significant association between senior manager's characteristics and initiating strategic orientation in the SMEs. Establishing a scanning system as part of strategic management process, is necessary for the formulation and planning of business strategies; increasing profit; and growth rate of the firm, and developing the firm's adaptability with unexpected environmental changes in a turbulent marketplace. Generally speaking, successful entrepreneurial SMEs emphasis on long term plans, objectives and ongoing evaluation in strategic planning. They employ a multi-disciplinary management team in strategic decision-making process and increase employees' motivation through involvement of them in the strategic activities. Finally this research suggests that suggest that management should develop a strategic orientation in the business as it grows through the implementation of an effective strategic management process.

Azhdar Karami

Acknowledgments

The author wishes to acknowledge the contributions of colleagues who have been either directly or indirectly involved in the presentation of this volume. I would like to thank Professor F. Analoui from Bradford University, UK for his professional comments and reviewing this book. Professor N. Kakabadse from Northampton Business School, Northampton University, UK and Professor M. Branine form Dundee Business School, University of Abertay Dundee, UK for their valuable comments. I would like to thank Department of Economics, University of Tabriz, Iran for supporting the original work. Last but by no means least, I would like to offer my sincere thanks to Janet Analoui for undertaking unenviable task of editing the final copy of the book.

Chapter 1

Introduction to Strategy and Entrepreneurship

Introduction

Strategic Entrepreneurship has been recognized as an important factor that contributes to a firm's success. Despite the potential benefit of strategic entrepreneurship for sustaining entrepreneurial firms, this area has been under researched in the small and medium enterprises literature. However research into strategy formulation and implementation, particularly in small and medium-sized enterprises (SMEs), recently has become one of the main focuses of both academia and industry (Berry, 1998; Beal, 2000; Hitt, 2000; Krishnan, 2001). Perhaps this is because, the key role of SMEs is in generating employment, promoting innovation, creating competition and generating economic wealth (Smith, 1998; Bridge and Peel, 1999). Strategic management is fundamentally about setting the underpinning aims of an organization, choosing the most appropriate goals towards those aims, and fulfilling both over time (Thompson, 1996). David (1995) holds that strategic management can be defined as the art and science of formulating, implementing, and evaluating cross-functional decisions that enable an organization to achieve its objectives. As this definition implies, strategic management focuses on integrating managerial abilities and techniques to achieve organizational success.

It has been discussed (Analoui and Karami, 2003) that the dominant paradigm in strategic management is a prescriptive, rational and analytic model characterized by two principle functions: strategy formulation and implementation. The major contributors to this approach are Ansoff (1965); Andrews (1986) and Porter (1979, 1980, p. 1985) from Harvard University. It has been argued that strategic management is about how the strategy is developed and implemented (Cole, 1994). Strategy formulation is how the firm chooses to define strategy and how it approaches implementation through strategic management (Collin, 1995; Bowman, 1998). The approach to strategy formulation dictates the eventual management style. The nature of the strategy formulation will therefore result in the adoption of a specific approach to strategic management. The development of a strategy can be formal or rational (Mintzberg, 1994), emergent or progressed (Whittington, 1993), under a logical incremental path. Strategic management handles how a strategy is developed and where the organization's environment is analysed before the appropriate strategy is selected and implemented (Hambrick, 1981; Wheelen and Hunger, 1998).

Even though some have concluded that small firms do not commonly practice strategic management (Gable and Topol, 1987), there have been several studies that have found a positive relationship between strategic planning and performance in these companies. For example, Robinson (1982) found that small businesses that employed consultants to help with strategic planning performed better than firms that did not. Bracker, Keats and Pearson (1988) found that small electronics firms that engaged in sophisticated strategic planning performed better than unstructured planners. Several other studies have reported positive relationships between formal strategic planning and financial performance in small firms (Wood, Johnston and DeGenaro, 1988; Watts and Ormsby, 1990). Still others have reported positive relationships among various measures of strategy content and small firm performance (Miller and Toulouse, 1986; Bracker, Keats and Pearson, 1988). Proponents of strategic management in SMEs have suggested that the type of planning employed will be contingent upon its stage of development and that this activity will evolve and become more formal and sophisticated over the life cycle of the business (Robinson et al., 1984; Scott and Bruce, 1987). The literature suggests that as the activities and supporting functional areas of the organizations become more complex, strategic management will develop through various stages from its initial beginnings as simple financial plans and budgets, through to forecast-based planning, externally orientated planning where the managers begin to think strategically, proactively planning the firm's future and formal strategic management techniques (Goodwin and Hodgett, 1991; Foster, 1993; Berry, 1998; Apfelthaler, 2000; Beal, 2000). It is often argued that the managers must make this necessary progression toward a strategic orientation and more sophisticated strategic management techniques as the business grows in order to ensure the future survival and long term success of the company (Hitt, 2000; Wolff, 2000).

Finally, it is important to recognize that in studying strategic management practice in small and medium-sized firms, the role of the entrepreneur is critical (McGrath and MacMillan, 2000; Meyer and Heppard, 2000). In business, preparation comes through strategic planning (Analoui and Karami, 1993). Many owners and managers of small businesses routinely plan their day-to-day operations, but do not believe that strategic planning applies to them. However, it has been discussed that, no business is too small to require a sound strategy, and few strategies are so simple that they need not be developed into a strategic plan (Robinson and Pearce, 2001). The entrepreneur's personal goals, characteristics and strategic awareness will all significantly impact on the development of the business (Daft, Sormunen and Parks, 1988; McKenna, 1996). Previous studies have already shown that whether or not an effective strategy development process is implemented will be heavily influenced by the firm's owner manager and that the ability to comprehend and make appropriate use of sophisticated strategic management practice is a function of the entrepreneur's previous experience (McKenna, 1996; Berry, 1998; Chan and Foster, 2001).

Origin of Strategy

Before reviewing the core research background related to strategic management in entrepreneurial small and medium sized enterprises, it is necessary to clarify the term because of the troublesome intellectual terrain that strategy in management occupies. Let us first be clear as to what strategy is. What is the origin of strategy? Where does the word strategy come from? In the case of the origin of strategy,

Luttwak (1987) has contended that as in the case of many scientific terms, the word "strategy" (French *strategie*; Italian *strategia*) is derived indirectly from the Greek *strategos* (general), which does not carry the connotation of the modern word. The Greek equivalent for our "strategy" would have been *strategike episteme* (general's knowledge) or *strategon sophia* (generals' wisdom). On the other hand *strategemata* (*strategematon* is the Greek title of the Latin work by Frontinus) describes a compilation of *strategema*, precisely "stratagems" or tricks of war (ruses de guerre). Characteristically, a modern American definition of official military origin is much more inclusive: 'The art and science of developing and using political, economic, psychological and military forces as necessary during peace and war, to afford the maximum support to policies, in order to increase the probabilities and favourable consequences of victory and to lessen the chances of defeat' (Luttwak, 1987, pp. 239–240).

Definition of Strategy in Management

The word strategy has long been used implicitly in different ways (Bowman and Kakabadse, 1997; Mintzberg and Quinn, 1998). The term strategy has been conceptualized in diverse forms according to the parent social science discipline of numerous authors (Mintzberg, 1994; Marsh, 1999). The concept of strategy in business and management is analogous to that in war. Strategy as an area of management that is concerned with the general direction and long-term policy of the business as distinct from short-term tactics and day to day operations. Hence, the strategy of business may be defined as it's long-term objectives and the general means by which it intends to achieve them (Segal-Horn, 1998). Explicit recognition of multiple definitions can help us to manoeuvre through this field. Accordingly, some definitions of strategy in management are presented here and their relevant interrelationships are then considered. One early definition of strategy was provided by the American business historian, Chandler (1962), who suggested:

> strategy is the determination of the basic long term goals and objectives of an enterprise, and the adaption of courses of action and the allocation of resources for carrying out those goals (1962, p. 13).

He subscribes to the widely-held view that strategy is as much about planning and defining goals and objectives as it is about providing the means for achieving them. A more continuous and interactive definition of strategy, has been offered by Hofer and Schendel (1978):

> strategy is a fundamental pattern of present and planned resource deployments and environmental interactions that, indicates how the organization will achieve its objectives (1978, p. 25).

Another commentator Andrews (1986) defines strategy as:

> ...a pattern of decisions... (which represent)... the unity, coherence and internal consistency of a company's strategic decisions that position a company in its environment

> and give the firm its identity, its power to mobilise its strengths, and its likelihood of success in the marketplace (Andrews, 1986, p. 112).

Mintzberg and Quinn (1998) identified interrelated definitions of strategy. Strategy as a plan: by this definition, strategies have two essential characteristics. They are made in advance of the actions to which they are applied and they are developed consciously and purposefully. A strategy is the means used to achieve the objectives of the organization. A strategy is not just a plan, it ties together all the parts of the organization. Strategy covers all major aspects of the firm and through strategy all parts of the firm are compatible with each other and fit together well. As a plan strategies may be general or they can be specific. 'A strategy is the pattern or plan that integrates an organization's major goals, policies, and action sequences into a cohesive whole. A well-formulated strategy helps to marshal and allocate an organization's resources into a unique and viable posture based on it's relative internal competencies and shortcomings, anticipated changes in the environment, and contingent moves by intelligent opponents' (Mintzberg and Quinn, 1998, p. 3).

Strategy as pattern: defining strategy as a plan is not sufficient; we also need a definition that encompasses the resulting behaviour. Thus, strategy is proposed as a pattern, 'specifically a pattern in a stream of actions' (Mintzberg and Quinn, 1998, p. 11). The definition of strategy whether as plan or pattern can be quite independent of each other: plans may go unrealized, while patterns may appear without preconception. Mintzberg, Quinn and Ghoshal (1995) argued that, 'if we label the first definition *intended* strategy and the second *realized* strategy, then we can distinguish deliberate strategies, where intentions that existed previously were realized, from *emergent* strategies, where patterns developed in the absence of intentions, or despite them which went *unrealized*' (1995, p. 15).

Strategy as position: the third definition is that strategy is a position-specific, a means of locating an organization in what organization theorists like to call an 'environment' (Mintzberg and Quinn, 1998, p. 13). By this definition, strategy becomes the mediating force or match between organization and environment, that is between the internal and the external context. Strategy as a position looks outside the organization, seeking to locate the organization in the external environment and place it in a concrete position.

Strategy as perspective: a fourth definition of strategy looks inside of the organization. Strategy in this respect is to the organization what personality is to the individual (Mintzberg, Quinn and Ghoshal, 1995). The definition of strategy as a perspective, suggests that strategy is a concept. In this case strategy is a perspective shared by the members of an organization through their intentions and/or by they actions (Mintzberg and Quinn, 1998). Strategy as both *position* and *perspective* can be compatible with strategy as *plan* and/or *pattern*. But in fact, the relationship between these different definitions can be more involved than that.

Johnson and Scholes (1993) describe strategy as being concerned with:

- the full scope of an organization's activity,
- the process of matching the organization's activities to its environment,
- the process of matching the organization's activities to its resource capabilities,

- having major resource implications and,
- being affected by the values and beliefs of those who have power in an organization.

Johnson and Scholes (1993) in their empirically-grounded text on exploring corporate strategy, categorize a number of different approaches to strategy as follow:

- A 'natural selection' view, that is where organizations are under great environmental pressure and have constantly to adapt to changes in their environment.
- A 'planning' view, that is where strategy comes about through highly systematized forms of planning; this is the rational approach to strategy.
- A 'logical incremental view', that is an evolutionary step-by-step approach to strategy; it is an adaptive approach but one which is more controlled by them than the natural selection example mentioned above.
- A 'cultural view', that is an approach to strategy based on the experiences, assumptions and beliefs of management over time and which may eventually permeate the whole organization.
- A 'political view', that is where strategy emerges after a variety of internal battles, in which managers, individuals and groups bargain and trade their interests and information.
- A 'visionary view', that is where the strategy is dominated by one individual, or sometimes a small group, who have a particular vision of where the organization can and should be; this is a particularly intuitive approach.

Chaffee (1985), whose tripartite classification of strategy is presented in Table 1.1, attention should be thus focused more on means, with goals seen as an alignment of the organization and its environment. Lower level changes in style, marketing of quality, are seen as strategically important. Although top managers are still seen as responsible for guiding strategy, other managers are clearly involved in the process (Chaffee, 1985).

Of the associated terms that are regarded as important variables by Chaffee, strategic management appears in each of his three classifications of strategy. When strategy is linear, strategic management takes the form of long range planning; when strategy is adaptive, strategic management balances strategic fit to company predisposition. Finally, when strategy is interpretive, strategic management can be regarded as a vital capability for the continuous improvement of quality performance.

Evolution of Strategy Theory

Over the last 30 years there have been many developments in the field of strategic management. Many of the concepts that form the current approaches were developed over the recent decades. Among the main concepts developed during the 1960s and 1970s were the product life cycle, the experiences curve, the strategic business unit (SBU), and the growth share (portfolio) matrix. The Boston Consulting Group was

Table 1.1 Three models of strategy

Variable	Linear Strategy	Adaptive Strategy	Interpretive Strategy
Sample definition	"...determination of the basic long term goals of an enterprise, and the adaption of courses of action and the allocation of resourcesnecessary for carrying out these goals" (Chandler, 1962, p.13)	"strategy is fundamental pattern of present and planned resources deployments and environmental interactions that, indicates how the organization will achieve its objectives" (Hofer and Schendel, 1978, p.25).	Orienting metaphors constructed for the purpose of conceptualising and guiding individual attitudes of organizational participants (Chaffee, 1985, p. 94).
Nature of strategy	Decisions, actions, plans integrated	Achieving a "match" Multifaceted	Metaphor Interpretive
Focus for strategy	Means, ends	Means	participants and potential participants in the organization
Aim of strategy	Goal achievement	Coalignment with the environment	Legitimacy
Strategic behaviour	Change markets, products	Change style, marketing quality	Develop symbols, improve interactions and relationships
Associated terms	Strategic plannin, strategy formulation and implementation	Strategic management, strategic choice, strategic predisposition, strategic trust, strategic design, strategic fit, niche	Strategic norms, emergent strategic management, strategy flexibility
Associated measures	Formal planning, new products, configuration of products or business, market segmentation and focus, market share, merger/ acquisition, product diversity	Price, distribution policy, marketing expenditure and intensity, product differentiation, authority changes, proactiveness, risk taking, multiplexity, integration, futurity, adaptiveness, uniqueness	Measures must be derived from context, may require qualitative evaluation, demand responsiveness

Source: Adapted from Chaffee, (1985) Three models of strategy, *Academy of Management Review*, Vol. 10, no.1, pp. 89-98.

the dominant influence (Leavy, 1996) in forming the above views. In the 1960s and 1970s the emphasis was primarily on strategies for growth, diversification and vertical integration. The 1980s were dominated by the contribution of Michael Porter in the field of strategic management including the five-force model (1979), generic strategies (1985) and the value chain (1985).

During the low-growth 1980s, the emphasis in the field of strategy shifted towards competitivism and renewal, particularly in the core, and often in the nature of the business. There is a growing belief that the business world in 2000s is facing a whole new set of priorities such as the increasing globalization of competition, new information and technology (Leavy, 1996). These developments are changing the nature of business and competition in several ways. Perhaps strategy is the main essence of management, pulling together all of the strands required to run any organization in response to competition in the operative environment. The scholars in the field of strategy (Ansoff, 1965; Williamson, 1991; Stacey, 1993; Whittington, 1993; Mintzberg, 1994) have produced a variety of definitions of business strategy reflecting in some cases significantly differing approaches to the subject. Whittington (1993) identified four main approaches in strategy. These consist of the classical (traditional) approach, the evolutionary approach, the processual approach and the systemic approach. The classical and evolutionary approaches see profit maximization as the natural outcome of strategy-making; the systemic and processual approaches are more pluralistic, envisioning other possible outcomes as well as just profit.

The four discussed approaches to strategy differ widely in the ways they provide advice to top management. The Classical school confidently prescribes a rational and sequential approach offered as a universal form. The Evolutionary and Processual approaches are more cautious, each sceptical of the strategist's capacity to direct strategy in this rational hierarchical way. And System theorists take a more relativists stance insisting that both the ends and means of strategy depend on the character of prevailing social systems (Whittington, 1993) (see Table 1.2).

Table 1.2 Four perspectives on strategy

	Classical	Processual	Evolutionary	Systemic
Strategy	Formal	Crafted	Efficient	Embedded
Rational	Profit Maximization	Vague	Survival	Local
Focus	Internal (Plans)	Internal (Political/ Cognitions)	External (Markets)	External (Societies)
Key Influence	Economic/Military	Psychology	Economics/ Biology	Sociology
Key Authors	Chandler Ansof Porter	Cyert & March Mintzberg Pettigrew	Hannan & Freeman Williamson	Granovetter Marris
Key Period	1960s	1970s	1980s	1990s

The main characteristics of the four approaches are illustrated in Table 1.2 The Classical approach stresses rationality and analysis. For the classical approach strategy should be formal and explicit, it's objective unambiguous profit maximization. The Evolutionary approach stresses the unpredictability of the environment which makes irrelevant much of what is traditionally regarded as strategic analysis (Segal-Horn, 1998). Evolutionarists believe that high profitability and efficiency are essential for survival. Processual theorists too dismiss Classical formality, viewing strategy as 'crafted', it's goals are vague and any logic often emerging in retrospect (Whittington, 1993). In contrast, the Systemic approach stresses the importance and to an extent, the uniqueness of social systems within which diverse attitudes to and conceptualization about strategic issues occur (Segal-Horn, 1998).

Changing Paradigm of Management

Mintzberg, Quinn and Ghoshal (1995) argued that, if you ask managers what they do, they will most likely tell you that, they plan, organize, coordinate and control. The fact is that, these four words, which have dominated management vocabulary since the French industrialist Henry Fayol first introduced them in 1916, tell us little about what management is. So let us shed light on some definitions of management. Koontz and Weihrich (1990) have defined management as,

> ...the process of designing and maintaining an environment in which individuals, working together in groups, efficiently accomplish selected aims (Koontz and Weihrich, 1990, p. 4).

It was suggested that, as managers, people carry out the managerial functions of planning, organizing, staffing, leading and controlling. Moreover, managing is concerned with productivity; this implies effectiveness and efficiency. Daft (2000), contends that, management often is considered to be a universal phenomena, because it uses organizational resources to accomplish goals and attains high performance in all types of profit and non-profit organizations. He has therefore defined it as,

> "management is the attainment of organisational goals, in an effective and efficient manner through planning, organizing, leading, and controlling organizational resources" (Daft, 2000, p. 7).

Two important points are: 1) the four functions of planning, organizing, leading, and controlling and 2) the attainment of organizational goals in an effective and efficient manner. Managers, as we are all aware, use a multitude of skills to perform these functions (Analoui, 2000).

The world of organizations and management is also changing (Stoner, Freeman and Gilbert, 1995; Daft, 2000). Rapid environmental changes are the cause for fundamental transformations with a dramatic impact on the managers' job. These transformations in turn, represent a shift from a traditional to a new paradigm of management (see Table 2.1). A paradigm is a shared mind-set that represents a fundamental way of thinking about, perceiving, and understanding the world (Daft, 2000). Traditionally, the whole organization has been coordinated and controlled through the vertical hierarchy, with decision making authority residing with upper-level managers. Within the new paradigm, the primary responsibility of managers is not solely defined as making decisions, but rather to create learning capability throughout the organization (Jordan and Jones, 1997).

In the learning organization, top managers are leaders who create a vision for the future that is widely understood and imprinted throughout the organization. Employees are empowered to identify and solve problems because they understand the vision and long-term goals of the organization (Pfeffer, 1995). The most striking change now affecting organizations and management is globalization. Taking a global view of the world has become a necessity for virtually every company and manager (Kakabadse, Kakabadse and Myers, 1996). Global competition has also triggered a need for new management approaches that emphasize empowerment of workers and involvement of employees. Today managers have to understand cross-cultural patterns and often work with team members from many different countries. Diversity of the workforce has become a fact of life for all organizations, even those that do not operate globally. Another significant shift in management paradigm is that, technology is electronic rather than mechanical. Information technology facilitates new ways of working, such as virtual teams and telecommunications that challenge traditional methods of management and control (Daft, 2000). In the face of these rapid transformations, organizations are learning to value change over stability. The fundamental paradigm during much of the twentieth century was a belief that things can be stable and efficient. In contrast, the new paradigm is based on the presence of change and chaos as the natural order of things (Tetenbaum, 1998). The change to the new paradigm of management means that managers now must rethink their approach to organizing, directing, and motivating workers (Daft, 2000).

The Strategy in Management Context

For almost two decades, managers have been learning to play a new set of roles (Shay and Rothaermel, 1999). It is advocated that, companies must be flexible to respond rapidly to competitive and changing market (Porter, 1998). In order to understand the problems which result in success or failure for a company, it is necessary to begin by defining some concepts. Terms such as business policy, corporate strategy, strategic planning, and strategic management seem to be used interchangeably, while the various component terms relating to strategy formulation are not clearly defined. A concept which takes in the full scope of management tasks at both corporate and functional level is that of the 'strategy' concept (Marsh, 1999; Webb and Pettigrew, 1999). The term 'strategy' has been defined as 'the pattern of objectives, purpose or goals, and major policies and plans for achieving these goals, stated in such a way as to define what business the company is in or is to be in and the kind of company it is or is to be' (Luffman et al., 1991, p. 4). Strategy is the way in which a corporation endeavours to differentiate itself positively from it's competitors, using it's relative corporate strengths to better satisfy corporate needs (Ohmae, 1983, p. 93).

To understand what strategic management is all about, it is helpful to look at its history and review its core ideas. Strategic management grew out of both teaching and research in business administration. On the teaching side, the roots were the business policy or general management classes that by the 1960s most business schools required as the 'capstone' course at the end of the business curriculum (Goldsmith, 1995). Business policy professors were forced to try to think systematically about companies strategies which eventually led them into the self-styled study of strategic management (Schendel and Cool, 1988). On the research side, four main periods can be distinguished in the evolution of strategic management theories (Figure 1.2). Theoretically, the recent theories of strategic management such as the resource-based view of the firm (Boxall, 1996), have turned attention towards the internal aspects of the firm, its characteristics represented the crucial research domain in the early development of strategic management (Hoskisson et al., 1999). Early strategy researchers such as, Andrews (1986) and Ansoff (1965) were more concerned with identifying firms' 'best practices' that contribute to the firm's success. The researchers in this stream share an interest in pondering the inner growth engines or 'the black box' of the firm, and argue that, a firm's continued success is chiefly a function of its internal and unique competitive resources (Hoskisson et al., 1999).

During the next development period, strategic management departed, theoretically and methodologically, from the early period to the industrial organization (IO) economics period. Developments in the field, beginning in the 1970s, fostered a move toward IO economics (Porter, 1980, 1985), with its theoretical roots based on Mason (1939) and Bain (1968); Hoskisson et al. (1999) argued that, this swing shifted the attention externally toward industry structure and competitive position in the industry. Industrial organization economics considers the structural aspect of an industry, whereas works on strategic groups are largely focused on firm grouping

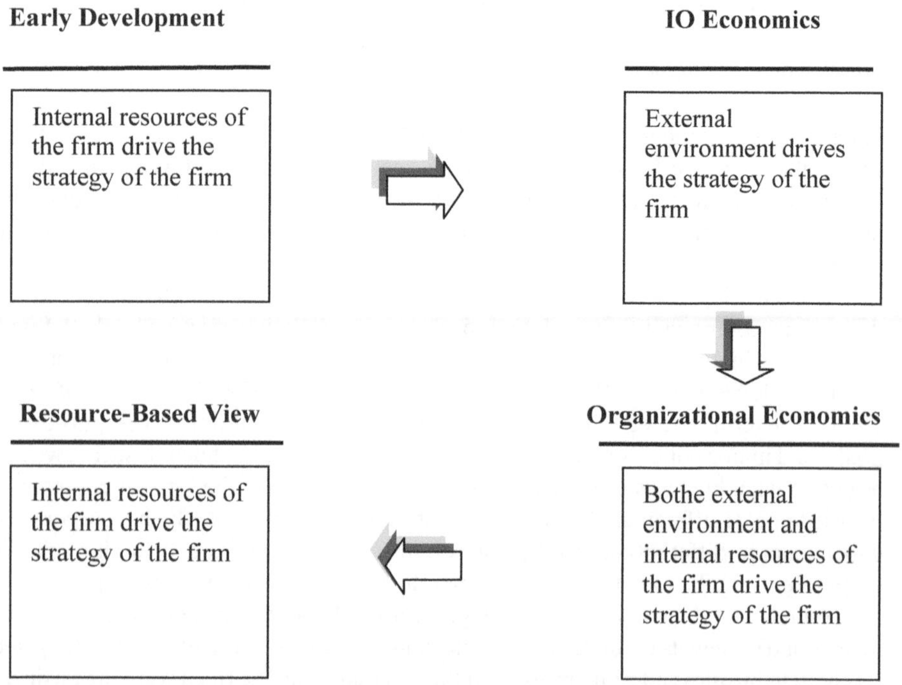

Figure 1.1 Evolution in strategic management theories

within an industry (Hoskisson et al., 1999). Strategic groups and competitive dynamics are popular research areas in the current field of strategic management.

Within the third period of developing strategic management theories, a swing back toward the firm can be clearly observed. The re-emergence of internal firm characteristics is evident in the emphasis which has been placed on competitive dynamics and boundary relationships between the firm and its environment (Hill and Jones, 1995; Heene, 1997; Hoskisson et al., 1999). Compared with industrial organization economics, strategic management moves much closer to the firm and direct competitive rivalry between specific firms in the competitive environment (Chen, 1996). Finally, and more recently, the popularity of the resource-based view of the firm has once again returned the focus to the inside of the firm. Theoretically, the central premise of the resource-based view of the firm addresses the fundamental questions of why firms are different and how firms achieve and sustain competitive advantage (Boxall, 1992, 1996; Grant, 1998; Hoskisson et al., 1999).

Strategic Management

Goldsmith argued that 'the area had its genesis in the findings from the study of business case studies in the 1950s and 1960s, that companies in the same industry could succeed following different approaches, while other companies that followed approaches similar to each other were not equally successful' (1995, p. 2). Orthodox economic theory could not explain these anomalies; corporate strategy could. For example, several companies might do well in one line of trade by employing strategies of purchasing different market niches. Other companies however, might fail with similar strategies because their strategies did not match the unique assets and talents these other firms brought to bear. The question raised therefore is, what is this powerful force called 'corporate strategy'? One of the pioneers of strategic management Kenneth Andrews has noted 'corporate strategy is the pattern of major objectives, purposes or goals, and essential policies and plans for achieving these goals, stated in such a way as to define what business the company is in or is to be' (1986, p. 28). Subsequent writers have also argued that the word organization can be substituted for corporate in definition so that the notion of strategy can be applied to any formal human collectively (Hitt, 1985; Goldsmith, 1995). If organization strategy is a key to organization performance, it follows that managers ought to work in a methodical way to develop sound strategies for their organizations. Many managers started to do sophisticated long term planning; this activity was rechristened strategic planning in the 1970s to evoke the new concern for figuring out how to gain an edge in the marketplace, and more importantly, how to keep it (Goldsmith, 1995). Strategic planning involved more than forecasting. From strategic planning it was a small step to today's field of strategic management – with greater stress on management (Ansoff, 1965). Managing strategy is not just a matter of plotting actions in advance, as the strategic planners soon learnt. It was realized that the long term course of an organization could hardly be left to a planning unit alone. Strategic management gave one answer to the problem of hollow plans. Goldsmith (1995) argued that, rather than being preoccupied with analysis of the firm and its environment and the formulation of strategies, the emerging sub-field began to feature implementation and evaluation as critical components of organization success. These are the action and assessment phases of the strategic management process. He further asserted that 'strategic management, to sum up, is a broad activity that encompasses mapping out strategy, putting strategy into action, and modifying strategy or its implementation to ensure that the desired outcomes are reached' (Goldsmith, 1995, p. 4).

Strategic management is fundamentally about setting the underpinning aims of an organization, choosing the most appropriate goals towards those aims, and fulfilling both over time. David (1995) holds that strategic management can be defined as the art and science of formulating, implementing, and evaluating cross-functional decisions that enable an organization to achieve its objectives. As this definition implies, strategic management focuses on integrating managerial abilities and techniques such as, marketing, financial/accounting, human resource management, production management, research and development to achieve organizational success. Early theories of strategy concentrated on sequential models of corporate planning whereby sound forecasting enabled organizations to set realistic objectives and then to evaluate strategies to achieve them. Such models implied that, organizations could and should manage changes, but they were criticized for concentrating on planning and for ignoring, to a large extent, how the plans would be implemented. In other words, the managerial aspects were not sufficiently considered, mainly because the planning was often carried out by specialist planners who sold their plans to the board of senior managers. Nevertheless, corporate planning was popular in the 1960s. This period was one of economic stability and planners were able to convince both themselves and their directors that they could predict the future several years ahead. The oil crisis of 1973 proved them wrong. The outcome was that corporate planning was criticized as organizations found themselves in turbulent change, and long-range plans were of limited use. Ansoff and McDonnell (1990) separated goal-setting (concerned with ends) from strategy (concerned with means). On the subject of strategic management they provided the following definition: '… strategic management is a systematic approach for managing strategic change which consists of the following:

- Positioning the firm through strategy and capability planning
- Real-time strategic response through issue management
- Systematic management of resistance during strategic implementation.'

This definition favours an adaptive approach to strategic management. Accordingly, Cole (1994) provides the definition 'strategic management is a process directed by top management, to determine the fundamental aims or goals of the organisation, and ensure a range of decisions which will allow for the achievement of those aims or goals in the long-term, whilst providing for adaptive responses in the shorter term'.

Therefore, strategic management is that set of managerial decisions and actions that determines the long term performance of a corporation (Wheelen and Hunger, 1998). Wheelen and Hunger contend that, strategic management includes environmental scanning (both internal and external), strategy formulation (strategic or long range planning), strategy implementation, and evaluation and control (1998). The study of strategic management emphasizes on the monitoring and evaluation of external opportunities and threats in light of a corporations strengths and weaknesses.

Strategic Management Process

Thompson argued that the area addressed by strategic management has been defined as 'the management processes and decisions which determine the long term structure and activities of the organization' (1996, p. 6). This definition incorporates five key themes including management process, management decisions, time scales, structure of the organizations, and activities of the organizations. What, then, is strategic management? Johnson and Scholes (1993) suggest that, it is not enough to say that it is the management of the process of strategic decision making. It should be pointed out that the nature of strategic management is different from other aspects of management. An individual manager is most often required to deal with problems of operational control, such as the efficient production of goods, the management of a sale force, the monitoring of financial performance or the design of some new system that will improve the efficiency of the operation. These are all very important tasks, but they are essentially concerned with effectively managing a well defined part of the organization within the context and guidance of a more all embracing strategy. These tasks are vital to the effective implementation of strategy but they are not the same as strategic management. Johnson and Scholes (1993) propose that strategic management is concerned not only with taking decisions about major issues facing the organization. Also it is concerned with ensuring that the strategy is put into effect. 'It can be thought of as having three main elements within it including strategic analysis, strategic choice and strategy implementation' (1993, p. 16).

There are different models of the strategic management process. Pitts and Lei (1996) assert that, a management process designed to satisfy strategic imperatives that push forward the firm's vision and mission is called a strategic management process. It consists of four major steps: Analysis, Formulation, Implementation, and Adjustment/Evaluation. The strategic management process thereby begins with careful analysis of a firm's internal strengths and weaknesses and external opportunities and threats. This effort is commonly referred to as SWOT analysis. Information derived from SWOT analysis is used to construct strategies that will enable the firm to pursue its mission. Similarly, Pearce, and Robinson (1991) in their strategic management model (see Figure 1.2) have started the process by defining company mission in light of the company profile and external environment and operating industry analysis. Strategies must now be formulated in a way that they match the external opportunities found in the environment with the firm's internal strengths.

For each firm this match-up is likely to be different. Pitts and Lei (1996) tell us that, in order to gain maximum competitive advantage, individual firms need to identify the activities they perform best and seek ways to maximize their effect. Effective strategy formulation is based on identifying, understanding, and using the firm's distinctive competencies and strengths in a way that other firms can not do as well (Ansoff and McDonnell, 1990; Pitts and Lei, 1996; Bowman, 1998; Mintzberg

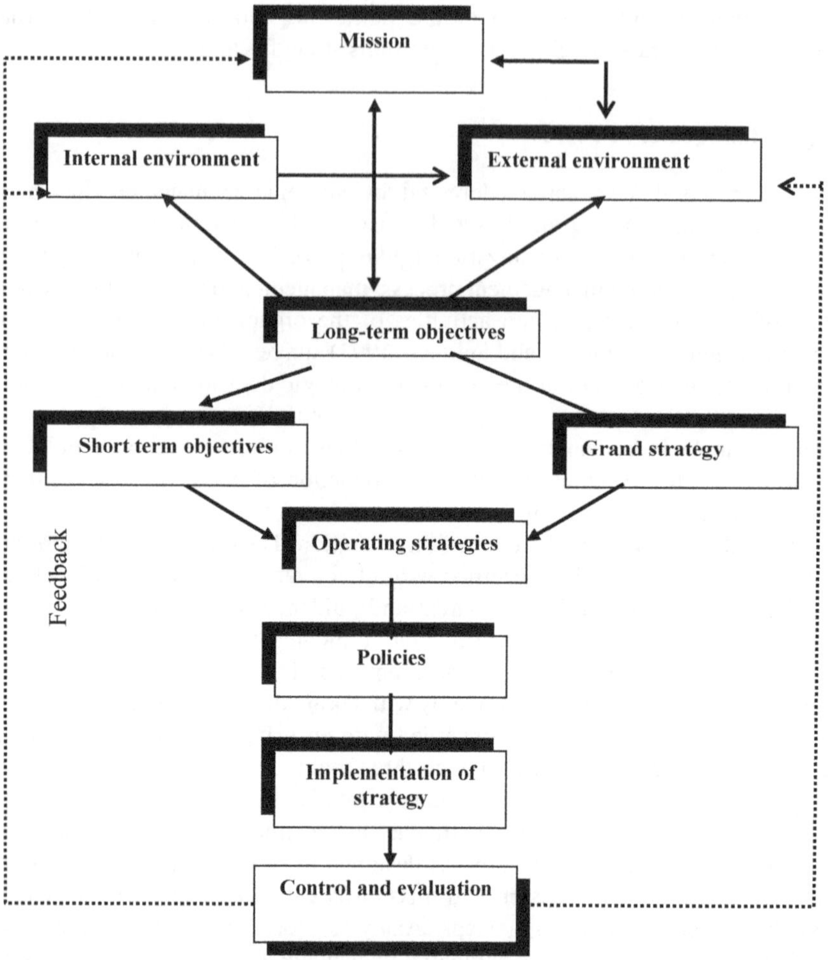

Figure 1.2 Strategic management process

and Quinn, 1998). In some models, the strategy formulation is the first step towards the formulation of the strategic management process. The third element of the strategic management process is implementation. Implementation measures include organizing the firm's tasks, hiring individuals to perform designated activities properly, and rewarding them to for carrying out those responsibilities effectively.

Finally, the industry environment within which a firm operates inevitably changes over time (Bowman and Faulkner, 1997). Also a firm's performance may occasionally fall below desired levels. Either event compels a firm to re-examine its existing approach and make adjustments that are necessary to regain high performance. Mechanisms must be put into place to monitor potential environment changes and alert managers to a development that requires modification or adjustment of mission, goals, strategies, and/or implementation practices (Collin, 1995;

Pitts and Lei, 1996). In order to compare and identify the strategic management model characteristics, three strategic management models were selected. These, have proved to be particularly seminal to the development, by the researcher, of a three stage strategic management model. The latter will be described in detail in this chapter. Despite differences in details and variations in wording, the three models selected for comparison show the following common features. First, strategy formulation: in this stage, there is an emphasis on company mission, business goals, and their relationship to the international nature of the external environment in which opportunities and threats are present. Second, strategy implementation: in this stage, there is an emphasis on leadership, organization structure, and their relationship to functional policies, resource allocation decisions, and the impact of operational management on organizational culture. And third, strategy evaluation: in this stage, there is an emphasis on control of activities, using performance appraisal to provide positive feedback, motivating improvement of policies and operational procedures in line with grand strategy.

Stages of Strategic Management

Strategies constitute a means to an end and these ends are concerned with the purpose and objectives of the organization. They are the things that businesses do, the paths they follow, and the decisions they take, in order to reach certain points and levels of success. Strategic management is a process which needs to be understood more than just as a discipline. It is the process by which organizations determine their purpose, objectives and desired levels of attainment; decide upon actions for achieving these objectives in an appropriate time scale, and frequently in a changing environment; implement the actions; and assess progress and results. Whenever and wherever necessary the actions may be changed or modified. The magnitude of these changes can be dramatic and revolutionary, or more gradual and evolutionary (Thompson, 1996). It is possible to interpret the sequence of elements that comprise the (three selected) strategic management models as being arranged to understand the strategic situation, choosing suitable strategies, and making the chosen strategies happen. The strategic management process can thus be claimed to consist of three stages: awareness, strategy formulation, and strategy implementation.

Awareness

In order to formulate effective strategies, strategists need to diagnose the firms internal strengths and weaknesses and the opportunities and threats of the firm. So strategists employ different techniques such as SWOT analysis to analyse the internal factors such as culture, structure, resources, leadership style and external factors of the firm such as economical and social factors, technology, and competitors (Zajac, 1995).

Strategy Formulation

Strategy formulation includes developing a business mission, deciding both short term and long term objectives, and prioritizing strategies to pursue. Strategy formulation is concerned with resource allocation, decisions about diversifications, entry into international markets, merging with suppliers or sale agencies, and participation in joint ventures. Strategy commits an organization to specific products, markets and technologies over an extended period of time. They determine long term competitive advantages. Top managers bear responsibility for the ramification of strategic formulation decisions: this reflects their authority to commit company resources for implementation of strategy (Rumelt, 1991; Analoui and Karami, 2003).

Strategy Implementation

Strategy implementation seeks to create the right circumstances within organizations so that formulated strategies can be executed. Implementation of strategy is achieved by developing a strategy-supportive culture, creating an effective organizational structure, and motivating individuals to learn new ways of contributing to improved performance. Often considered to be the most difficult stage in strategic management, strategy implementation requires personal discipline, commitment and sacrifice. Successful strategy implementation relies on managerial ability to lead employees, assist redesign of products, improve organizational process, and adjust to environmental constraints (Ansoff and McDonnell, 1990).

Evaluation

Strategy evaluation culminates the activity inherent in the design, application and eventual assessment of strategy. Strategy evaluation is needed because current success does not guarantee that such success will continue in the future: an organization which becomes complacent loses the drive required for survival in an increasingly competitive environment. Essential to realistic evaluation of company performance is the development of performance indicators linked to key improvement factors and attributes that influence improvement of people, product, and process elements of organizational performance. Strategic evaluation begins by noting external and internal circumstances, continues by measuring performance, and ends by critical assessment of achievement against strategic objectives (Hill and Jones, 1995; Wheelen and Hunger, 1998).

Environmental analysis, strategy formulation, strategy implementation and evaluation activities occur at three managerial levels in a large organization: corporate, Strategic Business Unit (SBU), and functional levels. By fostering effective communications and interaction among managers and employees across hierarchical levels, strategic management helps a firm to function by virtue of team structure that links corporate, SBU, and functional levels of the strategically-driven organisation. Most small business do not have divisions or business units.

What is Entrepreneurship?

Among the many engaged in entrepreneurship area, Stevenson (1983) defined entrepreneurship as the pursuit of opportunity beyond the tangible resources that you currently control. With this definition, emphasis is placed upon how opportunity can be recognized, the process of committing to an opportunity, gaining control over the resources, managing the network of resources that may or may not be within a single hierarchy, and the way in which participants are rewarded (Stevenson, 1985; Stevenson and Jarillo, 1991). The entrepreneurial organization focuses on opportunity, not resources. Entrepreneurs must commit quickly, but tentatively, to be able to readjust as new information arises. The process of commitment becomes multi-staged, limiting the commitment of resources at each stage to an amount sufficient to generate new information and success before more resources are sought. The entrepreneurial organization uses the resources that lie within the hierarchical control of others and, therefore, must manage the network as well as the hierarchy.

Approaches to Entrepreneurship

Many different and useful approaches have been used to describe and to analyse entrepreneurship. Austin et all (2006) argued that perspectives on entrepreneurship have tended to fall within three main streams of research, which include a focus on:

- The results of entrepreneurship: this stream is the domain of economists and explains the effects of entrepreneurship on the economic system.
- The causes of entrepreneurship: this stream explains why entrepreneurs act. This stream is the domain of sociologists and psychologists.
- The entrepreneurial management: this stream is the domain of management theorists. It discusses how entrepreneurs act and behave.

In the first stream of research, economists have explored the impacts and results of entrepreneurship. One of the early studies in entrepreneurship (Schumpeter, 1934) examined entrepreneurship as a key process through which the economy as a whole is advanced. The impact of entrepreneurship on the economic system is an important issue in economics which is neglected. Perhaps the reason for this is that entrepreneurship is not readily compatible with the equilibrium framework that has come to dominate the field of economics (Birkinshaw, 2000). The importance of entrepreneurship on economics has been investigated from different perspectives. For example, Dean and McMullen (2007) in their study investigated how entrepreneurship can help resolve the environmental problems of global socio-economic systems. They argued that environmental economists conclude that, environmental degradation results from the failure of markets, whereas the entrepreneurship literature argues that opportunities are inherent in market failure. As Dean and McMullen (2007) discussed, a synthesis of this literatures suggests that environmentally relevant market failures represent opportunities for achieving profitability while simultaneously reducing environmentally degrading economic behaviours. It also implies conceptualizations of sustainable and environmental entrepreneurship which detail how entrepreneurs seize the opportunities that are inherent in environmentally relevant market failures.

The second stream of research has focused on the entrepreneurs themselves. Research in this stream examines entrepreneurship from a psychological and sociological perspective (McClelland, 1961; Collins and Moore, 1964). For example, Harada (2004) studied the relationship between entrepreneurs' characteristics and firm performance. Harada (2004) estimated the production function of new Japanese firms and examined whether the total factor productivity is affected by the human capital and gender of entrepreneurs. Empirical results show decreasing returns to scale of production, which verifies the assumption of production functions in many previous studies on entrepreneurship. The findings of this research have also illustrated that the entrepreneur's age has a significantly negative effect on productivity, and the negative effect increases after 60 years of age. Although related business experience before start-up has a significantly positive effect, the magnitude is limited and cannot overcome the negative effect of age. In another study Serarols-Tarres et al. (2006) investigated the influence of entrepreneur characteristics on the success of pure dot.com firms. They argued that cyber-traders companies known as dot.com firms, are playing an increasingly significant role on the Internet, although the majority have not yet achieved much success. Despite this, there have been few studies focusing on the factors that affect the success of these companies. Serarols-Tarres et al. (2006) attempted to determine whether the characteristics of the entrepreneur may constitute a success' factor for such firms, and if so, to what extent. They analysed 23 cases of Spanish dot.coms and a model to explain the influence of the entrepreneur characteristics on the success of pure dot.com firms was proposed.

Finally, the third stream has focused on the entrepreneurial management process. This diverse literature includes research on how to foster innovation within established corporations (Gray and Mabey, 2005), start-ups and venture capital (Timmons and Bygrave, 1986), organizational life cycles (Quinn and Cameron, 1983), and predictors of entrepreneurial success (Dollinger, 1984). For example, Gray and Mabey (2005) investigated the role of leadership and management in boosting efficiency, productivity and innovation in European entrepreneurial firms. They argued that small firm participation in formal management development has been significantly lower than that of large organizations. The main contrasts in management development practices were partly due to size effects but also partly due to key differences in strategic approaches to management development.

Clearly from these three streams of research, earlier conceptualizations of entrepreneurship have often focused on either the economic function of entrepreneurship or on the nature of the individual who is 'the entrepreneur,' whereas in recent years, significant research has focused on the 'how' of entrepreneurship.

Studying Strategy in Entrepreneurial SMEs

As discussed in the previous section, small and medium-sized firms in the UK make a large contribution to the economics of the country (McKiernan and Morris, 1995;

Webb and Pettigrew, 1999). Research reveals that small companies are responsible for a large proportion of innovations in products and services, job creation and employment (Wheelen and Hunger, 1998). Despite the overall successes of small businesses, however, every year a lot of small companies fail. The propensity for small business failure in the early years is well documented (Storey, 1994). However, as well as a high failure rate, it is further estimated that at a given point in time approximately 40 per cent of businesses are experiencing neither growth nor decline. A variety of reasons have been identified for the lack of growth in micro enterprises. For example, Curran (1996) identified that for many owner-managers, employment growth is not an objective for the business and Hakim (1989) suggested that the majority have no plans for growth.

There are also numerous studies to explore gaps or market failures associated with lack of finance (Binks and Ennew, 1996; Devins, 1999). According to a new report by chartered accountants Kidsons Impey (see Anonymous, 1999), many of the UK's small and medium-sized businesses (SMEs) are failing to plan strategically for the future. Its Facing the Future survey of fast growing business (turnover growth in excess of 10 per cent p.a. over three years) from a variety of industry sectors found that almost one-third (32 per cent) of respondents had no business plan at all. Statistics tell us that small to medium-sized enterprises (SMEs) fail at a staggering rate. These are hard statistics to digest, knowing that the *SME* sector employs millions of employees and contributes significantly to the British economy. Indeed, a reduction in the failure rate of small businesses would lead to tremendous economic benefits. It is estimated that, there were approximately 3.7 million active businesses in the UK at the start of 2000. Of the entire population of 3.7 million enterprises only 7,000 were large (for details see Small Business Services, 2000). More than 1 million of these are statistically destined to fail, just imagine the impact of saving a reasonable percentage of them. Consider also the impact if a larger percentage of SMEs were not only able to survive, but grow to be competitive players in the global marketplace. There are many reasons for the failure rate of start-up businesses, including lack of adequate working capital, poor market selection, and rapidly changing external market conditions. However, the most significant reason for this high failure rate is the inability of SMEs to make adequate use of essential business and management practices. Many small firms fail to develop an initial business plan, and those that do establish a business plan fail to continually adjust and use it as a benchmarking tool (Robinson, 1982; Hitt, Gimeno and Hosskisson, 1998). This apparent lack of concern over the importance of business plans was further underlined. The underlying problem appears to be an overall lack of strategic approach, beginning with an inability to plan a strategy to reach the customer and ending with a failure to develop a system of controls and evaluation to keep track of performance.

Previous researches in the field of strategic management in small businesses, suggest several issues of significance that merit further investigations. For instance there are various arguments as to which type of strategy is the more effective for SMEs, should strategy be formal and written or informal? What is the association between strategic planning and performance in small businesses? The overall aim of this research is to explore senior managers' perception and attitudes, and contribution to the strategic management process in British small and medium sized enterprises in the electrical and electronic industry. This study therefore sought to answer the following questions in an attempt to highlight important considerations for managers of small and medium-sized firms.

- What are the senior managers' perceptions and attitudes to the strategic management process including: environmental scanning, strategy formulation, implementation and evaluation of strategy in small and medium sized enterprises.
- Which factors are associated with the effective strategy formulation and implementation process in small and medium sized enterprises and what is their impact on firm performance?
- What are the characteristics of a dynamic strategic management model in SMEs as an extension to the basic strategic management model, to assist decision making of the stages of formulation, implementation, and evaluation of strategy?

The Rationale for Studying Strategy and Entrepreneurship

While the volume of literature on strategic management in large organizations is extensive (Stacy, 1993; Pearce and Robinson, 1994; Collin, 1995; Hitt, Gimeno and Hosskisson, 1998; Wheelen and Hunger, 1998; Hoskisson, 2000), the literature on small and medium sized enterprises strategic management is more limited (McKiernan and Morris, 1995; Berry, 1998; Smith, 1998; O'Gorman and Doran, 1999; Chan and Foster, 2001; and Beal, 2000). Strategic management as a field of study typically deals with large, established business corporations, however, SMEs cannot be ignored. In the UK, small and medium sized enterprises (*SME*) have been defined as one firm that employs up to 250 people and has up to £50 million turnover (Amboise and Muldowney, 1988; Berry, 1998; and Beal, 2000).

Some writers have argued forcefully that formal strategic management procedures are particularly inappropriate for small and medium-sized firms, which have neither the management nor financial resources to indulge in elaborate strategic management techniques (Cragg and King, 1988; Shrader et al., 1989; Watts and Ormsby, 1990). Also for companies operating within the turbulent environment of high technology industries where conditions changes so fast that environmental forecasting becomes meaningless and long range planning of questionable value (Smith and Fleck, 1987; Shrader et al., 1989). A number of studies have concluded that there is little or no significant relationship between strategic planning and the performance of small firms (Unni, 1981; Robinson and Pearce, 1984; Shrader et al., 1989; Watts and Ormsby, 1990). These studies report mixed planning/performance relations, and most suggest that the value of planning is mitigated by factors such as environmental uncertainty, managerial expertise, and stage of firm development.

This study explores the application of strategic management in small and medium sized enterprises in the UK. The electronic industry has been selected as the main focus in the *SME* sector. The rational for that is the significant role of the SMEs in the UK economy and the dynamic nature of the electronic industry. Small and medium-sized enterprises are key drivers of economic growth and job creation in the UK (Bryson et all, 1992; McKiernan and Morris, 1995; Webb and Pettigrew, 1999). The shift to a knowledge-based, global economy is opening up new opportunities and challenges for these small businesses.

Generally speaking, it could be conclude that, small businesses are the backbone of the economy (for example Schwenk and Shrader, 1993) accounting for more than half of total employment and over 80 per cent of employment growth in the past decade (Wheelen and Hunger, 1989). Small firms in the electronic industry are also often innovative and challenging to manage strategically (Bracker et al., 1988). Consequently, it is important to assess the value of approaches like strategic management for improving the performance of these firms.

Integration of Strategic and Entrepreneurial Thinking

While the fields of strategic management and small businesses, have developed largely independently of each other, they both are focused on how firms adapt to environmental change and exploit opportunities created by uncertainties and discontinuities in the creation of wealth (Hitt and Ireland, 2000; Venkataraman and Sarasvathy, 2001). As such, several scholars have recently called for the integration of strategic and entrepreneurial thinking (for example McGrath and MacMillan, 2000). Accordingly, Meyer and Heppard (2000) argue that the two are really inseparable. McGrath and MacMillan (2000) argue that strategists must exploit an entrepreneurial mindset and, thus, have no choice but to embrace it in order to sense opportunities, mobilize resources, and act to exploit opportunities, especially under highly uncertain conditions. Venkataraman and Sarasvathy (2001) use a metaphor based on Shakespeare's Romeo and Juliet. They suggest that strategic management research that does not integrate an entrepreneurial perspective is like the balcony without Romeo. Alternatively, they argue that entrepreneurship research without integration of a strategic perspective is like Romeo without a balcony.

In the 1990s, the small business became one of the mainstays of the economy (Webb and Pettigrew, 1999). One of the reasons for this can be attributed to an increasing number of employees, who, because of being laid off by the larger corporations in the 1980s and early 1990s, had joined the small business workforce. Second, has been the trend in large firms to outsource some of their activities to smaller firms, facilitated, to some extent, by the growth of the Internet. Third, the relative stability of the economy since the early 1990s has encouraged entrepreneurial activity. Fourth, the emergence of new economies around the world has accelerated global development, and this has also encouraged entrepreneurial activity in the UK. Small businesses will, therefore, continue to play a major role in both job creation and economic growth in the next decade. Recognizing the importance of small businesses as major contributors to job creation and economic growth, especially during the past decade, academic research on small business management practice has grown dramatically in the recent past. In particular, topics involving the strategic growth of small businesses have received much attention from researchers (for example see Krishnan, 2001).

The total numbers of SMEs make them an important constituent of local, regional and national economics and subsequently a potential target for policy intervention. According to the Official UK Labour Market Statistics (1998) small businesses account for 84 per cent of all business units of UK. Business support policy interventions have shifted from a focus on job creation through business start-ups in the 1980s towards increasing the competitiveness of existing businesses with a view to their growth and development in the 1990s. The recent Competitiveness DTI, White Paper (1998) with its focus on the provision of advice to at least 10,000 start-ups a year by the year 2001, suggest once again, an increased emphasis on business formation. The importance of SMEs to the economy depends on the abilities of SMEs to fulfil these roles. Economic strategies to support SMEs will focus on the factors that encourage their growth or inhibit their growth. Company strategies for SMEs to grow and be successful will be based upon a technological or commercial innovation, or on a focused niche strategy with a differentiated product or services. Evan with these strategies any growing company will face severe problems as it proceeds through the different phases of its life cycle (Hitt and Ireland, 2000; Venkataraman and Sarasvathy, 2001).

Structure of the Book

The book is organized into seven separate but interlinked chapters. Chapter 1 introduces the objectives and scope of the study. This chapter provides an overview of the major works in the areas of strategy and management. It also provides a brief description of the key concepts of strategy and entrepreneurship.

Chapter 2 reviews the existing theories of strategy formulation in entrepreneurial small and medium sized enterprises. The theories differ greatly in their scope and purpose, and inevitably both have been the subjects of, at times, fierce academic debate that is outlined in the chapter.

Chapter 3 provides a conceptual framework of the research. Accordingly, this chapter describes how the research design was developed and in doing so draws together all of the proceeding chapters. The chapter begins by outlining the research questions through the development of the framework and the resulting hypothesis about the process of strategic management in SMEs.

Chapter 4 introduces the major findings of the research in connection with research propositions and hypotheses. The hypotheses offered by the conceptual framework of the research is compared with the findings of the study providing an interesting insight into the phases of the process of strategy formulation in entrepreneurial small and medium sized enterprises.

Chapter 5 discusses strategic entrepreneurship and the role of entrepreneurs in the strategy formulation process in SMEs. It starts with a discussion about exploring and examining the entrepreneurs' perception of the importance of the strategic management process in the studied firms. It explores the role of senior managers in the strategic management processes within small and medium enterprises in the next section of the chapter.

Chapter 6 continues with a discussion about the findings of the research into the existence and nature of environmental analysis in developing business strategies in the studied firms. Finally, the chapter discusses the findings on factors associated with effective strategy formulation and implementation process in SMEs.

Finally, Chapter 7 concludes the volume and as such is primarily concerned with the significance of the findings of the research and its implications for the future development of the subject. The chapter begins by revisiting the aims of the research and the research questions. Then considers each of the research propositions and hypotheses. The chapter aims to explain the final lessons; the theoretical and practical contributions as well as the implications for research in a wider context.

References

Amboise, G. and Muldowney, M. (1988), 'Management Theory for Small Business: Attempts and Requirements', *Academy of Management Review*, **13**(2), 226–240.

Analoui, F. (2000), 'What Motivates Senior Managers?' 'The Case of Romania', *Journal of Managerial Psychology*, **15**(4), 324–326.

Analoui, F. and Karami, A. (2003), *Strategic Management in Small and Medium Enterprises* (London: Thomson Learning).

Andrews, K. (1986) *The Concept of Corporate Strategy*, (Homewood, IL: Irwin).

Ansoff, H.I. and McDonnell, I. (1990), *Implanting Strategic Management* (Englewood Cliffs, N.J.: Prentice Hall).

Ansoff, H.I. (1965), *Corporate Strategy* (New York: McGraw-Hill).

Apfelthaler, G. (2000) Why Small Enterprises Invest Abroad: The Case of Four Austalian Firms with U.S. Operations, *Journal of Small Business Management*, 38 (3), 92–99.

Bain, J.S. (1968), *Industrial Organizations*, 2nd edn (New York: Wiley Books).

Beal, R.M. (2000), 'Competing Effectively: Environmental Scanning, Competitive Strategy, and Organisational Performance in Small Manufacturing Firms', *Journal of Small Business Management*, **38**(1), 27–47.

Berry, M. (1998), 'Strategic Planning in Small High-Tech Companies', *Long Range Planning*, **31**(3), 455–466.

Binks, M. and Ennew, C. (1996), *Financing Small Firms in Small Business and Entrepreneurship*, 2nd edn (London: Macmillan Business Books).

Birkinshaw, J. (2000), *Entrepreneurship in the Global Firm* (London: Sage Publications).

Bowman, C. (1998), *Strategy in Practice* (London: Prentice-Hall Inc.).

Bowman, C. and Faulkner, D. (1997), *Competitive Corporate Strategy* (London: Irwin).

Bowman, C. and Kakabadse, A. (1997), 'Top Management Ownership of the Strategy Problem', *Long Range Planning*, **30**(2), 197–208.

Boxall, P. (1992), 'Strategic Human Resource Management: Beginnings of a New Theoretical Sophistication?' *Human Resource Management Journal*, **2**(3), 60–79.

Boxall, P. (1996), 'The Strategic HRM Debate and the Resource-Based View of the Firm', *Human Resource Management Journal*, **6**(3), 59–75.

Bracker, J.S., Keats, B.W. and Pearson, J.N. (1988), 'Planning and Financial Performance Among Small Firms in a Growth Industry', *Strategic Management Journal*, **9**, 591–603.

Bridge, J. and Peel, M.J. (1999), 'Research Note: A Study of Computer Usage and Strategic Planning in the SME Sector', *International Small Business Journal*, **17**(4), 82–87.

Bryson, J., Keeble, D. and Wood, P. (1992), 'Business Networks, Flexibility and Regional Development in UK Business Services'. Working Paper, No. 19, Small Business Research Centre, University of Cambridge.

Chaffee, E.E. (1985), 'Three Models of Strategy', *Academy of Management Review*, **10**(1), 89–98.

Chan, S.Y. and Foster, J.M. (2001), 'Strategy Formulation in Small Business: The Hong Kong Experiences', *International Small Business Journal*, April/June.

Chandler, A. (1962), *Strategy and Structure* (Cambridge: MIT Press).

Chen, M.J. (1996), 'Competitor Analysis and Interfirm Rivalry: Toward a Theoretical Integration', *Academy of Management Review*, **21**, 100–134.

Cole, G.A. (1994), *Strategic Management, Theory and Practice* (New York, NY: DP Publication Ltd.).

Collin, C. (1995), *Cases in Strategic Management*, 2nd edn (New York, NY: Pitman Books).

Collins, O.F. and Moore, D.G. (1964), *The Enterprising Man* (East Lansing, MI: Michigan State University).

Cragg, P.B. and King, M. (1988), 'Organizational Characteristics and Small Firms' Performance Revisited', *Entrepreneurship: Theory and Practice*, **13**(2), 49–64.

Curran, J. (1996), 'Small Business Strategy' in *The Concise International Encyclopedia of Business and Management, London: International Thomson Business Press*. Warner, M. (ed.), 4510–4520.

Daft, R.L. (2000), *Management*, 5th edn (New York, NY: The Dryden Press).

Daft, R.L., Sormunen, L. and Parks, D. (1988), 'Chief Executive Scanning, Environmental Characteristics, and Company Performance: An Empirical Study', *Strategic Management Journal*, **9**, 123–139.

David, F.R. (1995), *Strategic Management*, 5th edn (London: Prentice-Hall).

Dean, T.J. and McMullen, J.S. (2007), 'Toward a Theory of Sustainable Entrepreneurship: Reducing Environmental Degradation Through Entrepreneurial Action', *Journal of Business Venturing*, **22**(1), 50–76.

Devins, D. (1999), 'Supporting Established Micro Businesses: Policy Issues Emerging From an Evaluation', *International Small Business Journal*, **18**(1), 86–96.

Dollinger, M.J. (1984), 'Environmental Boundary Spanning and Information Processing Effects on Organizational Performance', *Academy of Management Journal*, **27**, 351–368.

Foster, M.J. (1993), 'Scenario Planning for Small Businesses', *Long Range Planning*, **26**(1), 123–129.

Gable, M. and Topol, M.T. (1987), 'Planning Practices of Small-Scale Retailers', *American Journal of Small Business*, **12**(2), 19–32.

Glueck, W.L. and Jauch, L.R. (1988), *Business Policy and Strategic Management*, 5th edn (New York: McGraw-Hill).

Goldsmith, A. (1995), 'Making Managers More Effective: Applications of Strategic Management', *Working paper* No. 9, USAID March.

Goodwin, D.R. and Hodgett, R.A., '(1991) Strategic Planning in Medium Size Companies', *Australian Accountant*,. **61**(2), 71–83.

Grant, R.M. (1998), 'The Resource-Based Theory of Competitive Advantage: Implications for Strategy Formulation, Chapter 19, in Costin, H. (ed), (1998) *Reading in Strategy and Strategic Planning, The Dryden Press*.

Gray, C. and Mabey, C. (2005), 'Management Development – Key Differences Between Small and Large Businesses in Europe', *International Small Business Journal*, **23**(5), 467–485.

Hakim, C. (1989), 'Identifying Fast Growth Small Firms', *Employment Gazette*, **January**, 29–41.

Hambrick, D.C. (1981), 'Environment, Strategy, and Power Within Top Management Teams', *Administrative Science Quarterly*, **26**, 253–276.

Harada, N. (2004), 'Productivity and Entrepreneurial Characteristics in New Japanese Firms', *Journal of Small Business Economics*, **23**(4), 299–310.

Heene, A. (1997), 'The Nature of Strategic Management', *Long Range Planning*, **30**(6), 933–938.

Hill, C.H. and Jones, G.R. (1995), 'Strategic Management Theory', *An Integrated Approach*, 3rd edn (Boston: Houghton Mifflin Company).

Hitt, L. and Ireland, R.D. (1985), 'Corporate Distinctive Competence, Strategy, Industry, and Performance', *Strategic Management Journal*, **6**, 273–293.

Hitt, M.A. and Ireland, R.D. (2000), 'The Intersection of Entrepreneurship and Strategic Management Research' in *Handbook of Entrepreneurship*, Sexton, D.L. and Landstrom, H.A. (eds.) (Oxford: Blackwell Publishing), 45–63.

Hitt, M.A., Gimeno, J. and Hosskisson, R.E. (1998), 'Current and Future Research Methods in Strategic Management', *Organizational Research Methods*, **1**, 6–44.

Hofer, C.W. and Schendel, D. (1978), 'Strategy Formulation: Analytical Concept', *New* (York: West Publishing Company).

Hoskisson, R.E. (2000), 'Strategy in Emerging Economics', *Academy of Management Journal*, **43**(3), 249–268.

Hoskisson, R.E., Hitt, M.A., Wan, W.P. and Yiu, D. (1999), 'Theory and Research in Strategic Management: Swings of a Pendulum', *Journal of Management*, **25**(3), 417–456.

Johnson, G. and Scholes, K. (1993), *Exploring Corporate Strategy: Tex and Cases*, 3rd edn (London: Prentice Hall).

Jordan, J. and Jones, P. (1997), 'Assessing Your Company's Knowledge Management Style', *Long Range Planning*, **30**(3), 392–398.

Kakabadse, A., Kakabadse, N. and Myers, A. (1996), 'Leadership and the Public Sector: An Internationally Comparative Benchmarking Analysis', *Public Administration and Development*, **16**(4), 377–396.

Koontz, H. and Weihrich, H. (1990), *Essential of Management*, 5th edn (Columbus, OH:McGraw-Hill/Book Co.).

Krishnan, H.A. (2001), 'Supplier Selection Practices Among Small Firms in the United States: Testing Three Models', *Journal of Small Business Management*, **39**(3), 259–271.

Leavy, B. (1996), *Key Process in Strategy* (London: International Thomson Business Press Books).

Luffman, G., Sanderson, S., Lea, E. and Kenny, B. (1991), *Business Policy: An Analytical Introduction*, 2nd edn (Oxford: Blackwell Business Publication).

Luttwak, E. (1987), *Strategy the Logic of War and Peace* (Belknap: USA Harvard).

Marsh, I. (1999), 'Program Strategy and Coalition Building as Facets of New Public Management', *Australian Journal of Public Administration*, **58**(4), 54–68.

Mason, E.S. (1939), 'Price and Production Policies of Large Scale Enterprises', *American Economic Review*, **29**, 61–74.

McClelland, D.C. (1961), *The Achieving Story* (Princeton, NJ: D. Van Nostrand Books).

McGrath, R.G. and MacMillan, I. (2000), *The Entrepreneurial Mindset* (Boston, Mass.: Harvard Business School Publishing).

McKenna, S.D. (1996, November), 'The Darker Side of the Entrepreneur', *Leadership and Organizational Development Journal*, **17**(5), 41.

McKiernan, P. and Morris, C. (1995), 'Strategic Planning and Financial Performance in UK SMEs: Does Formality Matter?' *British Journal of Management*, **5**, 31–41.

Meyer, G.D. and Heppard, K.A. (2000), *Entrepreneurship as Strategy: Competing on the Entrepreneurial Edge* (Thousand Oaks, Calif.: Sage).

Miller, D. and Toulouse, J.M. (1986), 'Strategy, Structure, CEO Personality and Performance in Small Firms', *American Journal of Small Businesses*, Winter, 47–62.

Mintzberg, H. (1978), 'Patterns in Strategy Formations', *Management Science*, **24**(9), 934–948.

Mintzberg, H. (1994), *The Rise and Fall of Strategic Planning* (London: Prentice-Hall).

Mintzberg, H. and Quinn, J.B. (1998), *Reading in the Strategy Process*, 3rd edn (New Jersey: Prentice-Hall Books, Inc.).

Mintzberg, H., Quinn, J.B. and Ghoshal, S. (1995), *The Strategy Process*, (*European Edition*, New Jersey: Prentice Hall International (UK) Ltd).

O'Gorman, C. and Doran, R. (1999), 'Mission Statements in Small and Medium Sized Businesses', *Journal of Small Business Management*, **37**(4), 59–66.

Official UK Labour Market Statistics (1998) Annual Employment Survey, http://www.nomisweb.co.uk/news/april01.html#ABI.

Ohmae, K. (1983), 'The Mind of the Strategist', Harmondsworth: Penguin Books.

Pearce II, J.A. and Robinson, JR. R.B. (1991) (1991), *Formulation, Implementation, and Control of Competitive Strategy*, 4th edn (Boston: Irwin).

Pearce, J. and Robinson, R. (1994), *Strategic Management: Strategy Formulation and Implementation*, 5th edn (Boston, Mass.: Irwin).

Pfeffer, J. (1995), 'Producing Sustainable Competitive Advantage Through the Effective Management of People', *Academy of Management Executive*, **9**(1), 55–72.

Pitts, R.A. and Lei, D. (1996), *Strategic Management Building and Sustaining Competitive Advantage* (New York, NY: West Publishing Company).

Porter, M. (1979), 'How Competitive Forces Shape Strategy', *Harvard Business Review*, March/April.

Porter, M. (1980), *Competitive Strategy* (New York: Free Press).

Porter, M. (1985), *Competitive Advantage: Creating and Sustaining Superior Performance* (New York: Free Press).

Porter, M. (1998), *On Competition* (Boston: Harvard Business School Presses).

Quinn, R.E. and Cameron, K. (1983), 'Organizational Life Cycles and Shifting Criteria of Effectiveness', *Management Science*, **29**, 33–51.

Robinson, R.B. (1982), 'The Importance of Outsiders in Small Firm Strategic Planning', *Academy of Management Journal*, **25**(1), 80–93.

Robinson, R.B. and Pearce, J.A. (2001), 'Why Small Businesses Need a Strategic Plan?' *Business and Economic Review*, **48**(1), 12–15.

Robinson, R.B., Pearce, J.A., II (1984), 'Research Thrusts in Small Firm Strategic Planning', *Academy of Management Review*, **9**(1), 128–137.

Robinson, R.B., Pearce, J.A., Vozikis, G. and Mescon, T. (1984), 'The Relationship Between Stage of Development and Small Firm Planning and Performance', *Journal of Small Business Management*, **22**(2), 45–52.

Rumelt, R.P. (1991), 'How much Does Industry Matter?' *Strategic Management Journal*, March, 167–185.

Schendel, D.E. and Cool, K.O. (1988), Development of the Strategic Management Field, in *Strategic Management Frontiers,* ed, J. H. Grant, (Greenwich, CT: JAI Presses), 17–31.

Schumpeter, J.A. (1934), *The Theory of Economic Development* (Cambridge, Mass.: Harvard University Press).

Schwenk, C.R. and Shrader, C.R. (1993), 'Effects of Formal Strategic Planning on Financial Performance in Small Firms: A Meta-Analysis', *Entrepreneurship: Theory and Practice*, **17**(3), 53–72.

Scott, M. and Bruce, R. (1987), 'Five Stages of Growth in Small Businesses', *Long Range Planning*, **20**(3), 45–52.

Segal-Horn, S. (1998), *The Strategy Reader* (Oxford: The Open University, Blackwell Publishers Ltd.).

Serarols-Tarres, C., Padilla-Melendez, A. and del Aguila-Obra, A.R. (2006), 'The Influence of Entrepreneur Characteristics on the Success of Pure Dot.Com Firms', *International Journal of Technology Management*, **33**(4), 373–388.

Shay, J.P. and Rothaermel, F.T. (1999), 'Dynamic Competitive Strategy: Toward a Multi-Perspective Conceptual Framework', *Long Range Planning*, **32**(6), 559–572.

Shrader, C.B., Mulford, C.L. and Blackburn, V.L. (1989), 'Strategic and Operational Planning, Uncertainty, and Performance in Small Firms', *Journal of Small Business Management*, **27**(4), 45–60.

Small Business Services (2000), 'UK Small Business Services'. Available at www.sbs.gov.uk.

Smith, J.A. (1998), 'Strategies for Start-Ups', *Long Range Planning*, **31**(6), 857–872.

Smith, J.G. and Fleck, V. (1987), 'Business Strategies in Small High Technology Companies', *Long Range Planning*, **20**(2), 61–68.

Stacy, R.D. (1993), *Strategic Management and Organizational Dynamic* (London: Pitman Publishing).

Stevenson, H.H. (1983), *A Perspective on Entrepreneurship* Harvard Business School Working Paper No. 9-384-131. Boston: Harvard Business School.

Stevenson, H.H. (1985), 'The Heart of Entrepreneurship', *Harvard Business Review*, **63**, 85–94.

Stevenson, H.H. and Jarillo, J.C. (1991), 'A New Entrepreneurial Paradigm' in *Socio-economics: Toward a New Synthesis*. Etzioni, A. and Lawrence, P. (eds.) (Armonk, NY: M.E. Sharpe), 185–208.

Stoner, J.A.F., Freeman, R.E. and Gilbert, D.R. (1995), *Management* (London: Prentice-Hall/International Limited).

Storey, D.J. (1994), *Understanding the Small Business Sector* (London: Routledge Books).

Teece, D.J., Pisano, G. and Shuen, A. (1997), 'Dynamic Capabilities and Strategic Management', *Strategic Management Journal*, **18**, 509–533.

Tetenbaum, T.J. (1998), 'Shifting Paradigms: from Newton to Chaos', *Organizational Dynamics*, spring, 21–32.

Thompson, J.L. (1996), *Strategic Management: Awareness and Change*, 2nd edn (London: Chapman and Hall).

Timmons, J.A. and Bygrave, W.D. (1986), 'Venture Capital's Role in Financing Innovation for Economic Growth', *Journal of Business Venturing*, **1**, 161–173.

Unni, V.K. (1981), 'The Role of Strategic Planning in Small Business', *Long Range Planning*, **14**(2), 54–58.

Venkataraman, S. and Sarasvathy, S.D. (2001), 'Strategy and Entrepreneurship: Outlines of an Untold Story' in *Handbook of Strategic Management*. Hitt, M.A., Freeman, E. and Harrison, J.S. (eds.) (Oxford: Blackwell Publishing) (in press).

Watts, L.R. and Ormsby, J.C. (1990b), 'Small Business Performance as a Function of Planning Formality: A Laboratory Study', *Journal of Business and Entrepreneurship*, **2**(1), 1–8.

Webb, D. and Pettigrew, A. (1999), 'The Temporal Development of Strategy: Patterns in the UK Insurance Industry', *Organization Science*, **10**(5), 601–621.

Wheelen, T.L. and Hunger, J.D. (1998), *Strategic Management and Business Policy* (Reading, Mass.: Addison-Wesley).

Whittington, R. (1993), *What is Strategy and Dose It Matter?* (London: Routledge).

Williamson, O.E. (1991), 'Compatitive Economic Organisation: the Analysis of Discrete Structural Alternatives', *Administrative Science Quarterly*, **36**, 269–229.

Wolff, J.A. (2000), 'Internationalisation of Small Firms: An Examination of Export Competitive Patterns, Firm Size, and Export Performance', *Journal of Small Business Management*, **38**(2), 34–48.

Wood, D.R., Johnston, R.A. and DeGenaro, G.J. (1988), 'The Impact of Formal Planning on the Financial Performance of Real Estate Firms', *Journal of Business Strategies*, **5**(1), 44–51.

Zajac, E. (1995), SMJ 1994 Best Paper Prize to Birger Wernerfelt. *Strategic Management Journal*, **16**(3), 169–170.

Chapter 2

Strategy Formulation in Small and Medium-Sized Enterprises

Introduction

A wide range of conceptual frameworks exists for strategy formulation in small and medium-sized enterprises (SMEs). Early scholars (Chandler, 1962; Ansoff, 1965; Andrews, 1971) in the field of strategy regarded strategy as a rational decision-making process by which the organization's resources are matched with opportunities arising from the competitive environment. Others have stated that, environment has a strong deterministic influence on the strategy making process in organizations (Porter, 1980; Bourgeois and Brodwin, 1984; Flood et al., 2000).

In contrast, the proponents of the resource-based view, however, argue that, it is not the environment but the resources of the organization, which should be considered as the foundation of the strategy (Grant, 1991; Boxall and Steeneveld, 1999). Despite the apparent differences, these approaches to strategy have one thing in common; they all aim at maximizing performance by improving one organization's position in relation to other organizations in the same competitive environment. That is, how the organization is differentiated from its competitors. The existing presence of a wide range of approaches towards strategy reflects the different views taken in researching the subject and its evolution over time. This chapter aims to provide the reader with a comprehensive overview of the major works in the field of strategy formulation with particular concern for small and medium sized entrepreneurial firms.

Theoretical Background of Strategy in Entrepreneurial SMEs

Much has been written in recent years about the importance of strategic management in entrepreneurial small and medium enterprises. The success and rapid growth of many medium and small sized businesses have been largely attributed to their strategic planning capabilities. While some prominent writers have concentrated on exploring strategic planning theory and developing a conceptual framework upon which a discipline could be based, others have chosen to study company planning practices and the way in which management could more effectively apply strategic planning theory.

Though interest in small business management has sharply increased and indeed the literature available on strategic management in small businesses has grown over the past two decades, much of it remains conceptual in approach. The few empirical studies that do exist have been criticized on the grounds that they lack academic rigour and do not illuminate the perceived relationship between formal strategic management processes and organizational performance (Shrader et al., 1989).

Rational Model of Strategy

Traditional thinking on strategy tends to define it in terms of planning to arrive at the optimum strategy for a given context. Plans are naturally based on a linear model of decision-making (Chaffee, 1985), and the planning process is divided into two main stages: strategy formulation and implementation (Ansoff, 1965). The formulation of strategy is seen as the prerogative of top management (Chaffee, 1985) and more importantly it is seen as a rational exercise, involving the objective analysis of company resources and the external environment in which the company operates.

The planning model, therefore, focuses on the links between the organization and its external environment. Consequently, a myriad of sophisticated techniques have been developed to aid managerial decision-making. These included portfolio analysis (The Boston Consulting Group), the General Electric market attractiveness-business position matrix, Porter's model of industry attractiveness (Porter, 1980) and the product life cycle theory. Great faith is placed on the gathering of 'hard' factual information for planning and control purposes.

The planning model is adaptive in the sense that it suggests that the organization has to continually strive to keep up with an environment that moves ahead of it (Hamel, 1996). Other writers have presented the planning in the context of 'voluntarism', thus giving the impression of well-informed leaders choosing between clearly articulated alternatives. According to Hanlon and Scott (1995), the dominant perspective in relation to strategy in smaller organizations has been the rational planning model. Planning is often seen as the key to a company's success (Leidecker and Bruno, 1986; Monck et al., 1988), since it reduces uncertainty, it ensures that alternatives are considered and assists managers in dealing with investors (O'Gorman and Cunningham, 1997).

Other researchers focus on planning as being contingent upon the nature of the business itself (Monck et al., 1988; Berry, 1998), which includes the skills of the owner-managers and their predisposition to planning, company size and stage of development/life cycle (Robinson and Pearce, 1984; Scott and Bruce, 1987). A survey of 257 companies found that small high-tech firms do use strategic planning to direct their long-term growth, bearing in mind that the planning processes become more sophisticated as firms grow (Berry, 1998).

The value and applicability of strategic planning for the small firm has been questioned by some who argue that, for example, a lack of financial resources and constraints on management time are seen as obstacles to strategic planning (Bhide, 1994). It has been argued that strategic planning loses its meaning in a dynamic environment, where innovation, flexibility and responsiveness to perishable opportunities are key conditions for survival (Mintzberg, 1979). At the other extreme, writers like Carson and Cromie (1989) argue that most entrepreneurs use neither formal planning nor strategy. Thompson (1999) suggests that entrepreneurs require the ability to think and act strategically. While the majority of researchers share the view that formal planning is a necessity, they also acknowledge that planning in small firms tends to be different from that of large corporations (Carson and Cromie, 1989).

Within the rational planning school of thought, attempts have been made to identify the types of strategy associated with high growth SMEs (Covin, 1991; Smallbone, Leig and North, 1995). On the whole, the niche strategy (Miles and Snow, 1978) is seen as the accepted norm since it enables entrepreneurs to conserve resources and avoid direct confrontation with large firms. Managers have been advised to pay special attention to the development of new products and markets (Smallbone, Leig and North, 1995), to compete on the basis of product differentiation, innovation, high product quality, and to exploit the unique strengths of the small firm (Murray and O'Gorman, 1994).

It is therefore proposed that making the correct strategic choices at start-up is crucial since investments made in people, technology and fixed assets cannot be easily altered. Indeed, the links between the environment, strategy and performance have been explored (Covin and Slevin, 1990). Sandberg and Hofer (1987) nevertheless concluded that small firms should enter industries in the growth stage, or industries characterized by heterogeneous demand, supply shortages or evident disequilibria. Studies in the planning school of thought, while valuable, tend to embody an explicit, normative model of the strategy process. Hence, strategy formulation is assumed to be driven by the owner-manager.

Intuitive Learning Model of Strategy

Probably, McCarty and Leavy's recent work (2000) is the best example of work in the debate concerning the intuitive learning model of strategy. They provide a comparison between the rational planning and intuitive learning models of strategy (see Table 2.1). Over the years, several writers have taken the debate well beyond the normative, rational planning models that have dominated the strategic management field for so long.

Distinguished writers such as Mintzberg (1987) and Mintzberg and Waters (1982), see strategy not so much as the outcome of point-in-time planning exercises but more as a pattern in a stream of decisions made over time. Indeed, Mintzberg coined the term 'strategy formation' to highlight the empirical reality that strategies emerge over time and are often not realized as intended. Process theorists (Pettigrew and Whipp, 1991) have argued that a clear distinction between strategy formulation and implementation does not really exist. They have highlighted the non-linear nature of the strategy process. Thus, powerful political and cultural forces in large organizations tend to result in the convergence of planning and execution (Pettigrew, 1987; Johnson, 1992; Pfeffer, 1994). In this way strategies often reflect what will work in practice as much as what should be done (Quinn, 1980; Mintzberg, 1987).

Quinn (1980) argues that the development of strategies is a process of 'logical incrementalism' where managers implement strategies in a purposeful but gradual manner in order to minimize risk, hence remaining opportunistic, experiment and learn, and fashion a broad consensus for change. A study of Irish firms by Leavy and

Table 2.1 The differences between rational and learning models for strategic planning

The Rational Planning Model	The Intuitive Learning Model
Organization is guided by a formal plan.	Organization is not guided solely by a formal strategy and strategy may be deliberate and/or emergent in nature.
Focus is on the external environment: characteristics of the industry and market.	Focus is on the internal dimension of the organization: policies, culture, learning, organizational history, leadership.
Linear model of strategy formulation.	Non-linear model of strategy formulation.
Decision-making: hierarchical, top-down.	Decision-making: top-down and bottom-up.
Rational	Rational and emotional.
Adaptive	Inventive
Voluntaristic	Neither overly voluntaristic nor overly deterministic.

Adapted from McCarthy and Leavy, 2000.

Wilson (1994) illustrates the interplay between leadership the context (industry) and history in the shaping of strategic outcomes. They skilfully show how leaders might best be viewed as 'tenants of time and context'. Inevitably, new leaders have to deal with the strategic legacy of their predecessors, and the previous predictably made decisions and the changing nature of the business environment, which all serves to constrain leadership capacity. As a result, strategy formation is a continuous, interactive and uncertain process.

It is evident that process researchers are mainly concerned with exploring the relationship between internal processes and the degree of competitiveness (Leavy, 1996). The tacit assumption in this school of thought is that strategies are not the outcome of a highly analytical and rational process. Instead, strategists need to capture 'soft' data such as feeling, intuition, vision, learning and judgement as well as 'hard' data (Mintzberg, 1979; Quinn, 1980; Mintzberg, 1994). Several writers see the environment not as a neatly packaged, objective reality 'out there' but as an enacted and interpreted environment (Smircich and Stubbart, 1985; Isabella, 1990).

Psychologists illustrate that managers construct simplified mental models in dealing with complex problems. Without these simplifications, managers would become paralysed by the need to analyse extensive data. The process model of strategy also stresses invention as well as adaptation. For example, Hamel (1996) describes strategy as a prelude to 'revolution' where managers can 'enact' or 'create' their own environment and challenge industry conventions. While the planning model is primarily voluntarist in nature, the researchers on strategy process tend to adopt an intermediate world view, by being sensitive to how contextual forces can both enable and constrain leadership capacity (Leavy, 1996).

Several writers have focused on the internal dimensions of the firm (Hanlon and Scott, 1995; Meyer and Heppard, 2000). A study by Hanlon and Scott (1995) found that entrepreneurs were able to persuade others to 'buy into' their dream or vision that they believe shapes the development of the firm. Another study by Bouwen and Steyaert (1990), located in the resource-based school of thought, found that the values and core competencies of the firm tend to change in the growth phase. Not surprisingly, research in the small firm literature focuses on the personal characteristics of the founder; the entrepreneur is seen to have a crucial impact on company strategy, culture and performance (Kets De Vries, 1996). For example, it is argued that entrepreneurs are rarely strategists acting according to rational principles (Kets De Vries, 1996). Instead they are more likely to act on the basis of instinct, a master plan or vision, and impulse. Thompson (1999), however, believes that entrepreneurs possess the qualities of successful strategic leaders; they have to assess opportunities and threats in the environment and adopt strategic positions.

Several writers have called for further research on how strategies actually form in small firms (Hanlon and Scott, 1995; Hendry, Arthur and Jones, 1995; Boussouara and Deakins, 1999). For instance, Boussouara and Deakins (1999, 207) argue that, in the high technology arena, the formulation of marketing strategies and the learning process are not very well understood. In recent years, the organizational learning concept has emerged as a strong theme in the strategy in small firm literature (Hendry, Arthur and Jones, 1995; Boussouara and Deakins, 1999; Chaston, Berger and Sadler-Smith, 1999).

It is often assumed that learning, which underpins diverse activities such as new product development, productivity, customer service and management styles is associated with firm performance. However, not all studies provide clear statistically significant relationships between learning and performance (Chaston, Berger and Sadler-Smith, 1999). Organizational learning is often stimulated by crisis, although it has negative connotations for managers (Hendry, Arthur and Jones, 1995).

In summary, the treatment of strategy in the small business literature has lagged behind that of the mainstream strategic management. Most studies are deemed to be normative in orientation and thus firmly located in the rational-planning school of thought. Recent studies suggest that an optimal strategy for all firms in a given context does not exist. This is largely due to variations in learning, culture, personalities, experiences and goals of the actors involved in the process within the firms.

Conceptualization of Strategic Planning

While the term 'strategic planning' is the cornerstone for an entire discipline, there is remarkably little consistency in its operationalization (Boyd and Reuning-Elliott,

1998). The strategic planning construct has been used by researchers for over two decades, and is generally one element of a larger analysis or model. Consequently, the development of a common conceptualization and measurement scheme has received only sporadic attention (Boyd and Reuning-Elliott, 1998). The proposed table (see Table 2.2) is based on a review of selected works, published during the last decade, which have used the strategic planning construct.

There appears to be five problems associated with prior use of this construct. First, inconsistent measurement schemes have been used to describe and operationalize strategic planning. Numerous labels have characterized planning, and inconsistencies are found both within and across labelling schemes, that is studies using the same labels frequently use different indicators, and the same indicators are also used to represent multiple labels. Second, while planning is most frequently conceptualized as one dimensional, it has also been conceptualized with two, three and even seven dimensions. Third, studies often collapse interval or ratio level indicators to nominal or ordinal categories. The consequences of this transformation from a finer to cruder level of analysis include the loss of information and statistical power, and limiting the ability to effectively test hypotheses. Fourth, most of the prior studies do not report tests of the reliability or validity of their measures. The last concern with prior studies is parsimony. Since the willingness of executives to participate in a research is partially driven by survey length, a planning measure must balance precision vs. parsimony (Boyd and Reuning-Elliott, 1998)

To sum up, prior approaches to measuring planning have used inconsistent terminology, and have numerous methodological limitations. An important criterion, that is the content validity, also requires that proposed measures be grounded in theory. As seen previously, numerous approaches at both conceptual and operational levels have been used to develop measures for strategic planning. Organizational environment, for example, has been variously characterized as objects, elements, attributes and perceptions. Consequently, the first step in developing a model of strategic planning is to specify the underlying framework from which a measure can be operationalized.

Researchers have typically developed indicators intended to reflect how closely a firm's planning activities reflect those developed by normative strategy literature (Boyd and Reuning-Elliott, 1998). In most studies aspects of process, mission statements, trend analysis, long- and short-term goals, and organizational control systems have been selected to operationalize planning. While the choice of indicators has varied widely across studies, most studies seem to define planning as the formality of an importance associated with those indicators (Pearce and David, 1987). As a result, to be consistent with the prior studies Boyd and Reuning-Elliott (1998) in their study have, defined strategic planning as a normative process.

Strategy Formulation Phases in SMEs

The results of the comparative analysis show that the strategy formation process displayed a marked phase pattern over time. In general, strategy formation in SMEs does not conform in any way to the rational planning model of strategy. Rather,

Table 2.2 Comparison analysis of the use of strategic planning construct

Author(s)	Focus	Planning definition	Level	Indicators	Dimensionality tests	Reliability/ validity
Beal, 2000	Performance	Competitive strategy	Ordinal/ Interval		None	Alpha
Berry, 1998	Strategic Planning	Formality	Ordinal		None	Alpha
O'Gorman and Cunningham, 1997	Mission	Formality	Ordinal		None	Alpha
Priem *et al* (1995)	Contingency	Rationality	Interval	12	None	Alpha
Capon *et al* (1994)	Performance	Sophistication	Ordinal	500	None	None
Veliyath and Shortell (1993)	Generic strategies	Characteristics	Interval	12	Factor	Alpha
Powell (1992a)	Competitive advantages/ contingency	Goal setting, scanning and analysis	Interval	11	None	Alpha
Powell (1992b)	Contingency	Comprehensiveness	Interval	11	None	Alpha
Kukalis (1991)	Performance	Completeness and Areas	Ordinal	19	None	Reliability
Shortell and Zajac (1990)	Generic strategies	Formality and innovativeness	Interval	6	Factor	None
Sinha (1990)	Decision Making	Formality	Interval	2	None	Validity
Bracker *et al* (1988)	Performance	Sophistication	Ordinal	8	None	Reliability
Miller *et al* (1988)	Contingency	Analysis	Interval	5	None	Alpha
Odom and Boxx (1988)	Performance	Sophistication	Ordinal	6	None	None
Miller (1987)	Contingency	Rationality	Interval	12	Factor	Alpha
Venkatraman and Ramanujam (1987)	Planning effectiveness	Capabilities	Interval	12	Confirmatory factor	Reliability and validity
Ramanujam and Venkatraman (1987)	Effectiveness	Systems	Interval	34	None	Alpha
Bracker and Pearson (1986)		Sophistication	Ordinal	8	None	None
Grinyer *et al* (1986)	Contingency	Factors	Interval or ratio	19	Factor	None
Ginter *et al* (1985)	Descriptive	Process	Interval	8	None	None
Acklesberg and Arlow (1985)	Performance	Formality and analytical	Nominal/ interval	6	Factor	Alpha
Rhyne (1985)	Information use	Openness	Ordinal	8	Factor	Alpha
Fredrickson and Mitchell(1984)	Decision processes	Comprehensiveness	Interval	43	None	None
Welch (1984)	Performance	Strategy	Nominal	5	None	None
Javidan (1984)	Performance	Extensiveness	Ordinal	11	None	None
Robinson and Pearce (1983)		Formality	Ordinal	3	None	None
Leontiades and Tezel (1980)	Performance	Importance	Interval	1	None	Validity
Lindsay and Rue (1980)	Performance	Completeness	Ordinal	14	None	None

the companies seemed to evolve from an early fluid stage of strategy formation, referred to here as a quasi-strategic phase, to a stage where the enterprise becomes characterized by a more explicit and clearly defined strategy (see Figure 2.1). The first phase in the strategy formation process, as aptly illustrated by McCarthy and Leavy (2000), is characterized as a quasi-strategic phase, which is characterized by little planning formality, the pursuit of a multiplicity of goals, and a very individualistic management style with the founder's views predominating.

In general, the strategy formation process during the quasi-strategic phase is characterized by a short planning horizon and the absence of detailed goals; the planning process was informal in the sense that plans often resided in the minds of the founder and were communicated to others informally. None of the SMEs studied possessed a written strategy document. It is reported that all entrepreneurs stressed that getting the business off the ground in the early days was extremely difficult. It is clear that business start-up was typically an unstructured, uncertain and highly stressful phase.

Unlike leaders of established organizations who have to develop a strategy with reference to the past, entrepreneurs are in a position to be able to create their history. The founders' style of management can be described as 'individualistic' in the sense that they have control over the venture, have a tendency to be self-reliant and are able to persuade people to share their belief in their vision on account of their strong personalities.

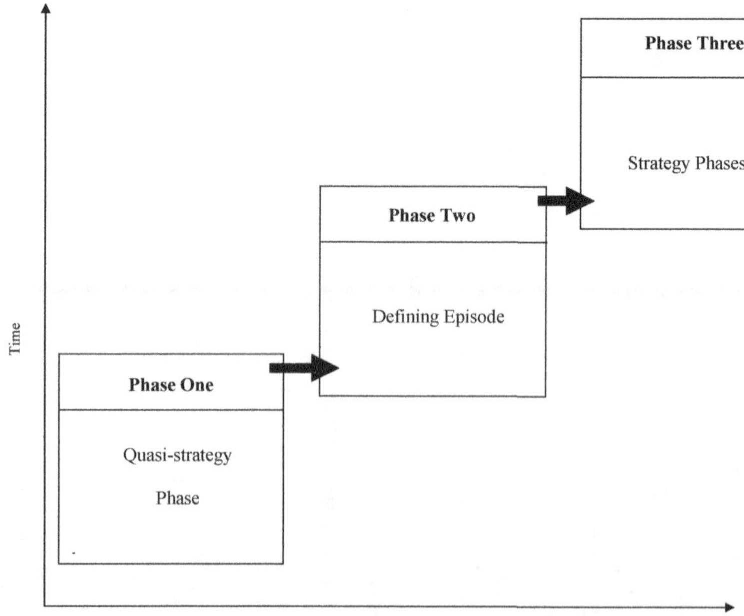

Figure 2.1 Three phases of strategy formulation in SMEs

The second phase has been referred to as the defining episode in the process of strategy formulation in SMEs. The term 'defining episode' is used to describe a period of transition. This could be a financial crisis or change in ownership, and in all cases it signifies a major break from the past. The business start-up phase is typically characterized by vision, imagination, unproven ideas, experimentation and opportunism. However, the onset of crisis usually results in the emergence of a more cautious outlook and a strong desire to safeguard the organization. During the crisis, people are more inclined to turn to hard reason, to ask 'why', to remember past experience of crisis and seek some justification for the proposed plans.

The third phase in the process is the strategic one. This phase seems to be characterized by greater planning and control, particularly of the financial side of the business. McCarthy and Levy report that in the company, long-term business strategies are put into place. Management moved from a service to more product-led strategy and it became more budget-orientated and more cost conscious. In the aftermath of crisis, management began holding formal meetings to review past performance and began to forecast the future over a 3-year period. Two companies were taken over after a crisis episode. Entrepreneurs suffered some loss of credibility during periods of crisis and the crisis showed that the risk-taking role played by the founding entrepreneur was no longer appropriate. The strategic phase of the business seems to demand a change in management style on the part of the entrepreneur.

Strategic Management Model for Entrepreneurial SMEs

The process involved in a typical model of strategic management was introduced. It includes environmental scanning, strategy formulation, strategy implementation and evaluation of strategy. Wheelen and Hunger (1998) have argued that, the above process does not fit small businesses and new entrepreneurial ventures. These companies must have a new mission, objectives, strategies, and policies out of a comparison of its external opportunities and threats to its potential strengths and weaknesses (see Figure 2.2).

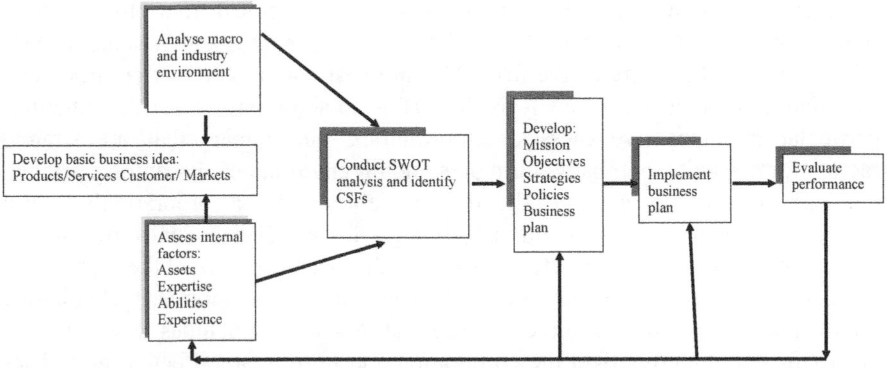

Figure 2.2 Strategy development model for new ventures

Consequently, they proposed a modified version of the strategic management model, which more closely suits the new entrepreneurial businesses and is composed of the following eight interrelated steps:

1. Develop the basic business idea, a product and/or service having target customers and/or markets. The idea can be developed from a person's experiences or generated in a moment of creative insight.
2. Scan and assess the external environment, to locate factors in the societal and task environments that pose opportunities and threats. The scanning should focus particularly on market potential and resource accessibility.
3. Scan and assess the internal factors relevant to the new business. The entrepreneur should objectively consider personal assets, areas of expertise, abilities and experience, all in terms of organizational needs for the new venture.
4. Analyse the strategic factors in light of the current situation using SWOT. The venture's potential strengths and weaknesses must be evaluated in light of opportunities and threats.
5. Decide go or no go. If the basic business idea appears to be a feasible business opportunity, the process should be continued. Otherwise further development of the idea should be cancelled unless the strategic factors change.
6. Generate a business plan specifying how the idea will be transformed into reality.
7. Implement the business plan through the use of action plans and procedures.
8. Evaluate the implemented business plan through comparison of actual performance against projected performance results. To the extent that actual results are less than or much greater than the anticipated results, the entrepreneur needs to reconsider the company's current mission, objectives, strategies, policies and programmes, and possibly make changes to the original business plan.

Environmental Scanning in SMEs

The purpose of environmental scanning is to identify strategic factors – those external (Opportunities and Threats) and internal elements (Strengths and Weaknesses) that will determine the future of the firm. The simplest way to conduct environmental scanning is through SWOT analysis. SWOT is an acronym used to describe those particular strengths, weaknesses, opportunities, and threats that are strategic factors for a specific company. In understanding environmental scanning, strategic managers must first be aware of the many variables within a corporation's external environment namely societal and task strategic forces. The societal forces include general forces that do not directly touch on the short-run activities of the organization but can influence its long-run decisions. These include economic, technological, political and socio-cultural forces. While, the task forces includes those elements or groups that directly affect the corporation and in turn, are affected by it. These are governments, local communities, suppliers, competitors, customers, creditors, employees and trade associations. A corporation's task environment is typically the industry within which that firm operates.

In contrast, the internal environment of the firm consists of variables that are within the organization itself and are not usually within the short-run control of top management. They include the corporation's structure, culture and resources. Key strengths form a set of core competencies, which the corporation can use for competitive advantage.

Previous research has identified the presence of three or four scanning stages or levels of complexity depending on the type of firms and their stage of development. Fahey, Kling and Narayanan (1981) found three types of scanning: 1) 'irregular scanning' 2) 'intermittent scanning' (partial integration of activities with objectives); and 3) 'continuous scanning' (structured opportunity-seeking). After verifying their typology with a sample of professionals and managers, these last researchers observed that the most complex scanning systems fell into the intermittent category. Similarly Jain (1984) found that, scanning practices are developed in four distinct types or phases:

1. the 'primitive phase' (no specific effort);
2. the 'situational phase' (awareness of the need to scan but no formal system introduced, or sporadic scanning);
3. the 'reactive phase' (unplanned, unstructured activities); and
4. the 'proactive phase' (rigorous, intensive practices).

Choo (1999), in his study contended that, environmental scanning includes both looking at information (viewing) and looking for information (searching). He offers four types of environmental scanning including: undirected viewing, conditioned viewing, informal search and formal search. In undirected viewing, the manager is exposed to information with no specific informational need in mind. The goal is to scan broadly in order to detect signals of forthcoming change early. Varied sources of information are used, and large amounts of information are screened. As a result, the individual becomes sensitive to selected areas or issues.

In conditioned viewing, as opposed to undirected, the individual directs viewing to selected topics or to certain types of information. The goal is to evaluate the significance of the information encountered in order to assess the general nature of the impact on the organization. The individual wishes to do this assessment in a cost-effective manner, without having to dedicate substantial time and effort in a formal search. If the impact is assessed to be sufficiently significant, the scanning mode changes from scanning to searching.

During informal search, the individual actively looks for information to deepen the knowledge and understanding of a specific issue. It is informal in that it involves a relatively limited and unstructured effort. The goal is to gather information to elaborate an issue so as to determine whether there is a need for action by the organization. If a need for a decision or response is perceived, the individual dedicates more time and resources to the search.

Finally, during formal search, the individual makes a deliberate or planned effort to obtain specific information or information about a specific issue. Search is formal because it is structured according to some pre-established procedure or methodology. The goal is to systematically retrieve information relevant to an issue in order to provide a basis for developing a decision or course of action. Formal searches could be a part of competitor intelligence gathering, patents searching, market analysis or issues of management, among other activities. Formal searches prefer information from sources that are perceived to be knowledgeable or from information services that make efforts to ensure data quality and accuracy.

In order to be effective, environmental scanning needs to engage all four modes of viewing and searching. Undirected viewing helps the organization to scan broadly and develop peripheral vision so that it can see and think 'outside the box'. Conditioned viewing tracks trends and gives the organization early warning about emerging issues. Informal search draws a profile of an issue or development, allowing the organization to identify its main features and assess its potential impact. Formal search systematically gathers all relevant information about an issue to enable intelligent decision-making (Choo, 1999).

One must also realize that SMEs do not necessarily evolve on a linear basis from stage to stage. Indeed, certain stages can be bypassed when a rapidly changing situation requires it. For instance, scanning can take on added importance and become more complex when the firm's environment becomes more uncertain or hostile, particularly when strong threats emerge (Raymond, Julien and Ramangalahy, 2001). Other factors such as the type of competitive advantage to be obtained by a firm, its level of technological development, the quality and level of education of its leaders, and its active participation in information networks (Organisation for Economic Co-operation and Development [OECD], 1993) can differentiate the type or level of scanning done by SMEs. In other words, a 'primitive' or a 'situational' scanning system can be perfectly justified if the information obtained allows the small firm to maintain or increase its competitiveness in a specific economic environment.

Recent studies have focused on environmental scanning as part of the planning processes in small and medium-sized enterprises (Larry, Fann and Nikolaisen, 1998). For instance, Larry, Fann and Nikolaisen (1998) conducted a study to investigate the environmental scanning practices and information sources of owner-managers of small firms not having planning departments. Using semi-structured interviews of 88 owner-managers in the USA, they found that, small businesses do analyse the environment prior to formulating their business strategies. They indicated that:

- most small business owner-managers who are responsible for both operational and strategic planning conduct environmental scanning regularly
- small business owners seek specialized information from magazines, while friends and family members act as personal advisers
- the owner-managers of the small businesses did not use or did not consider valuable the traditional sources of business information and advice for small businesses, such as accountants, bankers and lawyers
- owner managers perceived the business environment as stable.

Formal environmental scanning activity is emerging not only in large firms but also, as recently shown by Pollard and Hayne (1998), in SMEs. This includes SMEs' increasing use of computer-based systems (Raymond and Bergeron, 1997), even if their information and scanning practices vary depending upon the type of market and the level of competition.

In a recent enquiry in the land transport equipment industry, a majority of small firms considered their environmental scanning system, be it formal or informal, to be relatively effective, even if only a minority had at least one employee to which scanning responsibilities were formally assigned (Raymond, Julien and Ramangalahy, 2001). And while some of these firms required outside help to increase their scanning effectiveness, they did so for complex matters such as developing strategic alliances or networks in responding to international competition. Nonetheless, most studies initially assume that SMEs tend to have little scanning activity (Raymond, Julien and Ramangalahy, 2001). Another assumption is that there is 'one best way' for these firms to scan their environment, using prescriptive models usually taken from large organizations. However, these assumptions are too simplistic given that we still know too little about how SMEs, and above all their owner-managers, gather, select, interpret and analyse external information in conceiving their strategies and developing their operations. For instance, although some studies have shown the informal character of environmental scanning in small firms, in many cases scanning is a mix of informal and formal processes, depending upon the type of information sought or the urgency of the need (Raymond and Bergeron, 1997; Analoui and Karami, 2003).

Thomas, Clark and Gioia (1993) have found that, there is a positive relationship between environmental scanning and profit. Choo (1999) argues that, environmental scanning is the acquisition and use of information about events, trends and relationships in an organization's external environment, the knowledge of which would assist management in planning the organization's future course of action. Most empirical research on environmental scanning has focused on relationships between scanning behaviours (frequency, scope, sources used and interest) and environmental conditions such as environmental uncertainty, perceived threats and perceived opportunities (Sawyer, 1993; Lang, Calatone and Gudmundson, 1997). For instance Jennings and Lumpkin (1992) found support for their hypotheses that 1) firms following a differentiation strategy scanned their environments in search of opportunities; and 2) firms following a low cost strategy looked for threats to their survival. Results indicated that firms with effective scanning systems pursuing low cost leadership scanned their environments more frequently and more broadly than those firms with ineffective scanning systems pursuing the same competitive strategy. Furthermore, the findings suggest that firms employing effective scanning systems achieve alignment between strategy and environment. Niv, Jehiel and Isaac (1998) in their recent study interviewed CEOs in 46 firms with regard to the pattern of the environmental scanning they performed. The purpose of the theory is to form a fundament to organized environmental scanning.

Beal (2000), in his recent work, puts forward at least three plausible explanations for SME and their environmental scanning results. First, that the set of questions used to measure scanning frequency may lack content validity. Consequently, environmental scanning may be relatively infrequent. Relatively infrequent scanning should be reflected in low mean values in the frequency-of-scanning indexes. Thus, scanning of the environmental sectors that arguably have the most impact on firm performance and the formulation/implementation of competitive strategy occurs relatively infrequently. This finding provides the most plausible explanation for the non-significant relationships found between frequency of scanning and external alignment. Third, the frequency at which CEOs of SMEs scan their environments may not be critical to aligning their firms' competitive strategies with the stage of the industry life cycle in which the firms compete. Other factors such as scope of scanning, accurate assessment of opportunities and threats, and effective use of competitive information may be the key.

Finally, it has been argued (Berry, 1998) that, the entrepreneurs' strategic awareness and their perception of the benefits arising from environmental scanning within the SMEs will be a significant determinant of the success and survival of the SME in the long term (Berry, 1998).

Developing a Meaningful Mission Statement

It is commonly believed that, 'if you don't know where you are going, any road can take you there' (Collis and Montgomery, 1997). A clear vision defines the rules for acting incrementally and opportunistically. If a business is going to be successful today, creating a vision is a necessity, not a luxury – because no organization can progress without an understanding of where it is going and what it should be trying to achieve (Kakabadse, 2001). It is better to distinguish the term vision from mission. Some people like to consider vision and mission as two different concepts: a mission statement describes what the organization is now; a vision statement describes what the organization would like to become (Campbell and Yeung, 1991).

In answer to the question, what is vision? Kakabadse (2001) explains that, in management terms, the word visioning is used to describe an agreement among directors about the future of their organization. It requires access to all relevant information, such as the present state of the company and its values. Everyone has some idea of where they are going and what they want to achieve, but their vision is often outdated, shortsighted or too long term. And when people have different visions there is dispute. A manager facing an unexpected situation can take a decision after asking himself or herself the question 'will such an action further the company's vision?' Vision statements often embody the core values of the founding entrepreneur, and say something about the inspiration behind the company that would not be obvious from a reading of its business plans (Bowman and Kakabadse, 1997).

Strategic vision occurs where all acquisitions begin. Management vision of the acquisition is shared with suppliers, customers, lenders, and employees as a framework for planning, discussion, decisions and reactions to change (Sirower, 1997). Sirower also contends that the vision must be clear to large constituent groups and adaptable to many unknown circumstances.

In addition, the vision must be a continuous guide to the actual operating plans of the company. If vision does not translate into real actions, it can provoke damaging reactions from competitors (Wit and Meyer, 1998). Bowman and Faulkner indicated that 'a vision is an image of a better future, however defined; it is a state to which the company aspires, and therefore can at least logically be achieved. What happens when Komatsu succeed in encircling Caterpillar? Clearly a new vision needs to be adapted if the company is not to sink beneath the competitive waves, enthusiastically telling stories of past triumphs. For an ongoing sense of purpose a mission statement is needed' (Bowman and Kakabadse, 1997, 181).

The literature on mission statements in large firms and SMEs is both descriptive (Ackoff, 1987; Peters, 1988; Falsey, 1989; Campbell, Devine and Young, 1990; Pearce and Robinson, 1994) and prescriptive (Want, 1986; Pearce and David, 1987). Perhaps the research carried out by Pearce and David (1987) formed the first attempt to study empirically the relationship between mission statement and organizational performance in 500 SMEs. It was discovered that, higher performance firms tend to have comparatively more comprehensive mission statements. It has been posed that; a good mission statement captures an organization's unique and enduring reason for being, and energizes stakeholders to pursue common goals (Rarick and Vitton, 1995; Bart, 1998). It also enables a focused allocation of organizational resources. Accordingly, we have witnessed some empirical researches in the fields of definition and analysis of mission statements content in either large firms or small and medium-sized enterprises (Campbell et al., 1990; Bart, 1998). For instance, Bart (1998) introduced the content of a good mission statement, based on the results of his research, as the following:

- purpose, values/philosophy, vision, general corporate goal, and one big goal,
- distinctive competence, desired competitive position and competitive strategy
- mention stakeholders and behavioural standard
- general business definition, specific financial objectives and non financial objectives
- Specific market/customers served and specific product/service offered
- self concept, desired public image
- location of business, technology defined
- concern for survival, customers, employees, suppliers, shareholders and society.

There is ample evidence from the literature that the benefits which organizations derive from mission statements address many of the organizational and leadership problems that characterize growing SMEs (Analoui and Karami, 2003). A mission statement allows the firm to articulate a strong vision for the organization and to communicate it to its growing number of employees and professional managers (Klemm, Sanderson and Luffman, 1991). The mission statement can also increase the firm's legitimacy with new stakeholders such as financial institutions and shareholders. The detailed literature and comparative analysis of the mission statements in SMEs is provided in the conceptual framework of the research (Kakabadse, 2001).

In light of their mission, entrepreneurs develop the objectives and goals for their business. Objectives are the end result of planned activity. Business objectives convert the mission statement into specific goals that shape the direction and activities of the business (Lowry, Avila and Baird, 1999). If the vision describes what the corporation wishes to become in many years' time, an effective corporate strategy must also have a set of shorter-term goals and objectives so as to sustain a 40 per cent equity ratio. Objectives refer to specific short and medium-term quantitative targets. On the other hand, goals refer to qualitative intentions such as to improve new product development capabilities or becoming a global organization (Collis and Montgomery, 1997).

The process of setting objectives for the corporation, Bowman and Kakabadse (1997) have argued, and subsequently for the business unit, is the process of translating the corporation's strategies into specific and, if possible, measurable objectives, the achievement of which will signal that the corporation's adapted strategies are working successfully. They argued that objectives are frequently, but not always, financial. They need not even be measurable, but obviously it helps the monitoring process if they are measurable. As discussed, there are typical objectives that a corporation might set for itself in order to provide behavioural signposts regarding the implementation of strategy. Therefore, to be of worth to an *SME*, objectives should be measurable, achievable, realistic, explicit, internally consistent with each other, and communicable to others (Luffman et al., 1991).

Developing Business Strategies for SMEs

As discussed, the strategy of a corporation forms a comprehensive master plan stating how the corporation will achieve its mission and objectives. It maximizes competitive advantages and at the same time, minimizes competitive disadvantages (Wheelen and Hunger, 1998). The typical business firm usually considers three linked and interdependent levels of strategy consisting of corporate strategy, business strategy and functional strategy. Corporate strategy, essentially and simply is deciding what businesses the organization should be in, and how the overall group of activities should be structured and managed (Thompson, 1995). The second level of strategy is business strategy, which is concerned with creating and maintaining a competitive advantage in each and every area of the business. It can be achieved through any one function, or a combination of several (Thompson, 1995). Accordingly, the third level of strategy is functional strategy. Functional strategy is concerned with functional areas of the firm such as, marketing, financial, human resource, and research and development. Developing business strategies is discussed below.

Specialization and Diversification

When a firm diversifies, it moves out of its current products and markets into a new area. Clearly, this will involve a step into the unknown and will carry a higher degree of business risks (Lynch, 2000). However the firm may minimize this risk if it moves into related markets (see Figure 2.3).

Accordingly, when a firm moves to unrelated markets, it runs the risk of operating in areas where its detailed knowledge of the key factors for success is limited. Specialization and diversification have been central topics in strategy studies

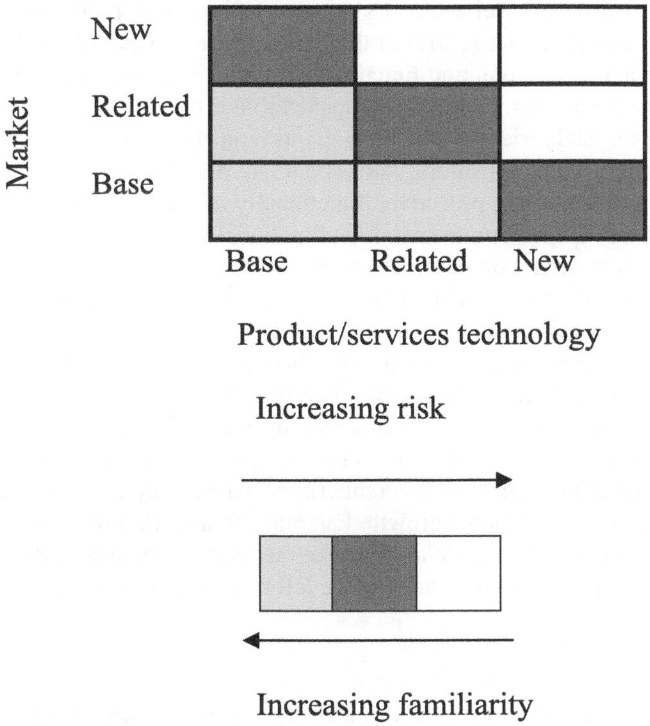

Figure 2.3 The product market matrix

(Ramanujam and Varadarjan, 1989; Hoskisson and Hitt, 1994). Specialization and diversification are two fundamental strategies at corporate level and describe the diversity of the activities of the firm. Very often diversification and specialization are defined by the diversity of the product, and industries or strategic business units (SBU) the firm is in.

The importance of diversification is clearly related to its widespread adoption in many firms in market economies (Hitt, Hoskisson and Kim, 1997). Different studies of the diversification of SMEs reach the conclusion that the strategic situation of SMEs is characterized by a number of related products or product groups rather than by several discrete businesses. Many scholars tried to study the link between diversification and other organizational factors. For instance, theoretical explanations linking diversification and performance stem mainly from efficiency gains due to economies of scale and scope (Chandler, 1990), learning and domain redefining (Mintzberg, 1987); risk reduction (Chandler, 1962) and top managers' strategic leadership abilities (Ohmae, 1982).

The large body of literature in this field provides important insights into the motivation for diversification and its subsequent performance consequences (Ramanujam and Varadarjan, 1989; Datta, Rajagopalan and Rasheed, 1991; Hoskisson and Hitt, 1994). The results of other studies of diversification in SMEs (Bamberger, 1998) show that, diversification is a basic for growth in SMEs. It also has been found that, rising firm size is related to rising diversification of related product groups. Bagchi-Sen and Kuechler (2000) in their recent research examined the association between strategic planning and functional diversification (services and markets) in SMEs. They found that, SMEs face considerable difficulty in overcoming both in-house and external barriers in accessing clients requiring non-traditional services (for example management consulting) and clients involved in international businesses. They reported that, the proactive, functionally diversified, and/or international orientated firms outperform the reactive, functionally concentrated and local market orientated firms. The competitive advantage for the former categories is based on flexible specialization such as customization of services for specific groups of clients, speed of delivery and specialized skills.

Another study of diversification in the banking industry in Europe (Bamberger, 1998) found a significant relation between intended diversification and the bank's size, the CEO perception of competitive intensity and changing market preferences, and the bank's past variability in profitability. Finally, developing a market niche by differentiating a business from its competitors is a strategy that offers smaller firms a better chance of sustainable growth. Establishing a market niche is most effective when aimed at a narrowly defined market segment. Sometimes this can involve concentrating on gaps in the market place left by the larger companies.

Internationalization

Internationalization means that, a firm is acting in one or several foreign markets and thus, is working in an international context. For SMEs, it is a component of growing importance in their strategic behaviour and therefore all three proposed levels of strategies must be considered. Here, only internationalization strategies at the level of corporate strategy will be dealt with. These are concerned with the choice of foreign target markets, product or services to offer in the chosen foreign markets and the market entry strategies. Market entry strategies in the international field concern export, licensing and management contracts, as well as the establishment of sales or production subsidiaries. Forms and phases of internationalization for SMEs are illustrated in Figure 2.4. With respect to SMEs export is mostly discussed. Market entry strategies are also concerned with internal development (development of resources, potentials within the firm) versus acquisition (buying of companies and merger) strategies and different owner strategies.

As far as ownership strategies are concerned, the use of joint ventures is of particular interest. Despite the importance of exporting for SMEs, it is only one element and very often only the first step in the internationalization process. The process includes in addition to indirect or direct exportation, the creation of distribution agencies in the foreign countries, the creation of own production facilities abroad, different production strategies, as well as organizational strategies and internationalization of management and capital. The strategies and the level of internationalization should also be studied in relation to the entrepreneurial motivations, values, attitudes and objectives of the SME manager. For instance in a study of the internationalization plans of Swiss SMEs (Bamberger, 1998), with the prospect of the Western European economic integration, it has been found that, most of the companies planned to push

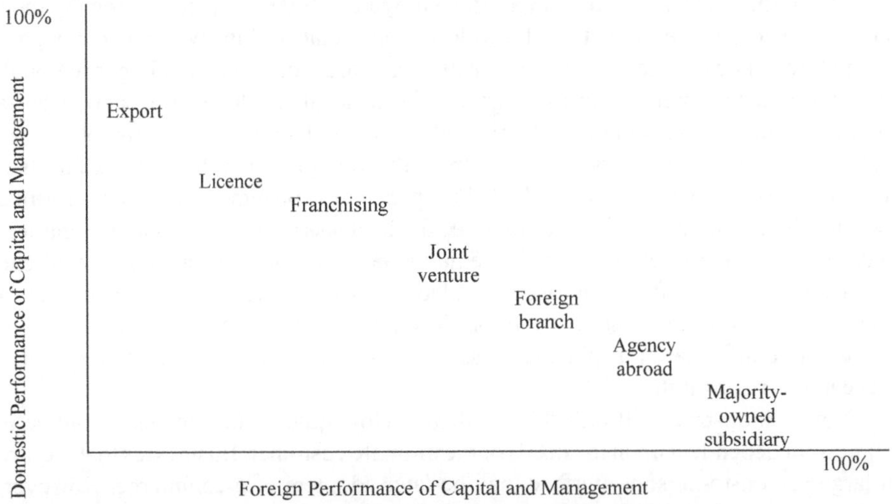

Figure 2.4 Phases and forms of internationalization for SMEs

their exports to the EC and only a few planned to establish production facilities abroad.

Competitive Strategies for SMEs

The first fundamental determination of a firm's profitability is industry attractiveness. In any industry, whether it is domestic or international, or produces a product or services, the role of the competition is embodied in five competitive forces: the entry of new competitors, the threats of substitutes, the bargaining power of buyers, the bargaining power of suppliers and the rivalry among the existing competitors (Porter, 1985). The collective strength of these five competitive forces determines the ability of firms in any industry to earn, on average, rates of return on investment in excess of the cost of capital. The strength of the five forces varies from industry to industry, and can change as an industry evolves. The five forces determine industry profitability, because they influence the price, costs, and the required investment of the firm in an industry. The strength of each of the five competitive forces is a function of industry structure (Porter, 1985).

The five-force framework allows the firm to see through the complexity and pinpoint those factors that are critical to competition in its industry as well as identify those strategic innovations that would most improve the industry's profitability. It directs manager's creative energies toward those aspects of industry structure that are most important to long-run profitability. Finally, the framework aims in the process, to raise the odds of discovering a desirable strategic innovation (Wit and Meyer, 1998). The five-force model has recently been used to analyse the industry structure in SMEs (Kleindl, 2000).

The traditional barriers to competition enjoyed by SMEs, created largely by their ability to serve niche markets and develop strong relationships with customers, are being threatened by Internet enabled businesses. Threat of entry from larger regional, national and international firms is greater because of the lower transaction costs involved when entering markets dominated by SMEs. These new entrants sometimes represent industries quite far removed from those with which the SME is familiar. For first movers with an established Web presence, consumers may have formed relationships with that business or may see the business as the brand name. Suppliers have an incentive to eliminate intermediaries because of the cost savings that can be incurred. This pattern has been enabled because of Web based efficiencies in both information flows and distribution flows. The easy access that buyers have to competitive information is placing pressure on prices and is encouraging customers to search for substitutes.

Not all industries will face this challenge. How quickly businesses go online is somewhat dependent upon the needs of the ultimate customer. Businesses that require a large person-to-person interface may be later adopters of e-commerce. However, online communication through email and Web pages, developing Extranet links to suppliers, and changing internal communication systems are having an impact on almost all businesses.

Competition is at the core of the success or failure of the business. As Porter has discussed, competition determines the appropriateness of a firm's activities that can contribute to its performance, such as innovations, a cohesive culture, or good implementation. Competitive strategy is the search for a favourable competitive position in an industry, the fundamental arena in which competition occurs (Porter, 1985).

The business side of the corporate strategy framework refers to the industries in which a firm operates, as well as to the competitive strategy it adopts in each. Industry choice is critical to the long-term success of a corporate strategy. It has repeatedly been demonstrated that the best predictor of firm performance is the profitability of the industries in which it competes (Rumelt, 1991). A set of industries in which a firm operates also influences the extent to which it will be able to share resources across its business. The notion of relatedness may be used as a surrogate for a firm's ability to create synergy among its business.

The particular competitive strategy a firm pursues in each industry also has an impact on corporate performance. While it may be unusual to find a corporation that pursues exactly the same source of competitive advantage in every one of its businesses, it is important to recognize that a corporation's resources are often only valuable when applied to similar generic strategies (Collis and Montgomery, 1997).

To understand how to achieve competitive advantage and how to generalize about the relative position of individual firms within an industry, Porter (1985) developed the concept of generic strategies, categories of strategy that follow a particular pattern. There are two basic types of competitive advantage, which the firm can process: low cost or differentiation (Porter, 1985). The two basic types of competitive advantages combined with the scope of activities that a firm seeks to achieve, lead to three generic strategies for achieving an average performance in an industry: cost leadership, differentiation and focus. The focus strategy has two variants; cost focus and differentiation focus (see Figure 2.5).

Porter has suggested that each of the generic strategies involves a fundamentally different route to competitive advantage, combining a choice about the type of competitive advantage sought with the scope of the strategic target in which competitive advantage is to be achieved (Porter, 1985). The cost leadership and differentiation strategies seek competitive advantage in a broad range of industry segments, while focus strategies vary widely from industry to industry, as do the feasible generic strategies in a particular industry.

Competitive advantage is argued by Wit and Meyer (1998) as being at the heart of any strategy, and achieving competitive advantage requires a firm to make a choice about the type of competitive advantage it seeks to attain and the scope within which it will attain it. It is also reported that the idea of generic strategies emphasizes the consistency of a firm's activities and the need to tie each to the firm's overall mission. This stresses the importance of not getting stuck in the middle and ultimately failing to build a distinctive competence that creates a competitive advantage (Collis and Montgomery, 1997).

Developing an effective competitive strategy is vital for small and medium-sized enterprises. Burns and Harrison (1996) considered a number of generic strategies, whilst Porter (1985) contends that, there are only three fundamental ways of achieving sustainable competitive advantages.

Cost leadership This assumes that, costs can be reduced, for example through economics of scale and this is important to customers. This is an inherently unattractive alternative for smaller firms as they can rarely achieve the economics of scale of large firms and seldom have the capital to invest constantly in new technology.

Differentiation Where the firm sets out to be unique in the industry along some dimensions that are widely valued by customers. This is called developing a unique

	Competitive Advantage	
Competitive Scope	Cost leadership (not attractive) NA	Differentiation (attractive) A
	Cost focus (possibly attractive) PA	Differentiation focus (very attractive) VA

NA: Not Attractive
PA: Possibly Attractive
A: Attractive
VA: Very Attractice

Figure 2.5 Generic competitive strategies and their attraction to SMEs

selling proposition (USP). The firm sets out to establish itself as unique and different from its competitors in some ways. It can then charge a premium price. The risks associated with this are that the differentiation cannot be sustained as competitors imitate or the USP becomes less important to customers. If the premium charged is too high, customers may decide not to purchase. This is an attractive strategy for smaller firms, particularly when combined with the third generic strategy.

Focus Where the firm focuses on a narrow target market segment combined with either of the other strategies. If the firm adopts a strategy of focused differentiation it is said to pursue a niche strategy. This is a very attractive strategy for SMEs. Focuses can also be used with cost leadership, where concentrating on certain market segments offers some cost advantages.

In a survey of some 1500 smaller companies across Europe, Burns and Harrison (1996) reported that, those companies that had seen their sales and/or profit grow in the 1990s, were those that had better or different products or services, and this led to weak-to-normal levels of competition. Another survey into 3,500 of Britain's 'Supper League Companies' concluded that most of these high growth companies served niche markets. In other words, successful firms follow a strategy of differentiation, probably focused on target market segments.

Electronic Commerce (EC) and SME Business Strategies

The strategic management of technological innovation and IT are lively, contemporary topics within rapidly changing business environments with frequent technological change and globalized competition. Small and medium-size firms face special problems in the formulation of their strategies due to their deficiencies arising from their limited resources and range of technological competencies.

The Internet and the World Wide Web (WWW) are having a major impact on how businesses operate. The Web allows customers to easily search and find competitive information and new sources of supply. Internet Protocols (IP) are allowing for close contact between firms by linking companies and supply-chains through Extranets. As the Internet Technology (IT) revolution continues to expand, cellular phones will act as convenient links to information and ordering. Moving into e-commerce may require a major change in the commerce models that businesses use. Not surprisingly, many businesses are waiting to see if these virtual marketing commerce models are viable because of the transaction costs involved in developing online businesses. They may find that they do so at their own peril.

Electronic commerce has been defined from different perspectives. From a communications perspective: EC is the delivery of information, products/services, or payment over telephone lines, computer networks, or any other electronic means. From a business process perspective: EC is the application of technology towards the automation of business transactions and work flow. From an online perspective: EC provides the capability of buying and selling products and information on the Internet and other online services (Turban et al., 2000). The notable types of ECs are as follow.

- Business-to-Business (B2B): most of EC today is of this type. It includes information flow among two or more organizations.
- Business-to-Consumer (B2C): these are retailing transactions with individual shoppers. The typical shopper at Amazon.com is a consumer.
- Consumer-to-consumer (C2C): in this category consumer sells directly to consumers. Examples are individuals selling in classified ads and selling residential property, cars and advertising personal services on the Internet and selling knowledge and expertise.
- Consumer-to-business (C2B): this category includes individuals who sell products or services to organizations, as well as individuals who seek sellers, interact with them and conclude a transaction.
- Non-business EC: An increased number of non-business institutions such as academic institutions, not-for-profit organizations, religious organizations, social organizations and government agencies are using various types of EC to reduce their expenses or to improve their operations and customer services.
- Intra-business (organizational) EC: this category includes all internal organizational activities, usually performed in intranet, that involve exchange of goods, services or information.

Regarding the benefits of EC to the organizations, EC expands the marketplace to national and international markets and decreases the cost of creating, processing, distributing, storing and retrieving paper-based information. It allows reduced inventories and reduces telecommunication costs, and the time between the outlay of capital and the receipt of product and services (Komenar, 1997; Turban et al., 2000).

Electronic commerce has more benefits to consumers. It enables customers to shop or carry out other transactions 24 h a day, all year round, from almost any location. It provides the customer with more choices; they can select from any vendor and from more products and with less expensive products and services by allowing them to shop in many places and conduct quick comparisons. It allows quick delivery and customers can receive relevant and detailed information in seconds, rather than days or weeks. EC also makes it possible to participate in virtual auctions. It allows customers to interact with other customers in electronic communities and exchange ideas as well as compare experiences and finally; it facilitates competition, which results in substantial discount (Adam and Yesha, 1996).

Market economics, technological and societal pressures force organizations to respond. Traditional responses may not be sufficient due to the magnitude of the pressures and the frequent changes involved (Turban et al., 2000). Therefore, organizations frequently must use innovations and reengineering of their operations. In many cases, EC is the major facilitator of organizational responses. While SMEs typically do not have the capital and human resources of larger competitors, many appear to be making significant investments in information technology. Companies with 500 or fewer employees spent over $200 billion on technology products and services in 1998, over five times as much spent by larger companies (Caldwell and Wilde, 1998; Wilde, 1998).

SMEs are developing websites, Intranets and using email at close to the same percentages as larger businesses. However, they have been slower to adopt e-commerce applications (Wilder, 1999). This hesitancy could be due to the high cost of setting up and maintaining e-commerce applications. A viable option for SME e-commerce is to outsource to third party companies (De Soto, 1998). Table 2.3 summarizes findings from a survey of over 400 information technology managers worldwide (Engler, 1999).

Major technology strategies are recommended for SMEs attempting to compete in the contemporary global environment. Relative to larger firms, smaller businesses who make effective use of Internet opportunities may also find that they can be more innovative, faster in responding to environmental demands and better able to quickly change or adapt business models to gain competitive advantage. Using IT in order to improve customer services through online systems can be considered as a new strategy for SMEs. Online systems allow channel members and consumers to gain access to product and inventory information. Globalization and internationalization push SMEs to use electronic commerce. Electronic commerce allows SMEs access to larger markets without the cost of setting up new distribution systems. It also allows SMEs to target narrow markets faster than larger competitors. Lower overhead costs can be carried over to lower prices to customers.

Online connections between the SME and its customers increase the speed of response and allow for close to instant communication. Linked extranets allow SMEs

Table 2.3 Strategies used by SMEs

Strategy	*Advantages*
Improved customer services POR: 80%	Online system allows channel members and consumers to gain access to product and inventory information.
Electronic commerce POR: 60%	This allows SMEs access to larger markets without the cost of setting up new distribution systems. It also allow SMEs to target narrow markets faster than larger competitors. Lower overhead costs can be carried over to lower prices to customers.
Customer relationship management application POR: 50%	Online connections between the SME and its customers increase the speed of response and allow for close to instant communication. Linked extranets allow SMEs to act as virtual partners with other businesses.
Increased business to business connections (extranets) POR: 40%	SMEs can act as a virtual making intermediary linking larger businesses with very small suppliers. Online access to inventory and suppliers helps control access.

POR: Percent of Respondents
Adapted from Kleindl, 2000.

to act as virtual partners with other businesses. Increased business to business (B2B) connection has been considered as another strategy for SMEs (Engler, 1999). SMEs can act as a virtual intermediary linking larger businesses with very small suppliers. Online access to inventory and suppliers helps to control access.

In summary, SMEs are facing constant change in their competitive environment that will force them to modify or completely abandon many current business practices. They must consider new business models that take advantage of existing and emerging Internet-based technologies in order to stay competitive. Their willingness to adopt new technologies is also likely to influence their ability to hire and retain new talent. While internal development may not be feasible for many resource-poor SMEs, the use of IT can provide SMEs with the ability to compete.

Strategy implementation in SME

The third aspect of strategic management in SME is implementation and control of strategy (Oladeji, 1998; Voss, 1998; Noble, 1999). It has been argued that, well – formulated strategies only produce superior performance for the firm when they are successfully implemented (Robinson and Pearce, 1984; Noble, 1999). The implementation of business strategy has been the subject of increased study and search for solutions, especially since the process from strategy formulation to strategy implementation is not efficient and is, certainly in the present business environment, inadequate (Hauc and Kovac, 2000). Kalai and Ledyard (1998) compared traditional and new paradigm of strategy implementation in the organizations. They stated that, in the case of traditional static implementation it is often impossible for strategists to enforce their optimal outcomes. And when restricting the choice to dominant-strategy implementation, only the dictatorial choices of one of the participants are implementable (Kalai and Ledyard, 1998). Recently, the strategy implementation in SMEs is considered as a dynamic activity within strategic management process. For instance, Wheelen and Hunger (1998) consider strategy implementation as a process, which might involve changes within the overall culture, structure, and/or, management system of the entire organization. Grundy (1998) in his work investigated the strategy implementation in project management. He concluded that, a number of tools from strategic management, value management and from organizational change can be imported into project management to enrich traditional techniques considerably. These tools are particularly powerful when applied to complex and multi-functional projects which are entailed when attempting to turn business strategy into implementation. A review of literature reveals few formal definitions of strategy implementation. Some of the different views of strategy implementation are as follow:

- Implementation is a series of interventions concerning organizational structure, key personal actions, and control systems designed to control performance with respect to desired ends (Hrebiniak and Joyce, 1984).
- The implementation stage involves converting strategic alternatives into an operating plan (Aaker, 1988).

- Implementation refers to the 'how-to-do-it' aspects of marketing. Implementation deals organizational issues, with the development of specific marketing programs, and with the execution of programs in the field (Cespedes, 1991).
- Implementation is the managerial interventions that align organizational action with strategic intention (Floyd and Woolridge, 1992).
- Strategy implementation is the process by which strategies and policies are put into action through the development of programs, budgets, and procedures (Wheelen and Hunger, 1998).

The literature shows that, many scholars highlighted three main factors in strategy implementation mainly the structure, leadership style, and resources (Hrebiniak and Joyce, 1984; Lorange, 1998; Noble, 1999; Hauc and Kovac, 2000).

Organizational structure

Formulating strategy is very difficult, but the more problematic task confronting the CEOs in small and medium-sized enterprises (*SME*) is the successful implementation of strategy (Miller, 1988). To implement strategy successfully, attention must be paid to a number of organizational issues, especially organizational structure (Miller, 1988; Hrebiniak, 1990). The CEO must be concerned with a number of areas that are important for strategy implementation in SME, such as carefully considering the role of structure, and exercising appropriate leadership. Although, extensive research has examined the relationship between strategy formulation and organizational structure, only limited attention has been given to the contingency between organizational structure and implementation process (for example Porter, 1980; Smith and Fleck, 1987; Berry, 1998; Noble, 1999). Given the earlier arguments, it is expected that performance in small and medium-sized firms is correlated with the use of structural features that, must support the strategy (Miller and Toulouse, 1986; Miller, 1988). Goldsmith (1995) indicated that, implementing strategy is critical. It has two main aspects, one formal, and the other informal: they are organizational structure and organizational culture. For instance, Gupta (1987) examined the relationship between SBUs' strategies, aspects of the corporate-SBU relationship, and implementation and found that, structures that are more decentralized produce higher level of SBU effectiveness, regardless of the strategic context. Drazin and Howard (1984) suggest that, a proper strategy-structure alignment is a necessary precursor to the successful implementation of new business strategies.

Leadership style

The leadership style of the senior managers including CEOs can have a significant effect on implementation of strategy. Nutt (1983) considers the link between the organizational climate and various approaches to implementation. In this view, the management of the implementation process generally requires a driving force in the organization in order to succeed. Another aspect of implementation style considered by Nutt (1986) is the base of power used in the implementation process. The power base employed is closely tied to the technique used to guide implementation. He suggests that, managerial tactics and leadership style can play a critical role in overcoming the lower-level obstructionism that is prevalent to some extent in many implementation efforts. Gupta and Govindarajan (1984) address the relationship between the characteristics of an SBU's general manager and the perceptions of effectiveness in strategy implementation. The result of this research show that successful SBUs should have general managers with greater marketing/sale experiences, greater willingness to take risk, and greater tolerance for ambiguity. Best (1997) highlights three major forces that affect the successful implementation of strategic marketing plans:

1. ownership of the plan,
2. supporting the plan, and
3. adaptive planning.

Ownership becomes more complex in team-orientated implementation, but ownership also enhances the process by leveraging the unique talents of team members. In this regard the role of owner/managers or entrepreneurs in SMEs can not be ignored. Noble (1999) argued that, senior management can alleviate problems that result when groups of individuals interact to implement corporate strategy. Through an understanding of the fundamental stages and elements of an implementation effort, they can build an effective cross-functional implementation network (Noble, 1999). Parsa (1999) investigated, the impact of source of power on franchisees' strategy implementation process and eventual performance. Results from the study indicate that financial performance of the franchisees was affected by the method of implementation they chose. This study demonstrates that interaction of power sources and strategy implementation could impact a firm's performance and satisfaction. The results demonstrate that a proper match between the implementation methods and the desired outcomes is essential. Congruence between the sources of power and implementation and its effect on eventual performance was documented (Parsa, 1999).

Human Resources

It has been discussed that (Analoui, 2000; Rousseau and Rousseau, 2000) successful strategy realization is determined by the coherence of decisions and actions of all employees at all levels of the organization, and not just by the people who originally defined the strategy. This is also the reason why efficient and effective communication of an SME's strategy, for example, to all people within the organization is fundamental. Rousseau and Rousseau (2000) reported that, in a recent survey conducted in association with Robert Kaplan of the Harvard Business School and Business Intelligence, more than 40 per cent of senior managers and more than 90 per cent of all employees stated they did not believe they had a clear understanding of their company's strategy. In too many cases, when looking at the 'big picture,' if all decisions made throughout an organization are consolidated, it becomes clear that those decisions are often inconsistent in their objectives, or may even have conflicting objectives (Fulmer, 1990; Bowman and Kakabadse, 1997). To ensure that strategy is realized at all levels of the organization, a mechanism is necessary to direct all employees towards the same strategic performance management. In recent years, there has been a growing awareness that human resource management (HRM) is a factor that can, or at least should, play an important role in the development and implementation of effective strategic plans in SMEs (Fulmer, 1990; Beer, 1997; Boxall and Steeneveld, 1999). It is in strategy implementation that HRM may be able to play its most significant role. In this regard, the SMEs' senior managers would view human resources activities as equal to finance, operations and marketing. The firm's HRM would be involved from the outset in developing and implementing strategic plans. Both technical (task-related) and managerial skills (people and self-related) are necessary to formulate and implement strategic planning (Fulmer, 1990). The review of the literature in Chapters 2 also indicates that, most researchers (Bennett, Ketchen and Schultz, 1995; Boxall, 1996) seem to have emphasized on HR as a factor in determining the effective implementation of strategies in the firms. Generally, the business strategies were successfully implemented when, top managers viewed employees as the strategic resources.

Strategy Evaluation and Control

Evaluation and control is the process by which corporate activities and performance results are monitored so that actual performance can be compared with desired performance. Senior managers of SMEs use the resulting information to take corrective action and resolve problems. Although evaluation and control are the final major element of strategic management, they also can pinpoint weakness in previously implemented strategic plans and thus stimulate the entire process to be again. For evaluation and control to be effective, managers must obtain clear, prompt, and unbiased information from the people below them in the *SME*'s hierarchy (Wheelen and Hunger, 1998). It has been argued that, employing control system by SMEs managers depends on their awareness of strategy (Lorange, 1998). For instance, Emotional Intelligence (EI) testing done on a group of SME owner-managers showed clearly that owner/mangers with low EI held back their company's growth by trying to hold onto total control. It was found that they tended to have high independence, low trust, low empathy high aggression scores, and also tended to have extremely high stress levels. Managers who let their people take responsibility and did not hold onto control had high score on consideration for others, tolerance and sociability. They were also much less stressed than the other owner managers-and they had profitable, booming companies (Lorange, 1998). The evaluation and control of performance completes the strategic management model. Based on performance results, management may need to make adjustments in strategy formulation, in implementation, or in both.

Summary and Conclusion

Research into strategy formulation has come a long way since the early work in the 1960s. Nevertheless, many of the earlier concepts are still valid today and still their reflections can be seen in the assumptions employed by contemporary researchers. While earlier work, by and large, was directed at identifying reasons for superior performance, the focus later shifted towards the processes involved in formulating and the search for sources of competitive advantage in small and medium-sized enterprises.

With the increasing level of dynamics in the competitive environments, researchers have realized the need for adopting a dynamic approach to strategy formulation in entrepreneurial firms. However, there is no integrated framework with which dynamic strategy formulation and implementation can be realized. In this chapter a realistic strategic management process in entrepreneurial firms has been put forward. It is posed that the first step in strategic management for entrepreneurial firms is environmental scanning. Most small business owner-managers who are responsible for both operational and strategic planning conduct environmental scanning regularly. The literature suggests three types of scanning. These include; irregular scanning, intermittent scanning, and continuous scanning.

There is ample support for the view that firms with effective scanning systems pursuing low cost leadership scanned their environments more frequently and more broadly than those firms with ineffective scanning systems pursuing the same competitive strategy. The second aspect is the formulation of strategies. The typical business firm usually considers three linked and interdependent levels of strategy consisting of corporate strategy, business strategy and functional strategy. The corporate strategy of a firm determines its different product/market combinations. By corporate strategy the firm defines the scope of its activities.

Business strategy is concerned with creating and maintaining a competitive advantage in each and every area of the business. The firm's strategy at the functional level, include R&D, marketing, HR, financial, technology, production and operation strategies. Developing an effective competitive strategy is vital for small and medium-sized enterprises. Competitive strategy is the search for a favourable competitive position in an industry, the fundamental arena in which competition occurs. The particular competitive strategy a firm pursues in each industry also has an impact on corporate performance. Increased business-to-business (B2B) connection and using IT have been considered as an important strategy for entrepreneurial firms.

Finally the third aspect of strategy in entrepreneurial SMEs is strategy implementation and control. Implementation is the managerial interventions that align organizational action with strategic intention. Strategy implementation is the process by which strategies and policies are put into action through the development of programs, budgets, and procedures. In this research three factors associated with effective strategy implementation including leadership, organizational structure, and human resources are considered.

References

Aaker, D.A. (1988)*Strategic Market Management*, 2nd, ed., New York: Wiley and Sons.

Ackoff, R.L. (1987), 'Mission Statements', *Planning Review*, **15**(4), 30–31.

Adam, N. and Yesha, Y. (1996), *Electronic Commerce: Current Research Issues and Implications* (New York: Springer).

Aguilar, F.J. (1967), *Scanning the Business Environment* (New York: John Wiley & Sons).

Analoui, F. and Karami, A. (2003), *Strategic Management in Small and Medium Enterprises* (London: Thomson).

Analoui, F. (2000), 'What Motivates Senior Managers?' 'The Case of Romania', *Journal of Managerial Psychology*, **15**(4), 324–326.

Andrews, K. (1971), *The Concept of Corporate Strategy* (Homewood, Ill.: Irwin).

Ansoff, H.I. (1965), *Corporate Strategy* (New York: McGraw-Hill).

Bagchi-Sen, S. and Kuechler, L. (2000), 'Strategic and Functional Orientation of Small And Medium-Sized Enterprises in Professional Services: An Analysis of Public Accountancy', *The Service Industries Journal*, **20**(3), 117–146.

Bamberger, I. (eds) (1998) *Product Market Strategies of Small and Medium Sized* Enterprises (Asldershot, UK: Ashgate Publishing Limited).

Bart, C.K. (1998), 'A Comparison of Mission Statements and their Rational in Innovative and Non-Innovative Firms', *International Technology Management Journal*, **16**(1) 3, 64–77.

Beal, R.M. (2000), 'Competing Effectively: Environmental Scanning, Competitive Strategy, and Organisational Performance in Small Manufacturing Firms', *Journal of Small Business Management*, **38**(1), 27–47.

Beer, M. (1997), 'The Transformation of Human Resource Function: Resolving the Tension Between a Traditional Administrative and a New Strategic Role', *Human Resource Management*, **36**(1), 49–56.

Bennett, N., Ketchen, D.J., Jr and Schultz, E.B. (1995), 'An Examination of Factors Associated with the Integration of Human Resource Management and Strategic Decision Making', *Human Resource Management*, **37**(1), 3–16.

Berry, M. (1998), 'Strategic Planning in Small High Tech Companies', *Long Range Planning*, **31**(3), 455–466.

Best, R.J. (1997), *Market-based Management* (Upper Saddle River, N.J.: Prentice-Hall).

Bhide, A. (1994), How Entrepreneurs Craft Strategies that Work, *Harward Business Review*, March/April, 150–161.

Bourgeois, L.J. and Brodwin, D.R. (1984), 'Strategic Implementation: Five Approaches to an Elusive Phenomenon', *Strategic Management Journal*, **25**, 241–264.

Boussouara, M. and Deakins, D. (1999), 'Market-based Learning, Entrepreneurship, and the High Technology Firm', *International Journal of Entrepreneurial Behaviour and Research*, **5**(4), 204–223.

Bouwen, R. and Steyaert, C. (1990), 'Construing Organisational Texture in Young Entrepreneurial Firms', *Journal of Management Studies*, **27**(6), 637–649.

Bowman, C. and Fauikner, D. (1997), *Competitive Corporate Strategy* (London: Irwin).

Bowman, C. and Kakabadse, A. (1997), 'Top Management Ownership of the Strategy Problem', *Long Range Planning*, **30**(2), 197–208.

Boxall, P. (1996), 'The Strategic HRM Debate and the Resource-Based View of the Firm', *Human Resource Management Journal*, **6**(3), 59–75.

Boxall, P. and Steeneveld, M. (1999), 'Human Resource Strategy and Competitive Advantage: A Longitudinal Study of Engineering Consultancies', *Journal of Management Studies*, **36**(4), 443–463.

Boyd, B.K. and Reuning-Elliott, E. (1998), 'A Measurement Model of Strategic Planning', *Strategic Management Journal*, **19**(2), 181–192.

Burns, P. and Dewhurst, J., eds. (1996), *Small Businesses and Entrepreneurship*, 2nd edn (London: Macmillan Publishing Ltd.).

Burns, P. and Harrison, J. (1996), 'Growth. Chapter 3' in *Small Businesses and Entrepreneurship*, Burns, P. and Dewhurst, J. (eds.), 2nd edn (London: Macmillan Publishing Ltd.).

Caldwell, B. and Wilde, C. (1998), 'Emerging Enterprises', *Information Week*, June 29, 53–60.

Campbell, A. and Yeung, S. (1991), 'Brief Case: Mission, Vision, and Strategic Intent', *Long Range Planning*, 24(4), 145–147.

Campbell, A., Devine, M. and Young, D. (1990), *A Sense of Mission* (London: Hutchinson).

Carson, D. and Cromie, S. (1989), 'Marketing Planning in Small Enterprises: A Model and Some Empirical Evidence', *Journal of Marketing Management*, **5**(1), 33–51.

Cespedes, F.V. (1991), *Organising and Implementing the Marketing Effort* (Reading, Mass: Addison-Wesley Publishing).

Chaffee, E.E. (1985), 'Three Models of Strategy', *Academy of Management Review*, **10**(1), 89–98.

Chandler, A.D. (1962), *Strategy and Structure* (Cambridge, Mass.: MIT Press).

Chandler, A.D. (1990), Scale and Scope: the Dynamics of Industrial Capitalism, (Cambridge: MA, Belknap Press of Harvard University Press).

Chaston, I., Berger, B. and Sadler-Smith, E. (1999), 'Organisational Learning: Research Issues and Application in SME Sector Firms', *International Journal of Entrepreneurial Behaviour and Research*, **5**(4), 191–203.

Choo, C.W. (1999), 'The Art of Scanning the Environment'. 'American Society for Information Science', *Bulletin of the American Society for Information Science Washington*, **45**(3), 21–24.

Collis, D.J. and Montgomery, C.A. (1997), *Corporate Strategy: Resources and the Scope of the Firm* (Chicago, IL: McGraw-Hill Books).

Copacino, W.C. (1999), 'A New Direction in Strategic Planning', *Logistic Management and Distribution Report*, **38**(10), 36.

Covin, J. (1991), 'Entrepreneurial Versus Conservative Firms: A Comparison of Strategies and Performance', *Journal of Management Studies*, **28**(5), 439–462.

Covin, J. and Slevin, D. (1990), 'New Venture Strategic Posture, Structure and Performance: An Industry Life Cycle Analysis', *Journal of Business Venturing*, **5**, 123–135.

Datta, D.K., Rajagopalan, N. and Rasheed, A.M.A. (1991), 'Diversification and Performance: Critical Review and Future Directions', *Journal of Management Studies*, **28**(5), 529–558.

De Soto, R. (1998), Creating an Active Internet Presence: A New Alternative, *Telecommunication Magazine*, December, 73–75.

Drazin, R. and Howard, P. (1984), 'Strategy Implementation: A Technique for Organisational Design', *Columbia Journal of World Business*, **19**(summer), 40–46.

Engler, N. (1999), 'Small but Nimble', *Information Week*, January 18, 57–62.

Fahey, L., Kling, W.R. and Narayanan, V.K. (1981), 'Environmental Scanning and Forecasting in Strategic Planning-The State of the Art', *Long Range Planning*, **14**(1), 32–39.

Falsey, T. (1989), *Corporate Philosophies and Mission Statements* (New York: Quorum Books).

Flood, P.C., Dromgoole, T., Carroll, S.J. and Gorman, L., eds. (2000), *Managing Strategy Implementation* (Oxford: Blackwell Publishers Ltd.).

Floyd, S.W. and Woolridge, B. (1992), 'Managing Strategic Consensus: The Foundation of Effective Implementation', *Academy of Management Executives*, **6**, 27–39.

Fulmer, W.E. (1990), 'Human Resource Management: the Right Hand of Strategy Implementation', *Human Resource Planning*, **13**(1), 1–11.

Goldsmith, A. (1995) *Making Managers More Effective: Applications of Strategic management*, Working paper No. 9, USAID March.

Grant, R.M. (1991), 'The Resource-Based Theory of Competitive Advantage: Implications for Strategy Formulation', *California Management Review*, **33**(3), 114–135.

Grundy, T. (1998), 'Strategy Implementation and Project Management', *International Journal of Project Management*, **16**(1), 43–50.

Gupta, A. (1987), 'SBU Strategies, Corporate-S.B.U. Relations, and SBU Effectiveness in Strategy Implementation', *Academy of Management Journal*, **27**, 25–41.

Gupta, A. and Govindarajan, V. (1984), 'Business Unit Strategy, Managerial Characteristics and Business Unit Effectiveness at Strategy Implementation', *Academy of Management Journal*, **27**, 25–41.

Hamel, G. (1996), 'Strategy as Revolution', *Harvard Business Review*, **74**(July/August), 69–82.

Hanlon, D. and Scott, M. (1995), 'Strategy Formulation in the Entrepreneurial Small Firms' in *International Entrepreneurship*. Birley, S. and MacMillan, I. (eds.) (London: Routledge), 17–38.

Hauc, A. and Kovac, J. (2000), 'Project Management in Strategy Implementation – Experiences in Slovenia', *International Journal of Project Management*, **18**(1), 61–67.

Hendry, C., Arthur, M. and Jones, A. (1995), *Strategy Through People: Adaptation and Learning in the Small-Medium Enterprises* (London: Routledge).

Hitt, M.A., Hoskisson, R.E. and Kim, H. (1997), 'International Diversification: Effects on Innovation and Firm Performance in Product-diversified Firms', *Academy of Management Journal*, **40**(4), 767–798.

Hoskisson, R.E. and Hitt, M.A. (1994), *Downscoping: How to Tame the Diversified Firm* (New York: Oxford University Press).

Hrebiniak, L.G. (1990), 'Implementing Strategy'. *Chief Executive*, **57**, 74–78.

Hrebiniak, L.G. and Joyce, W.F. (1984), *Implementation Strategy* (New York: Macmillan).

Isabella, L. (1990), 'Evolving Interpretations as a Change Unfolds: How Managers Construe Key Organisational Events', *Academy of Management Journal*, **33**(1), 7–41.

Jain, S.C. (1984), 'Environmental Scanning in United States of America Corporations', *Long Range Planning*, **17**(2), 117–128.

Jennings, D.E. and Lumpkin, J.R. (1992), 'Insights between Environmental Scanning Activities and Porter's Generic Strategies: An Empirical Analysis', *Journal of Management*, **18**, 791–803.

Johnson, G. (1992), 'Managing Strategic Change: Strategy Culture and Action', *Long Range Planning*, **25**(1), 28–36.

Kakabadse, A. (2001), 'Dynamics of Executive Succession', *Corporate Governance*, **1**(3), 9–15.

Kalai, E. and Ledyard, J. (1998), 'Repeated Implementation', *Journal of Economic Theory*, **38**(2), 308–317.

Kets De Vries, M.F.R. (1996), 'The Anatomy of the Entrepreneur: Clinical Observation', *Human Relations*, **49**(7), 853–883.

Kleindl, B. (2000), 'Competitive Dynamics and New Business Models for SMEs in the Virtual Marketplace', *Journal of Development Entrepreneurship*, **5**(1), 73–86.

Klemm, M., Sanderson, S. and Luffman, G. (1991), 'Mission Statements: Selling Corporate Values to Employees', *Long Range Planning*, **23**, 73–78.

Komenar, M. (1997), *Electronic Marketing* (New York: John Wiley and Sons).

Lang, J.R., Calatone, R.j. and Gudmundson, D. (1997), 'Small Firm Information Seeking as a Response to Environmental Threats and Opportunities', *Journal of Small Business Management*, **35**, 11–23.

Larry, S.L., Fann, G.L. and Nikolaisen, V.N. (1998), 'Environmental Scanning Practices in Small Businesses', *Journal of Small Business Management*, **26**(3), 55–63.

Leavy, B. (1996), *Key Process in Strategy* (London, UK: International Thomson Business Press).

Leavy, B. and Wilson, J. (1994), *Strategy and Leadership* (London: Routledge).

Leidecker, L. and Bruno, A. (1986), 'Identifying and Using Critical Success Factors', *Long Range Planning*, **17**(1), 23–32.

Lorange, P. (1998), 'Strategy Implementation: The New Realities', *Long Range Planning*, **31**(1), 18–29.

Lowry, J.R., Avila, S.M. and Baird, T.R. (1999), 'Developing a Niching Strategy for Insurance Agents'. 'Society of Chartered Property and Casualty Underwriters', *CPCU Journal*, **52**(2), 74–83.

Luffman, G., Sanderson, S., Lea, E. and Kenny, B. (1991), *Business Policy: An Analytical Introduction*, 2nd edn (Oxford: Blackwell) Business Publication.

Lynch, R. (2000), *Corporate Strategy*, 2nd edn (Harlow, Essex: Pearson Education Limited).

McCarthy, B. and Leavy, B. (2000), 'Phases in the Strategy Formulation: An Exploratory Study of Irish SMEs', *IBAR*, **21**(2), 55–80.

Meyer, G.D. and Heppard, K.A., eds. (2000), *Entrepreneurship as Strategy: Competing on the Entrepreneurial Edge* (London: SAGE Publications Inc.).

Miles, R.E. and Snow, C.C. (1978), *Organisational Strategy, Structure and Process* (New York: McGraw-Hill).

Miller, D. (1988), 'The Relationship of Porter's Business Strategies to Environment and Structure', *Academy of Management Journal*, **37**, 280–308.

Miller, D. and Toulouse, J.M. (1986), 'Strategy, Structure, CEO Personality and Performance in Small Firms', *American Journal of Small Businesses*, Winter, 47–62.

Mintzberg, H. (1979), 'An Emerging Strategy of Direct Research', *Administrative Science Quarterly*, **24**, 582–589.

Mintzberg, H. (1987), 'Crafting Strategy', *Harvard Business Review*, July/August, 66–75.

Mintzberg, H. (1994), *The Rise and Fall of Strategic Planning* (London: Prentice-Hall).

Mintzberg, H. and Waters, J. (1982), 'Tracking Strategy in an Entrepreneurial Firm', *Academy of Management Journal*, **25**, 465–499.

Mintzberg, H., Quinn, J.B. and Ghoshal, S. (1995), *The Strategy Process*. (*European Edition*) (London: Prentice-Hall/International Ltd.).

Monck, C., Porter, B., Quintas, P., Storey, D. and Wynarczyk, P. (1988), *Science Parks and the Growth of High Technology Firms* (Beckenham, Kent: Croom-Helm).

Murray, J. and O'Gorman, C. (1994), 'Growth Strategies for Smaller Businesses', *Journal of Strategic Change*, **3**, 175–183.

Niv, A., Jehiel, Z. and Isaac, M. (1998), 'Environmental Scanning and Information Systems in Relation to Success in Introducing New Products', *Information and Management*, **33**(4), 201–211.

Noble, C.H. (1999), 'Building the Strategy Implementation Network', *Business Horizons*, **42**(6), 19–28.

Nutt, P.C. (1983), 'Implementation Approaches for Project Planning', *Academy of Management Review*, **8**, 600–611.

Nutt, P.C. (1986), 'Tactics of Implementation', *Academy of Management Journal*, **29**, 230–261.

O'Gorman, C. and Cunningham, J. (1997), *Enterprise in Action: An Introduction to Entrepreneurship in an Irish* (Context, Dublin: Oak Tree Press).

Ohmae, K. (1982), *The Mind of the Strategist: the Art of Japanese Business* (New York: McGraw-Hill).

Oladeji, S.I. (1998), 'Technology Policy and the Development of Small and Medium Scale Enterprises in Contemporary Nigeria', *Technovation*, **18**(2), 125–128.

Organisation for Economic, Cooperation and Development (OECD) (1993), *Small and Medium Sized Enterprises: Technology and Competitiveness* (Paris: OECD).

Parsa, H.G. (1999), 'Interaction of Strategy Implementation and Power Perceptions in Franchise Systems: An Empirical Investigation', *Journal of Business Research*, **45**(2), 173–185.

Pearce, J. and David, F. (1987), 'Corporate Mission Statements: Te Bottom Line', *Executive*, **1**, 109–116.

Pearce, J. and Robinson, R. (1994), *Strategic Management: Strategy Formulation and Implementation*, 5th edn (Boston, Mass.: Irwin).

Pearce, J., Freeman, E. and Robinson, R. (1987), 'The Tenuous Link between Formal Strategic Planning and Financial Performance', *Academy of Management Review*, **12**, 658–675.

Peters, T. (1988), *Thriving on Chaos* (London: Pan).

Pettigrew, A. (1987), 'Context and Action in the Transformation of the Firm', *Journal of Management Studies*, **24**, 649–670.

Pettigrew, A. and Whipp, R. (1991), *Managing Change for Competitive Success* (Oxford: Basil Blackwell).

Pfeffer, J. (1994), *Competitive Advantage Through People* (Boston, Mass.: Harvard Business School Publishing).

Pollard, C.E. and Hayne, S.C. (1998), 'The Changing Face of Information System Issues in Small Firms', *International Small Business Journal*, **16**(3), 70–87.

Porter, M. (1980), *Competitive Strategy Techniques for Analyzing Industries and Competitors* (New York: Free Press).

Porter, M. (1985), *Competitive Advantage: Creating and Sustaining Superior Performance* (New York: Free Press).

Quinn, J.B. (1980), *Strategies for Change: Logical Incrementalism* (New York: Irwin).

Ramanujam, V. and Varadarjan, P. (1989), 'Research on Corporate Diversification: A Synthesis', *Strategic Management Journal*, **10**(6), 523–551.

Rarick, C. and Vitton, J. (1995), 'Mission Statements Make Cents', *The Journal of Business Strategy*, **16**, 11–12.

Raymond, L. and Bergeron, F. (1997), 'Global Distribution Systems: A Field Study of Their Use and Advantages in Travel Agencies', *Journal of Global Information Management*, **5**(4), 23–32.

Raymond, L., Julien, P.A. and Ramangalahy, C. (2001), 'Technological Scanning by Small Canadian Manufacturers', *Journal of Small Business Management*, **39**(2), 123–138.

Robinson, R.B. and Pearce, J.A. (1984), 'The Relationship Between Stage of Development and Small Firm Planning and Performance', *Journal of Small Business Management*, April, 45–52.

Rousseau, Y. and Rousseau, P. (2000), 'Turning Strategy into Action in Financial Services', *CMA Management* (Hamilton) Dec/ Jan, **73**(10), 25–29.

Rumelt, R.P. (1991), 'How Much Does Industry Matter?' *Strategic Management Journal*, March, **1991**, 167–185.

Sandberg, W., and Hofer, C. (1987) Improving New Venture Performance: The Role of the Strategy, Industry Structure, and the Entrepreneur, *Journal of Business Venturing*, **2**(1), 5–28.

Sawyer, O.O. (1993), 'Environmental Uncertainty and Environmental Scanning Activities of Nigerian Manufacturing Executives: A Comparative Analysis', *Strategic Management Journal*, **14**, 287–299.

Scott, M. and Bruce, R. (1987), 'Five Stages of Growth in Small Business', *Long Range Planning*, **20**(3), June, 45–52.

Sirower, M. (1997), *The Strategy Trap: How Companies Lose the Acquisition Game* (New York: Free Press).

Smallbone, D., Leig, R. and North, D. (1995), 'The Characteristics and Strategies of High Growth SMEs', *International Journal of Entrepreneurial Behaviour and Research*, **1**(3), 44–62.

Smircich, L. and Stubbart, C. (1985), 'Strategic Management in an Enacted World', *Academy of Management Journal*, **10**(4), 724–736.

Smith, J.G. and Fleck, V. (1987), 'Business Strategies in Small High Technology Companies', *Long Range Planning*, **20**(2), 61–68.

Thomas, J.B., Clark, S.M. and Gioia, D.A. (1993), 'Strategic Sense Making and Organisational Performance: Linkage Among Scanning, Interpretation, Action Outcomes', *Academy of Management Journal*, April, 239–270.

Thompson, J. (1999), 'A Strategic Perspective of Entrepreneurship', *International Journal of Entrepreneurial Behaviour and Research*, **5**(6), 279–296.

Thompson, J.L. (1995), *Strategy in Action* (London: Chapman and Hall).

Turban, E., Lee, J., King, D. and Chung, H.M. (2000), *Electronic Commerce: A Managerial Perspective* (London: Prentice-Hall International Limited).

Voss, C. (1998), 'Made in Europe: Small Companies', *Business Strategy Review*, **9**(4), 1.

Want, J. (1986) Corporate Mission: The Intangible Contribution to Performance, *Management Review* (August), 40–50.

Wheelen, T.L. and Hunger, J.D. (1998), *Strategic Management and Business Policy*, 6th edn (New York: Addison-Wesley).

Wickham, P.A. (2001), *Strategic Entrepreneurship: A Decision Making Approach to New Venture Creation and Management*, 2nd edn (Harlow, Essex: Pearson Education Limited).

Wilde, C. (1998), Internet Levels the Field, *Information Week*, June 29, 64–66.

Wilder, C. (1999), 'E-businesses Work Status', *Information Week*, January, **4**, 53–54.

Wit, B. and Mayer, R. (1998), *Strategy: Process, Content, Context,*. London: International Thomson Business Press.

Chapter 3

Researching Strategy

Introduction

This chapter sets out the various steps that are necessary in executing this study and thereby satisfy its objectives. It aims to explain in detail all aspects of the research programme, with particular reference to all the key theoretical and practical issues involved. This chapter will provide a review of the methodology of research, which consists of five major activity stages. First, in order to present the research approach within the literature, the chapter starts with a theoretical discussion on methodology and research in strategic management. The chapter will continue with a theoretical discussion on research design and consequently the chosen research design and research process for this research will be discussed. Second, the research objectives and research hypotheses will be discussed in some detail. In this section the sample and criteria for selecting sample firms will be discussed. Third, the literature on strategic management in SMEs will be synthesized and a dynamic model of strategic management in entrepreneurial SMEs will be introduced. Accordingly, a conceptual framework of senior managers' perceptions of strategic management in small and medium-sized enterprises will be provided. This section also provides details of the research variables. In the fourth section the data collection techniques, questionnaire construction and survey process will be described. Finally, in the last section data analysis methods and the statistical techniques employed will be discussed.

Methodology in Management Researches: A Positivistic Approach

Perhaps before discussing the methodology of strategic management research in general and the current research in particular, it would be useful to define research methodology (Curran and Blackburn, 2001). Remenyi et al. (1998) argued that, research methodology refers to the procedural framework within which the research is conducted. It describes an approach to a problem that can be put into practice in a research program or process. Accordingly, it has been argued (Robson, 1997; Malhotra, 1999; Burns, 2000) that, methodology is understood to be the general principles behind research, whereas methods are the practical techniques used to undertake research. From this point of view, methodology provides the link between technique and theory.

In general it has been argued (May, 1997) that, the 'aim of positivism is to collect and assemble data on the social world from which we can generalise and explain human behaviour through the set of our theories' (p. 10). In order to consider the importance of a positivistic approach in management studies, it is useful to see what is the nature of social science. All theories of organizations are based upon a philosophy of science and a theory of society (Burrell and Morgan, 1993; Root, 1996). Sociological scientists approach their subject via explicit or implicit assumptions about the nature of the social world and the way in which it may be investigated (Sayer, 1992). Smith argues that the purpose of science is to develop laws. To develop a scientific law you start from the observation of a particular set of objects and look for regularities. A scientific law which is one of general assumptions of positivism is a general statement which describes empirical regularities which occur in different places and at different times (Smith, 1998).

There are different assumptions about the nature of social science. Burrell and Morgan (1993) developed a scheme for analysing assumptions about the nature of social science. First, there are assumptions of an ontological nature -assumptions which concern the very essence of the phenomena under investigation. Social scientists are faced with a basic ontological question: whether 'reality' is of an objective nature or the product of individual cognition. Ontology involves the study of theories of being, the questions we ask about what can really exist (Smith, 1998). Associated with this ontological issue, is a second set of assumptions of an epistemological nature. These are assumptions about the ground of knowledge – about how one might begin into understand the world and communicate this as knowledge to fellow human beings. Epistemology involves the study of theories of knowledge, the question we ask about how we know (Smith, 1998). The epistemological assumptions in these instances determine extreme positions on the issue of whether knowledge is something, which can be acquired on the one hand, or is something, which has to be personally experienced on the other. Burrell and Morgan (1993) argued that there is a third set of assumptions concerning human nature and in particular the relationship between human beings and their environment. This view tends to be one in which human beings and their experiences are regarded as products of the environment: one in which humans are conditioned by their external circumstances.

The three sets of assumptions outlined above have direct implications of a methodological nature. Each one has important consequences for the way in which one attempts to investigate and obtain 'knowledge' about the social world. Different ontology, epistemologies, and models of human nature are likely to incline social scientists toward different methodologies. Positivism is a term with many uses in social sciences and philosophy. In particular, positivist science has a preference for empirical data, which can be observed and measured so that the various component parts can be compared for their relative frequency (Smith, 1998). It embraces the notion that human affairs ought to be conceived as belonging to a natural order open to objective enquiry (Hollis, 1994). The idea behind logical positivism is that, because knowledge of the world can be justified only by experience, we are never entitled to assert the existence of anything beyond all possible experiences (Hollis, 1994).

Positivism in social science may be broadly represented as depending upon the assertion that the concepts and methods employed in natural science can be applied to form a 'science of man' or a natural science of society (Giddens, 1978). It has been maintained that the word positivist has become more of a derogatory epithet than a useful descriptive concept (Giddens, 1978). Burrell and Morgan (1993) argued that, most of the descriptions of positivism in current usage refer to one or more of the ontological, epistemological or methodological dimensions of their scheme for analysing assumptions with regard to social science. They indicated that, we use 'positivist' here to characterize epistemologies, which seek to explain and predict what happens in the social world by searching for regularities and causal relationship between its constituent elements (Burrell and Morgan, 1993). Positivist epistemology is in essence based upon the traditional approaches, which dominate the natural sciences. Positivist may differ in terms of detailed approach. Some would claim for example, that hypothesized regularities can be verified by an adequate experimental research programme. Others would maintain that, hypotheses can only be falsified and never demonstrated to be true. It is argued that, both 'verificationists' and 'falsificationists' would accept that, the growth of knowledge is essentially a cumulative process in which new insights are added to the existing stock of knowledge and false hypotheses eliminated (Burrell and Morgan, 1993).

Positivist opposed by anti-positivist theory. The epistemology of anti-positivism may take various forms but is firmly set against the utility of a search for laws or underlying regularities in the world of social affairs (Douglas, 1970). For the anti-positivist, the social world is essentially relativistic and can only be understood from the point of view of the individuals who are directly involved in the activities which are to be studied (Donaldson, 1996). Anti-positivists, reject the standpoint of the 'observer', which characterizes positivist epistemology as a valid vantage point for understanding human activities (Burrell and Morgan, 1993). From this point of view social science is seen as being essentially a subjective rather than an objective enterprise.

Overview of Research Methods Employed in Strategic Management

The best place to overview and discuss about research methods in strategic management is Hoskisson et al.'s recent research work (Hoskisson et al., 1999). During the early development of the strategic management theories, scholars (Ansoff, 1965; Andrews, 1971) emphasized the normative aspect of business knowledge and were chiefly interested in identifying and developing the 'best practices' that were useful for managers. Their principal goal was to impart knowledge to practitioners, rather than to pursue knowledge for scientific advancement. The most appropriate method for accomplishing this objective is inductive in character: in-depth case studies of single firms or industries. Therefore, they concluded that, the most valid methodology to achieve their purposes was case studies.

This discipline has been criticized. For instance Learned et al. (1969) argued that, these disciplines may not be appropriate for strategy studies because 'knowledge generated for one set of ends is not readily applicable for another' (p.6). In comparison, Chandler's strategy and structure is less normative or prescriptive in nature, although the research methods employed are still inductive (Rumelt, Schendel and Teece, 1994). Unlike Andrews (1971) and Ansoff (1962), Chandler (1962) attempted to seek generalization across a wider population of firms. Overall, the approach used by prominent strategy scholars during this period was mainly normative or prescriptive in purposes, with in-depth case analysis as the primary research tool.

Tremendous changes in the methodology of strategic management occurred during the last three decades. Schendle and Hatten (1972) strongly advocated that strategic management needed empirical research to show a relationship between variables as 'the conceptual development of the field has outstripped the research derived evidence available to support, deny or modify it' (p.101). Furthermore, they pointed out the need for strategy research to go beyond the inductive approach and for more deductive studies with 'reliable data specially collected to allow the development of testable answers to strategic questions' (Schendle and Hatten, 1972, 102). Although normative, inductive case based studies had dominated the early history of strategic management, positivistic, deductive empirical research became dominant during this period. Therefore, concern with explanation and prediction, rather than prescription, was strongly advocated by strategy scholars with the aim to elevate the field to a more rigorous 'scientific' academic discipline. Although the sample size in most studies was usually less than 100 in the earlier period, a typical study now has at least 100 observations and can to as large as tens of thousands of observations (for example Chen and McMillan, 1992; Gimeno and Woo, 1996).

During this period, researchers have expanded significant effort to construct data sets by means of large-scale surveys. Also increasing the attention paid to the methodological issues helped to advance the research rigour in the strategic management field. The choice of quantitative methods or qualitative methods has been the subject of controversy and the apparent 'dominance' of more quantitative-based methodological tools in the development of the field does not mean that these tools are applicable to all research questions (Hoskisson et al., 1999; Curran and Blackburn, 2001). The research question and context should dictate the choice of appropriate method. Moreover, the integration of quantitative and qualitative methodological tools (Judge and Zeithaml, 1992; Hitt, Gimeno and Hoskisson, 1998) is likely to be a fruitful course, especially in strategic management research.

Research Design: Qualitative or Quantitative Research?

It is especially important to understand and to contract two kinds of evidence that may be collected in business and management studies – qualitative and quantitative (Curran and Blackburn, 2001). Qualitative research uses words to describe situations, individuals, or circumstances surrounding a phenomenon. While quantitative research uses numbers usually in the form of counts or measurement to attempt to give precision to a set of observations (Remenyi et al., 1998). The evidence can be essentially qualitative, for instance written company reports, and quantitative such as measurement of performance of the subject of interest.

It has been argued that, qualitative research is situational or contextual, often based on a case study and its particular circumstances (Bryman, 1988; Robson, 1997). Qualitative research is aimed at discovering meaning and involves both interpretation and a critical approach to social work. Research questions are posed, rather than hypotheses and theory is often grounded in data. Concepts are in the form of themes, rather than relationships. Data are often in the form of words from observation, documents, interviews and participation. For qualitative researchers the fundamental questions is not whether the data proves or disproves a given theory but how to go about theorizing and generalizing from data (Robson, 1997).

In contrast, the 'quantitative research method relies mainly on a hypotheses which is derived from theory deductively. The objective is to test the theory by way of observation and data collection, the findings of which, following analysis would either confirm or reject the theory' (Robson, 1997, 11). In quantitative research the causal relationship between variables are investigated. The primary data are collected mainly using questionnaire and structured interview. In business and management studies, quantitative research has been compared with the methodology that natural scientists use in their investigations, with the same core language of approach including terms such as variable, control, measurement, experiment, reliability, and validity (Bryman, 1988; Remenyi et al., 1998).

Considering different aspects of both qualitative and quantitative methodologies, this question is raised; which one is the most appropriate research method in strategic management research? In an attempt to answer this question different aspects of both methodologies will be overviewed.

Quantitative Research Method

Quantitative research is often conceptualized by its practitioners as having a logical structure in which theories determine the problems to which researchers address themselves in the form of hypothesis derived from general theories. These hypotheses are invariably assumed to take the form of expectations about likely causal connections between the concepts, which are the constituent elements of the hypotheses.

In quantitative research the researcher uses quantitative data. Normally, the data, which have been measured in interval level, is considered as quantitative data. However, the measured data in ordinal level can also be treated as quantitative data. The obvious benefits of quantitative data are that, the numerical form makes comparison easy, data are standardized, visible and amenable to the test of classical survey statistics (Hart, 1987).

In general, sample size is greater and controlled in such a way as to be representative of the population from which they are drawn. This allows greater confidence in accepting the reliability of or the ability to generalize, the findings. Figure 3.1 captures some of the main ingredients of the quantitative research process. One portion of quantitative research is the need to render observable the concepts which are rooted in the hypotheses derived from a prior theoretical scheme. Thus, the quantitative researcher tends to be concerned about relating those concepts to one another in order to investigate associations and to tease out causal processes.

The measurement of concepts tends to be undertaken through the use of questionnaire devices or some form of structured observation. Quantitative research is often highly preoccupied with establishing the causal relationships between concepts. The frequent use of the terms 'independent variable' and 'dependent variable' by quantitative researchers is evidence of the widespread tendency to employ causal

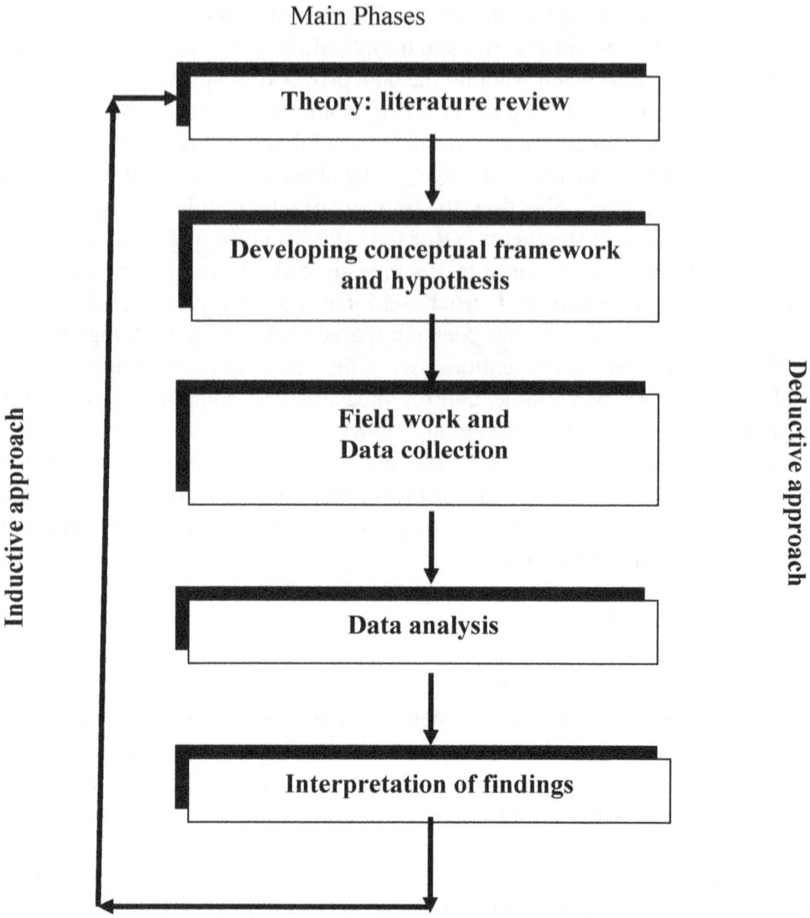

Figure 3.1 The structure of quantitative research process

imagery in investigations. Another aspect of quantitative research is that, the result of a particular investigation can be generalized beyond the confines of the research location. By verifying generality, the quantitative researcher draws nearer to the law-like findings of the science. Accordingly, the replication of established findings is often taken to be a characteristic of natural science. Replication can provide a means of checking the extent to which findings are applicable to other contexts. Finally, quantitative research tends to treat the individual as the focus or empirical enquiry.

Qualitative Research Method

Recently, a thoughtful and comprehensive discussion of the principal qualitative research methods and a convincing rationale for using them in management has been provided (Hurley, 1999). Van Maanen (1983) describes qualitative methods as an array of interpretative techniques, which seeks to describe, decode, translate, and otherwise come to terms with the meaning, not the frequency, of certain more or less naturally occurring phenomena in the social world. Similarly, Chisnall (1986) defines the essence of qualitative research as diagnostic attempt to discover what may account for certain type of behaviour, seeking a deeper understanding of factors, sometimes covert, which influence the decisions. Qualitative methods offer powerful and versatile techniques to examine the complexities and subtleties in the complicated sets of relationships in business and management studies.

In spite of the advantages of quantitative research, it has been argued that, it is not possible to use quantitative methods in some specific circumstances (Marshal, 1985; Bryman, 1988; Malhotra, 1999; Burns, 2000). For instance qualitative research is appropriate methodology in the following circumstances:

- Research that can not be done experimentally for practical or ethical reasons
- Research that delves into complexity and processes
- Research for which relevant variables have yet to be identified
- Research on unknown societies or innovative systems
- Research on informal and unstructured linkages and processes in organizations
- Research on real as opposed to stated organizational goals (Marshal, 1985).

Malhotra (1999) argues that, like secondary data analysis, qualitative research is a major methodology used in exploratory research. Researchers undertake qualitative research to define the problem or develop an approach. In developing an approach, qualitative research is often used for generating hypotheses and identifying variables that should be included in research. In business and management studies, qualitative research provides the fundamental understanding of peoples' language, perceptions, and values. Qualitative most often provides the understanding that allows us to decide on the information we must have to solve the research problem and how to properly interpret that information (Malhotra, 1999).

Choosing the Research Methodology

Research into strategy formulation and implementation should reflect the dynamics of change. In highly dynamic and uncertain environments there is no single generic method to research. Robson (1997) argued that, although qualitative and quantitative methodological approaches are different, it is wrong to oppose them as two competing methodologies. For some researchers however qualitative and quantitative research are simply different ways of conducting the research, each of which may be most appropriate to different kind of research questions. For instance, qualitative researchers may resort to some form of quantification in their work, and for a survey to be successful a quantitative researcher must integrate some qualitative knowledge into the survey's design and interpretation, and/or understand peoples frame of reference (May, 1997).

Different methods have different advantages and disadvantages but can be mutually supportive (Thomas, 1984). The difference between the two research methodologies in business and management studies, are summarized in Table 3.1.

Table 3.1 Qualitative versus quantitative research

	Qualitative Research	Quantitative Research
Objective	• To gain a qualitative understanding of the underlying reasons	• To quantify the data and generalize the results from the sample to the population
Sample	• Small sample size	• Large sample size
Data collection	• Unstructured	• Structured • Semi-structured
Data analysis	• Non-statistical	• Statistical
Outcomes	• Develop an initial understanding	• Recommend a final course of action

Qualitative research provides insights and understanding of the problem setting, whereas quantitative research seeks to quantify the data and typically uses some form of statistical analysis. While quantitative methods are necessary to test the validity and general applicability of research findings, the potential of in depth quantitative studies diminishes rapidly as the underlying conditions change in a dynamic environment. Researching strategy formulation and implementation therefore requires the right balance between qualitative and quantitative methods. Figure 3.2 presents a contingent research approach the aim of which is to identify such a balance.

Whenever a new management research problem is being addressed, quantitative research must be preceded by appropriate qualitative research. Langer (1999) argued that, qualitative research studies should always be followed by quantitative research to test the hypotheses.

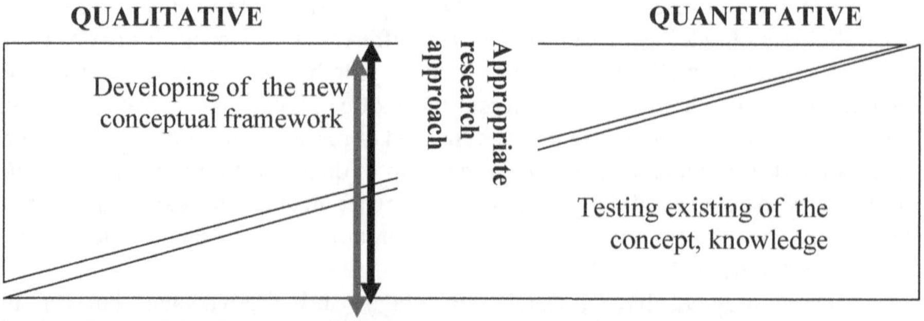

Figure 3.2 Contingent approach to research method

An example might be finding out what consumer needs are in order to create new product concepts, which will be shown in subsequent qualitative research. It is a principle of research in business and management studies, more especially strategic management, to view qualitative and quantitative research as complementary, rather than in competition with each other (Hunt, 1991). Using a combination of qualitative and quantitative research methods as a contingency approach in management researches, has been used by different researchers, for instance, Analoui (1990) and Feurer, Chaharbaghi and Wargin (1995). The degree to which quantitative and qualitative studies are used will depend on the environmental circumstances of the firms. In turbulent environments, research will focus on developing conceptual knowledge by relying on qualitative studies, whereas in more static environments quantitative studies are favoured for testing and validating existing conceptual knowledge.

Research Process

Developing an appropriate research process is considerable crucial point in research methodology, because there is no overall consensus about how to conceptualize the 'doing' of a research. There are different views about the place and role of theory; also about the sequence and relationship of the activities involved in a research, for instance, data collection and analysis are intertwined (Nachmias and Nachmias, 1996; Robson, 1997; Remenyi et al., 1998; Curran and Blackburn, 2001). Robson (1997) has classified the research processes into two categories. 'One is variously labelled as positivistic, natural science based, hypothetic-deductive, quantitative or even simply "scientific"; the other as interpretive, ethnographic or qualitative – among several other labels' (Robson, 1997, 18). The scientific approach is usually regarded as starting with theory and involving five sequential steps as follows:

- Deducting a hypothesis testable proposition about the relationship between two or more events or concepts from the theory.
- Expressing the hypothesis in operational terms (that is once indicating exactly how the variables are to be measured), which propose a relationship between two specific variables.
- Testing this operational hypothesis. This will involve an experiment or some other forms of empirical enquiry.
- Examining the specific outcome of the enquiry. It will either tend to confirm the theory or indicate the need for its modification.
- If necessary, modifying the theory in the light of the findings. An attempt is then made to verify the revised theory by going back to the first step and repeating the whole cycle.

In contrast, a major difference in the interpretive approach against the scientific approach is that, theories and concepts tend to arise from the enquiry. They come after data collection rather than before it. Because of this, it is often referred to as 'hypothesis generating' (as against 'hypothesis testing') research (Robson, 1997).

Reviewing the early studies in strategic management shows that, the most appropriate research methods for accomplishing strategy research objectives was inductive in character: in-depth case studies of single firms or institutes (Hoskisson et al., 1999). Overall, the approaches used by prominent strategy scholars during the foundation period were mainly normative or prescriptive in purpose, with in-depth case analysis as the primary research tool (Rumelt, Schendel and Teece, 1994).

There is some criticism of this approach (Silverman, 1998; Hoskisson et al., 1999). According to Hoskisson et al. (1999) 'generalisation was practically unfeasible or desirable, as each case is assumed to be complex and unique. These disciplines may not be appropriate for strategy studies because knowledge generated for one set of ends is not readily applicable to another' (p. 423).

The development of the research methods in strategic management studies within the last decade has been dramatic. While its roots have been in normative and inductive disciplines, the current field of strategic management research, is strongly empirical research and deductive. According to Hoskisson et al. (1999), 'although, normative, inductive case-based studies had dominated the early history of strategic management, positivistic, deductive empirical research became dominant during this period. Therefore concern with explanation and prediction, rather than prescription, was strongly advocated by strategy scholars with the aim to elevate the field to a more rigorous, scientific academic discipline' (Hoskisson et al., 1999, 431).

In this research the researcher employs a process which is based on the hypothetic-deductive discipline. According to McNeill (1990), the hypothetic-deductive research process, starts with the phenomena, out there in the world, which can be observed objectively. These sometimes-casual observations prompt ideas in the mind of the researcher, from which they develop and hypothesize. The researcher should try to prove the hypothesis wrong. An experiment is then carried out (or data collected in the field) and results are analysed. The hypothesis is then tested against the results. If the evidence does not support the hypothesis, it can be rejected or revised, and a fresh hypothesis developed. If the evidence supports it, then it can be seen as a contribution to theory (McNeill, 1990).

Objectives of Study and Research Questions

Although the economic benefits of planning have received much attention in the general management literature (for example, Kudla, 1980; Armstrong, 1982; Shrader, Taylor and Dalton, 1984; Rhyne, 1986; Pearce, Freeman and Robinson, 1987; Miller and Cardinal, 1994), the strategic planning-performance relationship appears to have been largely overlooked in the SME literature (Bracker and Pearson, 1986; Feltenstein, 1992; McKiernan and Morris, 1995). Recently, a few empirical attempts have been made to explore the dynamics of strategic management in the SME fields (Berry, 1998; Beal, 2000).

The above attempts have suggested several issues of significance which merit further investigation. There are various arguments as to which type of strategy is the more effective; for example, should the strategy be formal and written or informal? While Mintzberg (1994) favours the adaptive 'visionary' approach. Porter (1998) and subsequently, Niv, Jehiel and Isaac (1998) and Beal (2000) believe that formal planning is more effective. Mintzberg (1994) has criticized the formal planning procedures of strategic management as being too rigid, because they may restrict or prevent the use of judgement and intuition.

As discussed in Chapter 2, the role of senior managers and entrepreneurs in the development and implementation of strategies in SMEs is considerable. In this regard Beal (2000) indicated that, no strategic planning will be carried out in SMEs, unless the senior managers or entrepreneurs involved are aware of the importance of the process. Thus, the main objective of this research is to explore senior managers' perceptions, awareness and attitudes towards the formulation and application of strategic management in British small and medium-sized enterprises in the electronic industry. In order to achieve the objectives of the study, the following questions have been posed in an attempt to highlight the importance of the role of senior managers in so far as strategic management is concerned in small and medium-sized firms in the British electronic and electronic industry. These are:

1. What are the senior managers' perceptions and attitudes towards the strategic management process including: environmental scanning, strategy formulation, implementation and evaluation of strategy in small and medium-sized enterprises?
2. Which factors are associated with the effective process of strategy formulation and implementation in small and medium-sized enterprises and what are their likely impacts on firm performance?
3. What are the characteristics of a dynamic model of strategic management in SMEs and how can this assist the firms during the stages of formulation, implementation and evaluation of strategy?

Based on the above questions, a conceptual framework for analysing senior managers' perceptions of the planning and implementation of business strategies in small and medium-sized firms has been developed. It presents empirical evidence from the UK's electronic and electrical industry to describe the strategic management processes which they employ.

Research Hypotheses

The details of the objectives of the study and research questions of this study are linked to research propositions and relevant hypotheses stated. These are:

Proposition A To explore and examine CEOs' perceptions of the importance of the strategic management process in SMEs.

- H.1. CEOs of successful SMEs perceive employing a strategic management process as an important factor in running the business.

Proposition B To explore the role of senior managers in the strategic management processes within small and medium enterprises.

- H.2. There is a significant relationship between senior managers' age, work experiences, educational background and strategy formulation in SMEs.
- H.3. Strategic awareness of the senior managers in SMEs significantly impacts upon firm performance.

Proposition C To examine the existence and nature of environmental analysis in developing business strategies in small and medium-sized enterprises.

- H.4. CEOs of SMEs consider environmental analysis as a strategic activity when developing business strategies.
- H.5. There is a significant relationship between firm performance and having environmental scanning.

Proposition D To explore and examine the factors associated with effective strategy formulation and implementation process in SMEs.

- H.6. High performance firms use and put more emphasis on mission statement when developing their business strategies than do low performance firms.
- H.7. There are significant correlations between firm size, business life cycle, export activities, firm performance and employing formal strategic management techniques in SMEs.
- H.8. There is a positive association between CEOs perceptions of the importance of human resources and their involvement in the process of strategy formulation and implementation.

The Sample

Small and medium-sized enterprises play a key role in generating employment, promoting innovation, creating competition, and generating economic wealth. The importance of SMEs to the economy depends on their capabilities to fulfil these roles. An effective company strategy for SMEs' growth and success could be based either upon a technological or commercial innovation, or on a focused niche strategy with a differentiated product or service. Any growing company will face several problems as it proceeds through different phases of its life cycle.

Rigorously defining Small and Medium Enterprises (SME) has always been difficult. The term SME covers a variety of firms (Hertz, 1982) and most writers use it rather loosely (Amboise and Muldowney, 1988). Researchers and other interested parties have used specific criteria to convey SME as a construct: value added, value of assets, annual sales, and number of employees. The latter two are most often used to delimit the category (Amboise and Muldowney, 1988). For a growing number of researchers and reporting organizations, the SME is generally considered to employ no more than 250 persons and to have sales of less than £50 million per annum. According to Gupta (1988) the SME is one which is independently owned and operated, and which is not dominant in its field of operation. Quantitatively, the measure of sales revenue or number of employees are used as selection criteria, though a number of authors employ a variety of scales, and sectional differences among industries are sometimes recognized (Gupta, 1988).

In a more recent review of the financial assistance available to SME it is noted that, wide variations become apparent where quantitative parameters are applied to determine eligibility of small to medium sized firms: turnover limits range from £50,000 to £50 million; and the number of employees varies between 50 and 250 (Berry, 1998). In contrast, some scholars (Scott and Bruce, 1987; Gupta, 1988) suggest that, employing additional qualitative criteria can enhance the quantitative definition of SME. For instance, Scott and Bruce (1987) provided a qualitative definition of SME. They indicated that, an SME is one which has three characteristics:

1. management is independent; usually managers are also the owners;
2. capital is supplied and an individual or small group holds ownership; and
3. Area of operations is mainly local. Workers and owners are in one home community, but markets need not be located in the same community.

For statistical purposes, the Department of Trade and Industry (DTI) usually use the following definitions:

- micro firm: 0–9 employees
- small firm: 0–49 employees (includes micro)
- medium firm: 50–249 employees
- large firm: over 250 employees

However, in practice, schemes which are normally targeted at small firms, adopt a variety of working definitions depending on their particular objectives. In February 1996, the European Commission adopted a communication setting out a single definition of SMEs which has been illustrated in Table 3.2.

The communication also includes a (non-binding) recommendation to Member States, the European Investment Bank and the European Investment Fund encouraging them to adopt the same definitions for their programmes. The communication permits them to use lower threshold figures, if desired. Therefore, by examining the general consensus within the literature and through the combination of quantitative

Table 3.2 European Commission's definition of SMEs

Criterion	Micro	Small	Medium
Maximum number of employees	9	49	249
Maximum annual turnover	n/a	7 million euros	40 million euros
Maximum annual balance sheet total	n/a	5 million euros	27 million euros
Maximum % owned by one, or several enterprise(s) not satisfying the same criteria	n/a	25%	25%

Source: Small Business Services (2000)

and qualitative approaches, the following definition for SME was developed which has been employed throughout this research.

Small and medium-sized enterprises (SME) exhibit the following characteristics:

- Employing up to 250 employees.
- Having an annual turnover of up to £50 million.
- Management is independent and free from outside control in taking principal decisions.

Based on the above definition of SMEs, the final sample of the research has been framed.

The Dynamic SME Strategic Management Model

The literature review shows that, a number of models have been proposed for strategic management in SMEs (Linneman, 1980; Green and Jones, 1982; Shuman and Seeger, 1986; Aram and Cowan, 1990; Foster, 1993; Berry, 1998; Beal, 2000). The bases for all of these models are similar in their employed concepts. Many of the concepts and techniques dealing with strategic management have been developed and used successfully by business firms. As managers attempt to better deal with their changing world, a firm generally evolves through four phases of strategic management consisting of basic financial planning, forecast-based planning, externally orientated planning (strategic planning), and strategic management (Dyson and O'Brien, 1998).

Strategic management itself consists of four basic elements: environmental scanning, strategy formulation, strategy implementation, and evaluation and control (Wheelen and Hunger, 1998). Environmental scanning is the monitoring, evaluating, and dissemination of information, regarding the external and internal environment, to key people within the corporation. Its purpose is to identify strategic factors, those external end internal elements that will determine the future of the corporation. It is argued by Wheelen and Hunger (1998) that the simplest way to conduct environmental scanning is through analysis of strengths, weakness, opportunities, and threats (SWOT). Strategy formulation is the development of long range plans for the effective management of environmental opportunities and threats, in light of corporate strengths and weaknesses. It includes defining the corporate mission, specifying achievable objectives, developing strategies and setting policy guidelines. Strategy implementation is the process by which strategies are put into action through the development of programmes, budget, and procedures (Shrader, Taylor and Dalton, 1984; Phillips and Moutinho, 2000). The process might involve changes within the overall culture, structure, and management of the organization (Peel and Bridge, 1998).

Finally, evaluation and control is the process by which corporate activities and performance results are monitored so that actual performance can be compared with desired performance. Although evaluation and control is the final major element of strategic management, it also can pinpoint weaknesses in stages previously implemented and stimulate the entire process to begin again.

In this study, for the conceptual framework the basic strategic management model, which has been developed by Wheelen and Hunger (1998) will be adapted to the SMEs in the UK electrical and electronic industry. However, it must be noted that the conceptual model developed by Wheelen and Hunger is more related to large organizations where the strategists may not be aware of the processes involved in operations and implementations. Moreover, in the case of SMEs, the CEOs as the ultimate strategists, are more likely to be involved in corporate as well as operational levels of the decision-making process. The dynamic strategic management model in SMEs, provides a structured format for directing the examination of SME strategies under the heading of awareness; environmental scanning; strategy formulation; and strategy implementation and control.

Traditionally, the strategic management process models have attempted to answer six basic questions: what is our business? Where are we now? Where do we want to be? How are we going to get there? Which way is the best? And shall we do it? Most models of the strategic management process take a broad view of stakeholders, and are competitor-driven rather than customer-orientated. The dynamic SME's strategic management as an extension of basic strategic management model, introduces, a customer value-based model of strategic management (see Figure 3.3).

The dynamic SME strategic management model consists of three stages:

1. Awareness: understanding the strategic situation
2. Strategy formulation: choosing suitable strategies
3. Strategy implementation: making the chosen strategies happen.

The dynamic SME strategic management model is based on the process by which small and medium enterprises determine their purposes, objectives and desired levels of attainment; decide upon actions for achieving those objectives in an appropriate time scale, and frequently in a changing environment; implement the actions; and assess progress and results. It is therefore suggested that, the strategic management process illustrated here in small and medium enterprises is profiled by a dynamic sequence of the following activities:

- Vision and development of a meaningful mission statement.
- External environment analysis: assessing opportunities and threats in terms of its competitors, suppliers, the economy, socio-political influences and technology in order to improve customer value.
- Internal environment analysis: assessing internal capabilities, strengths and weaknesses.
- An analysis of the present situation of the SME in terms of its products, markets, its distinctive competitive advantages, and the personal objectives of the owner-manager, and consequently, defining the business in terms of mission, objectives, and values for meeting specified customer needs.
- Identifying key improvement factors and strategic issues of the company, which will influence the future direction of the SME.

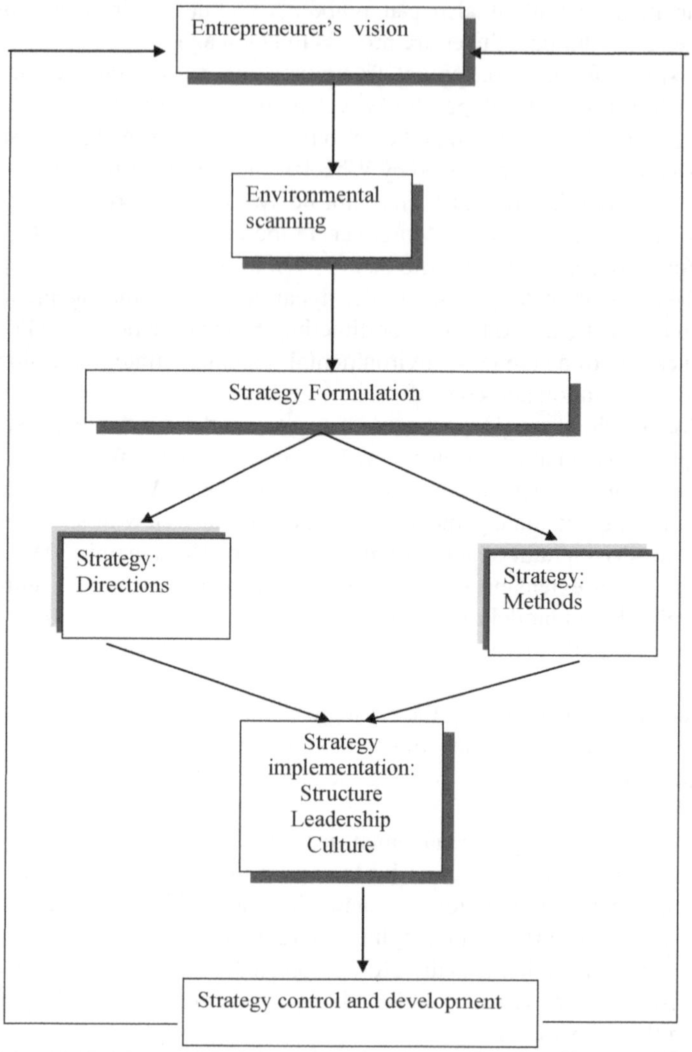

Figure 3.3 Dynamic strategic management model in entrepreneurial SMEs

- Strategy formulation and defining strategic alternatives in terms of objectives and grand strategies.
- Implementing change to enhance process and product by improving people capability.
- Monitoring improved customer value and business performance.

The basic questions referred to above are essentially aspects of a dynamic process. That is, they address the problem of deciding action priorities for companies that wish to prosper by developing and maintaining a competitive strategy by formulation, implementation, and evaluation of strategies that bring satisfaction to customers.

Defining Research Variables

In order to assess the validity of a hypothesis it is necessary to develop measurement of the constituent concepts. This process is often referred to as operationalization of variables (Bryman and Cramer, 1992). In deed what is happening here is the translation of the concepts into variables. In this research different sets of variables are used as below, for more details about the definition of variables see data dictionary.

Managerial and Corporate Characteristics

The first section of the questionnaire investigates the demographic characteristics of respondents. Respondents are asked about their age, sex, their status within the organization, experience, education, and functional background. Age is highly correlated with total work experience, organizational tenure and industry tenure. Hambrick and Mason (1984) maintained that firms with younger managers would be more inclined to pursue risky strategies than would firms with older managers. Education may be considered as indicative of one's knowledge and skill base. As noted by Hambrick and Mason (1984), a manager who has one type of formal education can be expected to have developed different management skills and mental model with which he or she evaluates situations than a manager with another type of formal education. With regard to their functional background, it could be supposed that managers define strategies largely in terms of the goals and tasks in their functional area.

External and Internal Environment Variables

The second section of the questionnaire investigates the firms' method for, and extent of environmental scanning. This examines both internal and external factors affecting the business in order to develop a picture of the managers' awareness of the environment in which his or her firm operates. The external environment of the firm consists of two distinguishable societal environments and task environment variables. Societal environment includes economic, technological, socio-cultural, and political legal variables. While task environment includes industry force variables. In contrast, the internal environment of the firm consists of structure, culture and resource variables. To measure the variables, for example external environment, they will be measured using the five-point Likert scale (low to high). For instance, each respondent is asked to describe the extent to which the external variables drive the company's strategy.

Strategy Formulation Variables

The formulation of strategies in the firm will be examined by direct reference to the variables such as mission, objectives, strategies and policies. The mission of a business is a statement of what the business stands for, what it hopes to achieve, its directions, aims and ambitions. Respondents are asked to indicate the main aim of their firm in terms of long term or short-term profit, survival, market share, growth and rate of return. The emphasis of some of the other variables such as mission statement, long term plans, and annual goals on firm strategy will be measured by using a five point Likert scale (no emphasis, moderate emphasis, strong emphasis).

Strategy Implementation and Control Variables

The main variables in this case consist of strategy implementation through leadership, IT, HR, programmes, budget and procedures. The majority of the variables will be measured by a five-point Likert scale (seldom, sometimes, always). The main variables for measuring the performance and control of the firm's strategy consist of financial variables, customer perspective variables, and innovation variable. For example, the use of accounting and financial variables such as ROI, is acknowledged to be important and used on a regular basis to good effect. Respondents are asked to identify customers feedback about the firm's products or services. Finally, they will be asked how often the firm's business strategy business strategy is reviewed.

The Methods of Data Collection

Data in social science in general, and in business and management studies in particular, are obtained in either formal or informal settings and involve either qualitative or quantitative formats. Robson (1997) argued that, a variety of combinations of these two settings for data collection results in three types of data collection: observation, interview and questionnaire survey. In this section the advantages and disadvantages of these three data collection methods are compared and in light of it the selected data collection method for this study is described.

Observation

Nachmias and Nachmias (1996) argued that, social science research is rooted in observation. A major advantage of observation as a technique is its directness. You do not ask people about their views, feelings, or attitudes; you watch what they do and listen to what they say (Robson, 1997). Moreover, data collected by observation may describe the observed phenomena as they occur in their natural setting. Other data collection methods introduce elements of artificiality in to the research environment. Observational methods might also be used when persons are unwilling to express themselves verbally. This appropriateness does not imply that observation is an easy or trouble -free option. There is a major issue concerning the extent to which an observer affects the situation under observation. There is also the very practical problem with observation that is, it tends to be time consuming (Robson, 1997). Based on the literature, there are very few examples of using observation as a data collection method in management studies.

Interview

One of the most effective methods of gathering primary data in strategic management research is interview. The research interview has been defined as 'a two-person conversation initiated by the interviewer for the specific propose of obtaining research relevant information, and focused by him on content specified by research objectives of systematic description, prediction or explanation' (Cohen and Manion, 1980, 244). Cohen and Manion argued that as a distinctive research technique, the interview might serve three purposes. First, it may be used as the principal means of gathering information having direct bearing on the research objectives. Second, it may be used to test hypotheses or as an explanatory device to help identify variables and relationships. Finally, the interview may be used in conjunction with other methods in a research undertaking (Cohen and Manion, 1980).

In the case of opinion and attitude questions, especially if they are presented in an open-ended format, the interviewer has the opportunity to ensure that the respondent understands the questions. Interviews are increasingly being used in strategic management research through which in-depth information about people's attitudes and values can be elicited. The researcher gains an impression of the respondent, is able to explore issues in greater depth and clarify concepts and definitions. There are more obvious advantages in the use of interview (Kohn and Dipboye, 1998). The process allows the interviewer to encourage the potential respondent to interpret complex questions, to correct the respondent's misunderstandings and to keep track of the interviewee's attention (Judd, Smith and Kidder, 1991).

Both questionnaire and interview are powerful instruments in collecting primary data. While for collecting qualitative data in management research, the in-depth interview is a considerable instrument. There are four types of interview. Based on research objectives, the researcher uses the appropriate type of interview. In the standardized or structured interview the wording of questions and the order in which they are asked is the same from one interview to another. The piece of paper, which is held by the interviewer, is the 'interview schedule' and that word 'schedule' seems to convey the formality of this type of interview (Gilbert, 1993). However, Gilbert has argued that the second type of interview is the semi-standardized type; here the interviewer asks certain major questions the same way each time, but is free to alter their sequence and to probe for more information. The interviewer is thus able to adapt the research instrument to the level of comprehension and articulacy of the respondent, and to handle the fact that in responding to a question, people often also provide answers to questions we are going to ask later (1993, p. 136). The third type of interview is unstructured or informal interviewing. It has been indicated that (Malhotra, 1999), what differentiates this form of interview from the structured or semi-structured interview is its open-ended approach. Based on a list of topics, which the interviewer wishes respondents to discuss, questions are flexible and phrased as the interviewer wishes. Context in this type of interview is very important. It is the most informal form of data collection and is often rich in content, which is why it is associated with a qualitative approach (Robson, 1997). Group interviewing is the fourth type of interview. Group interview have special value for those who want to assess how several people work out a common view, or the range of view, about some topic (Gilbert, 1993). In this type of interviewing the topic should be directed and it is up to the interviewer to maintain the focus so that the discussion does not deviate from the main topic. The researcher aims to encourage interaction in the group (Nachmias and Nachmias, 1996; Robson, 1997). Group interviewing allows the researcher to see how people interact when considering a topic, and how they react to disagreement.

Generally, there is no single best way of collecting data. In this research as will be discussed later, a combination of the different types of interviews, but more specially semi-structured for gathering the data have been used.

Personal interview: advantages and disadvantages The interview is a kind of conversation; a conversation with a purpose (Robson, 1997). Interviews carried out for research or enquiry purposes are a very commonly used approach, possibly in part because the interview appears to be a flexible and adaptable way of finding things out. The main advantage of interview lies in the quality of data. Interviews are the best instruments when as small number of high quality and detailed responses are considered. Nachmias and Nachmias (1996) argued that, flexibility in the questioning process; control of the interview situation; high response rate; and fuller or supplementary information are main advantages of interview. In contrast, higher cost; interviewer bias; and lack of anonymity are the main disadvantages of interview. Interviews offer more flexibility to the interviewer to probe for quality information. Personal interviews have a better chance of acceptance returns, with a low respondents-refusal rate. The sample is less distorted and a much wider range of questions can be covered (Gorton and Dool, 1983; Curran and Blackburn, 2001). Robson (1997) argued that, face-to-face interviews offer the possibility of modifying one's line of enquiry, following up interesting responses and investigating underlying motives in a way those postal and other self-administrated questionnaires cannot. In contrast, interviewing is time consuming. In addition in some fields it appears to be increasingly difficult to obtain co-operation from potential interviewees (Robson, 1997).

Interview is an unusual method in that it involves the gathering of date through direct verbal interaction between individuals. In this sense, it differs widely from the questionnaire. All tools of research have their own strengths and weaknesses. It is commonly agreed that interviewing is time consuming and costly, nevertheless, the process usually produces a good response rate (Judd, Smith and Kidder, 1991; Robson, 1997). It is held that interviewing allows flexibility and adaptability in the process of eliciting information from people (Robson, 1997). Although the interview allows more flexibility, at the same time such flexibility can lead to bias in the way questions are asked, prompts given, and answers recorded. Judd, Smith and Kidder (1991), argued that the source of bias lies in the personalities of both the interviewer and interviewee. The problem highlights the difficulties in ensuring validity and reliability in the interviewing process.

Questionnaire

It has been argued that, there are two main survey data collection models: questionnaire and interview. The main purpose of the research questionnaire is to obtain information that cannot be easily observed or that is not already available in written or computerized form. Evidence from the questionnaire survey is then used for one or more of the following purposes – description, explanation, hypothesis testing. Remenyi et al. (1998) argued that, the type of information sought when surveying individuals or objects, such as firms, usually include evidence on demographic and socio-economic variables. In addition, depending on the study, evidence may be sought on opinions or beliefs related to behaviours, experiences, activities and attitudes (Remenyi et al., 1998). The foundation of all questionnaires is the question. Nachmias and Nachmias (1996) argued that the questionnaire must translate the research objectives into specific questions; answers to such questions will provide the data for hypotheses testing. The question must also motivate the respondents to provide the information being sought. The major aspects of the questionnaire, which have been considered in formulating the questions of the postal questionnaire, consist of its content, measurement considerations, structure, and administration.

The mail questionnaire: advantages and disadvantages The mail questionnaire is an impersonal survey method. Under certain conditions and for a number of reasons, an impersonal method of data collection can be useful. Nachmias and Nachmias (1996) discussed the main advantages of the mail survey as follows:

- *Low cost*. Economy is one of the most obvious appeals of mail questionnaire. The mail questionnaire does not require a trained staff of interviewers; all it entails is the cost of planning, sampling, duplicating, mailing, and providing stamped self-addressed envelopes for the returns.
- *Reduction in biasing error*. The mail questionnaire reduces biasing error that might result from the personal characteristics of interviewers and variability in their skills.
- *Greater anonymity*. The absence of an interviewer also provides greater anonymity. The assurance of anonymity with mail questionnaires is especially helpful when the survey deals with a sensitive issue. On such matters, a mail survey may elicit a higher response rate than a personal interview.
- *Considered answers and consultations*. Mail questionnaires are also preferable when questions demand a considered answer or if an answer requires the consultation of personal documents or other people.
- *Accessibility*. Finally, the mail questionnaire permits wide geographic contact at minimal cost.

Although the mail questionnaire has its advantages, it also has some disadvantages in comparison with other survey methods. Nachmias and Nachmias (1996) listed the disadvantages of the mail survey as follows:

- *Required simple questions.* The mail questionnaire can be used when the questions are straightforward enough to be comprehended solely on the basis of printed instructions and definitions.
- *No opportunity for probing.* The researchers have no opportunity to probe beyond the given answer, to clarify ambiguous answers, or to appraise the non-verbal behaviour of respondents.
- *No control over who fills out the questionnaire.* With a mail questionnaire, the researcher has no control over the respondent's environment; hence they cannot be sure that the appropriate person completes the questionnaire.
- *Low response rate.* Perhaps the most serious disadvantage of mail questionnaire is that it is often difficult to obtain an adequate response rate. Nachmias and Nachmias indicated that, 'the typical response rate for a personal interview is about 95 percent, whereas the response rate for a mail survey is between 20 and 40 percent' (1996, p. 226).

From the listed disadvantages of the mail survey, the low response rate is crucial. In administrating the survey, it is important to consider the factors affecting the response rate. The difficulty of securing an acceptable response rate to mail questionnaires requires the use of various strategies that can be taken to increase the response rate. Three factors are important. First, the sponsorship of a questionnaire has a significant effect in motivating a respondent to fill it out and return it. Therefore, information on sponsorship must be included usually in the cover letter accompanying the questionnaire. Secondly, the researcher must be appeal to the respondents and persuade them that they should participate by filling out the questionnaire and mailing them back. In this case providing some facilities such as self addressed and stamped envelopes will be very useful.

Selection of Data Collection Techniques

As discussed earlier, data collection methods have been grouped into three categories consisting of observational methods, questionnaire surveys and interview (Nachmias and Nachmias, 1996). This study required the collection of both quantitative and qualitative data that would facilitate comparison and hypothesis testing. The data had to be collected from a population of 508 small and medium sized companies in the electronic industry all over the UK. Therefore, it was suggested that a mail questionnaire survey was the most appropriate data collection method (Curran and Blackburn, 2001). The mail questionnaire is the main research instrument in this study. The survey as the data collection method was selected when it became apparent that this method was superior, for our requirements, when compared with the other two methods.

Observational methods are suitable where the phenomena of interest can be observed, relevant events occur within a reasonable time and past events are irrelevant. In this research many of variables could not be observed. So this made the observational method inadequate for the research. However, although, the main data collection method was the survey method, during the follow up interviews the researcher did make some observations in the companies visited. In this research, where secondary data such as the annual reports of the companies, company documents, or published materials, were available, they also provided additional data.

The nature of data in strategic management research includes qualitative and quantitative. The collection of qualitative evidence usually involves interviews, which may be structured to a greater or lesser degree, in order to collect complex information about a particular aspect of the subject, for example, about how firms formulate and implement a business strategy (Remenyi et al., 1998). Because research into strategic issues requires the collection of complex evidence concerning 'why?', 'how?', and 'who?', simple survey techniques are not appropriate and the researcher has to engage in a more sophisticated research strategy. It has been emphasized that, qualitative and quantitative methods could be combined to reinforce each other in the same research project. For quantitative research it is usually obvious what evidence is required and this evidence may usually be collected within a tight structure (Remenyi et al., 1998). Thus, in social science in general and strategic management research in particular, evidence collection often involves the use of questionnaire.

The most important and main reasons for selecting the mail survey as the main research instrument in this study can be summarized as follows:

- *First*, abundant information can be gathered through a structured questionnaire. Meanwhile, the data obtained can have a moderate degree of complexity, if the questionnaire is of appropriate design. Since the required information in this research not only embodies the issues of planning and implementation of business strategies in SMEs, but also includes several organization characteristics, this tool could be used to gather information in an effective way.
- *Secondly*, the topic in this research itself is sensitive. Other methods may encounter a lot of problems during the data collection process and fail to gather enough good quality information. In addition, accuracy of data can be secured and interview bias can controlled by using mail survey.
- *Thirdly*, because of the large sample size, the information gathering process can be very efficient in a limited time. Accordingly, because of the nation wide focus of the study, the mail questionnaire was the most efficient instrument.
- *Finally*, owing to financial constraints, the mail questionnaire was the most appropriate and economical instrument to conduct the survey.

Questionnaire Construction

A questionnaire is a formalized set of questions for obtaining information from respondents. Regardless of the form of administration, a questionnaire is characterized by three specific objectives (Malhotra, 1999). First, it must translate the information needed into a set of specific questions that the respondents can and will answer. Second, a questionnaire must uplift, motivate and encourage the respondent to become involved in the interview, to cooperate and to complete the questionnaire.

Third, a questionnaire can be a potential source of response error, therefore the questions should be constructed in such a way as to minimize response error. In the present research the questionnaire was structured in six steps.

First step the was decision about what information was required. It is useful list all the items about which information is required. Based on the conceptual framework of the research, the subject area of discussion is mainly concerned with the following main notes:

- Strategic management process including formulation and implementation, in the corporate, business, and functional levels of the organization.
- Senior managers' attitudes, perception, and contribution to strategic planning and implementation of business strategies in small and medium-sized enterprises.
- Views of senior managers on the importance of environmental scanning for strategic management in SMEs.
- Importance of strategic management in increasing organizational performance.
- The requirements of managerial effectiveness and improved performance.
- Management style and its relation to developing corporate strategy.
- Criterion of managerial success and how it can be achieved.
- Nature of competitive advantages, core capabilities, competition, decision making and industry strengths analysis in SMEs.

Second step was to consider data collection alternatives. It is necessary to answer the question, is a survey research the best way of obtaining the information? In response to this question, and since in this research, both the primary qualitative and quantitative data were needed, then it was concluded that using a mail questionnaire and personal interview would be useful.

Third Step was the decision about the type of interview and the questions schedule. In management research as Bell (1993) has argued, once the researcher has decided what he or she needs to know, a decision will have to be made about the type of interview. A structured interview will produce structured responses, an open-ended interview will produce a wide range of responses. There is no single best way of collecting data; the method chosen depends on the nature of the research questions (Sapsford and Jupp, 1996). In summary the interview schedule consisted of both close-ended and open-ended questions.

The fourth step was refining the questions and considering how the questions would be analysed. Preparing an interview schedule or guide was *the fifth* step in structuring the questionnaire. This consists of considering the order of questions and preparing prompts in case the respondents do not provide essential information freely.

Finally, in the six step of structuring the questionnaire, revising the questionnaire, and avoiding bias were necessary.

As discussed earlier, the foundation of all questionnaires is the question. Survey questions may concern facts, opinions, attitudes, respondent's motivation, and their level of familiarity with a certain subject. Most questions however, can be classified into either of two general categories: factual questions and questions about subjective experience (Nachmias and Nachmias, 1996). Factual questions are designed to elicit objective information from the respondents regarding their background, environments, habits, and the like. The factual questions, which have been asked in the questionnaire, include such items as gender, age, education, experience, and organizational position. To increase accuracy the researcher has taken several steps, including encouraging respondents to answer the questions, asking more than one question about certain matters, repeating some of the questions, and making respondents feel comfortable when asking about events that they might found embarrassing.

In contrast, questions about subjective experiences involves the respondent's beliefs, feelings, opinions and attitudes that can incline a person to act or react in a certain manner when confronted with certain stimuli (Singleton et al., 1988). The main body of questionnaire investigated senior managers attitudes and perceptions about the formulation and implementation of strategies in business and at the functional level of manufacturing organizations. Although the answers to opinion and attitude questions were more sensitive to changes in wording, emphasis and sequence, than answer to factual questions, different methods and scaling of the questions such as Likert scale have been used to increase validity of questions. Importantly, types of questions were considered as a critical matter in questionnaire design.

Measurement Consideration

Questionnaire responses can be qualified by assigning numbers to the responses according to a given set of rules. This is what is understood by measurement (Cohen and Holliday, 1982). In this regard, operationalization of a concept refers to the whole process of selecting a working definition, choosing a unit of analysis, deciding on the variable name, and finally deciding on a level of measurement for that variable. It has been argued (Miller, 1991; Malhotra, 1999) that, the level of measurement describes the degree of accuracy and detail in a variable's possible value. Measurement can be made at three levels: nominal, ordinal, and continuous (interval and ratio). Table 3.3 illustrates some examples of the current research variables which have been measured in the three levels.

The first level of measurement is nominal level. Nominal scales, which are the least sophisticated level of measurement, are used to place variables into categories with respect to some characteristics. In this research some of variables such as gender and firm activity were measured by nominal scale. For example, numbers were assigned to categories, '1' for male and '2' for female. Also respondents were asked to indicate having written business plan or not by indicating '1' for yes and '2' for no.

The second level of data measurement is ordinal level. More importantly, ordinal scales were used when the respondents were asked for responses in the form of rank ordering. In ordinal scale while the evidence is put into categories, the numbers assigned indicate the ordering of the categories. However, while there is order in the numbers assigned, the intervals between the numbers have no meaning (Remenyi et al., 1998). For example, respondents were asked to rate the degree of emphasis

Table 3.3 Measurement level of the research variables, some examples

V.name SPSS	Variable Label	Measurement	Value Label
Demb	Respondents job title	Nominal	=1 managing director, =2 financial manager, 3= business manager
Demc	Age of respondents	Continuous	In years
Demd	Respondents sex	Nominal	=1 male, =2 female
Deme	Respondents work experience	Continuous	In years
Demh	Respondents formal management training	Nominal	=1 yes, =2 no
Demi	Employees of the firm	Continuous	Total number of employees
Demj	Turnover of the firm	Continuous	Total amount of the firm in last year
Ecoes15a	Impact of economic trends on business strategy	Ordinal	=1 poor, =2 below average, =3 average, =4 above average, =5 outstanding
Enscan8b	Environmental scanning	Ordinal	=1 not important, =2 limited importance, =3 important, =4 very important, =5 essential
Forwrbp1	Formal written business plan	Nominal	=1 yes, =2 no
Lbpprep2	Period of long-term business plan	Continuous	In months
Lbprrevw3	Reviewing long-term business plan	Continuous	In months
Missp10a	Emphasis on mission statement in strategic planning	Ordinal	=1 no emphasis, =2 weak emphasis, =3 moderate emphasis, =4 strong emphasis, =5 very strong emphasis

for each of following indicators within their organizations: mission statement, short term plans, long term plans, competitor analysis. Each item was measured on a 5-point Likert scale.

The third level of measurement level is continuous level. The third and final level of measurement is called the continuous, ratio, or interval scale. Remenyi et al. (1998) argued that, 'rating scales are strictly speaking ordinal. However, in practice, especially in the management area, these are treated as being measured at the interval level' (Remenyi et al., 1998, 153). Evidence based on interval scales can be analysed by virtually the full range of statistical procedures such as the mean, standard deviation, and Pearson's correlation coefficient. In practice, although the survey generally makes most use of the evidence at the ordinal level, some of the variables were measured in continuous scales. Variables such as the number of employees of the firm, amount of turnover of the firm and duration of the business plan preparation are examples of the variables which were measured in continuous scale.

The Process of Survey Questionnaire

Data were collected via mail surveys from 508 senior managers in the UK electronic manufacturing small and medium enterprises. The first phase of primary research involved the survey of the whole population of small and medium-sized enterprises in the electronic industry by means of mail questionnaire. Data were collected from each firm's managing director since they were viewed as the most accurate source for collecting the information required and for gauging data relating to the firm's strategic management processes. Questionnaires were sent out to all 508 companies, accompanied by a covering letter, addressed by name, to the managing director of each company.

The personalized cover letter explained the purpose of the study and provided assurances regarding the confidentiality of collected data. Managing directors were urged to personally participate in the survey. Participants in the survey were offered a summary analysis of the research. In order to minimize response bias, the participants were also provided with pre-addressed envelopes to enable them to return the completed questionnaires directly to the researchers without any risk of perusal within the firms. Potential respondents were assured that, no individual company data would be published and that all data generated would be aggregated. Thus, respondents were assured of the confidentiality of all data collected.

The first mailing generated 74 replies and a follow up letter together with another copy of the questionnaire was sent out two months after the first mailing to non-respondent companies in order to encourage an increased level of response. This second mailing generated a further 58 responses resulting in a total of 132 (27 per cent) completed questionnaires. In addition to the return of completed questionnaires, the survey generated the following alternative responses; 20 letters were returned by the Post Office, indicating that the companies targeted were in liquidation, 15 questionnaires were returned by companies indicating that, they were either unwilling to provide the required data, because of the company's policy involving such surveys, or that they did not engage in strategic management activities and therefore perceived that they were not suitable companies to take part in the survey. Companies indicating that, the managing directors targeted were no longer with then returned a further 20 questionnaires.

Therefore, out of the original 508 companies surveyed, 20 companies were discounted from original sample. From this sample of 488 companies a total of 132 (27 per cent) responses were generated. It is important to indicate that, a comparison of early-responding firms (those that responded before the follow-up letter was sent) and those that responded after the follow-up letter was sent showed that there was difference in terms of the number of employees, firms turnover, or any of the key parameters under study between the two groups and thus they were subjected to the same analytical treatment.

The Process of Research Interviews

As mentioned earlier, interviews are very time-consuming. Then, there is the use of the extra time needed to consider what has been said during the interview and the notes taken, to extend and clarify points that may have been raised. The validity of the data collected by the interview depends upon the effective establishment of a particular kind of social relationship between the interviewer and interviewee. Ackroyd and Hughes (1992) argued that the task of the interviewer is to obtain information, often a highly personal and private nature, from a respondent who is a stranger with little or no obligation to spend time and effort answering questions. In order to select the sub-sample of managing directors for conducting the personal interviews, the systematic sampling method was used.

As Nachmias and Nachmias (1996) argued, systematic sampling consists of selecting every *K*th sampling unit of the population after the first sampling unit is selected at random from the total of sampling units. Systematic sampling is more convenient than simple random sampling. Using the systematic sampling form, from the 60 managing directors (K = 5) who enclosed their business cards with the mail questionnaire and indicated that they were interested in being involved in the research, a total of 12 sub-sample were selected and interviewed. Based on the managers managerial level, their personality and the organizational culture, the initial contact is especially crucial. Obviously, if this fails there is no interview. The interviewer must give the respondents sufficient information about who the interviewer is, how the respondent came to be selected, what the questions will be about, assurances must be given as to confidentiality, and permission sought for the interview to take place (Ackroyd and Hughes, 1992).

In this research the appointment for interview was made through personal contact, and formal and informal channels. All interviews were individually conducted and started, first by briefing the interviewee about the background, importance, and objectives of the research for the development of senior managers and their organizations. The second phase in the process of interview was to establish a suitably relaxed and encouraging relationship between the interviewer and respondent. With this in mind the researcher communicated trust to the respondents and used small talk to ease the situation a little before embarking on the interviews proper. Since the creation of an atmosphere of mutual respect and trust is essential for a successful interview, the interviewees were then assured of the confidentiality of the entire discussion. During the interviews since the interview contains significant non-standardized items, the researcher aimed to place the respondents at ease so that they felt free to talk at some length. The final stage was bringing the interview to a close and disengaging from the scene. This can often be harder than it looks, especially if the relationship has been a rewarding one for the respondent (Ackroyd and Hughes, 1992).

Data Analysis

In order to analyse the data and consequently test the hypothesis, the collected data preliminarily was summarized using statistical graphs such as bar charts and histograms. In addition, various descriptive statistics including means, medians, modes, standard deviations, coefficient of skewness and kurtosis were calculated.

The main reason of such analysis was to get a clear picture of how the different variables were distributed.

The general picture which has been obtained was one of skewed and non-normal distributions. In order to cross check these observations regarding the distributions the Kolmogorove-Smirnove goodness-of-fit test was used on the data to check for normality. The result of the test confirmed that the majority of variables were not normally distributed. Accordingly, the finding had a big influence on the choice of statistical techniques that were used for testing the hypotheses.

Regarding the reliability of the data, reliability analysis on measurements has been carried out. Reliability refers to the extent to which a scale produces consistent results if measurement are made repeatedly (Wilson, 1995). The coefficient alpha is the average of all possible split-half coefficients resulting from different ways of splitting the scale item (Malhotra, 1999; Burns, 2000). Churchill and Peter (1984) argued that, this coefficient varies from 0 to 1, and a value of 0.6 or less generally indicates unsatisfactory internal consistency reliability. In saying this, they implied that, value of alpha above 0.6 were generally acceptable. In this research the coefficient alpha computed for the various variables. The value of alpha ranged from 0.65 to 0.89. This coefficient gave an indication of the internal consistency and therefore stability of measurement generated by research scales and indicated that, the data collected were quiet reliable.

Parametric or Non-Parametric Analysis

One of the unresolved issues in statistics is the question of when parametric rather than non-parametric tests should be used. There is an ongoing debate in research over the use of either parametric or non-parametric statistical analysis techniques. Siegel and Castellan (1988) argued that, a parametric statistical test specifies certain conditions about the distribution of responses in the population from which the research sample was drawn. Typically, parametric techniques assume the sample population has a probability distribution which is approximately normal. Since these conditions are not ordinarily tested, they are merely assumed to hold and thus the meaningfulness of the results of a parametric test depends on the validity of these underlying assumptions. Accordingly Cramer (1994) and Burns (2000) argued that, parametric tests should only be applied when the data fulfil the following three conditions:

- The variables are measured with an equal interval or ratio scale; and the samples are drawn from populations.
- Whose variances are equal or homogeneous.
- Whose distributions are normal.

These assumptions should hold true if parametric techniques are to be used. Violation of any of them means such tests should not be used. Instead, non-parametric techniques should be used. Cramer (1994) argued that, where the above assumptions are violated, non-parametric tests are almost as powerful as their parametric counterparts in detecting population differences. In such cases, it is advisable to use non-parametric tests. By and large, a non-parametric statistical test is based on a model that specifies only very general conditions and none regarding the specific form of the distribution from which the sample was drawn. Unlike parametric methods, non-parametric methods may be applied appropriately to data measured in an ordinal scale, and others to data in a nominal or categorical scale (Siegel and Castellan, 1988) where data are inherently in ranks or categories, they can not be treated by parametric methods (Cramer, 1994). In this research most of data captured by the postal survey were measured on nominal, categorical, and ordinal scales and were not normally distributed.

Statistical Tests Used

Hickey (1986) has developed the decision tree diagrams, which one can use when deciding upon the appropriate statistical tests to use. The choices to be made are based on the purpose of analysis, the number of samples being handled, the type of data available and the number of variables tested at a time. Similarly, Siegel and Castellan (1988) and Burns (2000) have developed tables of most non-parametric tests and conditions under which they can be used. Generally, in this research in order to analyse the data, parametric as well as non-parametric tests have been used. Table 3.4 provides the classification of the statistical test in terms of the level of the data measurement and research design. One-way analysis of variance technique ANOVA has been employed for the analysis of the data, when the data are measured in interval level, and an experimental design between subjects applied. In order to investigate the association between variables, the correlation analysis, Spearman rank order correlation for non-categorical data, and Pearson correlation for categorical data, have been used.

The Spearman's rank orders correlation coefficient were the ones calculated since the data were mainly ordinal and exhibited skewed distributions. In order to investigate the association between two samples in nominal level, Chi-square test

Table 3.4 Data analysis plan: Employed statistical tests

Type of Data	Experimental Design (Between Subjects)	Experimental Design (Within Subjects)
	Two Samples	
Nominal		McNemar test
Ordinal	Wilcoxon Mann-Whiteny Test	Wilcoxon signed ranks test
Interval	Independent Samples T test	Paired samples t-test
	Three Samples	
Nominal	Chi-square test	Cochran's Q test
Ordinal	Kruskal-Willis K-Sample Test	Friedman Test
Interval	One way ANOVA	Repeated measures ANOVA

has been used. While for ordinal variables the Mann-Whittney U test was used for detecting significant differences.

Consequently, independent sample T tests have been applied to the data, which was measured in interval levels. For investigating the relationship between variables in the case of more than three samples, Chi-square for nominal data, Kruskal-Wallis K-sample test for ordinal data, and ANOVA for interval data have been applied.

Summary and Conclusion

This chapter defines the conceptual framework of the study and discusses the ways of creating concepts, variables, hypotheses, and models in strategic management in small and medium-sized firms. An attempt has been made to synthesize the key themes apparent within the existing literature reviewed in Chapter 2. It presents a framework for analysing managers' attitudes and perceptions to strategic management, in British small and medium enterprises using empirical research methodology.

This chapter has reviewed a number of alternative approaches to the design of an appropriate methodology to meet the specific objectives of this study including qualitative and quantitative research methodologies, research process, data collection methods, and data analysis techniques. It has been concluded that, the objectives of this research require that rich, qualitative and quantitative data be collected; thus a methodology, which combines qualitative and quantitative approaches, was deemed appropriate. Management researchers use a wide range of techniques to collect their primary data. In order to gather the data, a combination of both mail questionnaire and personal interview survey techniques was judged to provide the most comprehensive means of capturing exploratory, descriptive and explanatory data pertinent to the stated research objectives. However, because of the nation wide focus of the study, mail questionnaire was the main survey instrument in this research.

Regarding data analysis the data were analysed using the SPSS package. Through preliminary analysis, it was found that, a portion of the data violated several of the assumptions underlying parametric analysis. Therefore, non-parametric analyses as well as parametric analysis has been used. Apart from that, in order to support the findings of the quantitative analysis, the research benefited from the results of qualitative analysis.

References

Ackroyd, S. and Hughes, J. (1992), *Data Collection in Context*, 2nd edn (Harlow, Essex: Longman).

Amboise, G. and Muldowney, M. (1988), 'Management Theory for Small Business: Attempts and Requirements', *Academy of Management Review*, **13**(2), 226–240.

Analoui, F. (2000), 'What Motivates Senior Managers?' 'The Case of Romania', *Journal of Managerial Psychology*, **15**(4), 324–326.

Andrews, K. (1971), 'The Concept of Corporate Strategy', (Homewood, IL: Dow Jones-Irwin Books).

Ansoff, H.I. (1965), *Corporate Strategy* (New York: McGraw-Hill).

Aram, D.J. and Cowan, S.S. (1990), 'Strategic Planning for Increased Profit in the Small Businesses', *Long Range Planning*, **23**(6), 63–70.

Armstrong, J.S. (1982), 'The Value of Formal Planning for Strategic Decisions: Review of Empirical Research', *Strategic Management Journal*, **3**, 197–211.

Beal, R.M. (2000), 'Competing Effectively: Environmental Scanning, Competitive Strategy, and Organisational Performance in Small Manufacturing Firms', *Journal of Small Business Management*, **38**(1), 27–47.

Bell, J. (1993), *Doing Your Research Project, A Guide for First-Time Researchers in Education and Social Science* (Berkshire: Open University Press Books).

Berry, M. (1998), 'Strategic Planning in Small High Tech Companies', *Long Range Planning*, **31**(3), 455–466.

Bracker, J. and Pearson, J. (1985), 'The Impact of Consultants on Small Firm Strategic Planning', *Journal of Small Business Management*, **23**, 23–30.

Bracker, J. and Pearson, J. (1986), 'Planning and Financial Performance of Small, Mature Firms', *Strategic Management Journal*, **7**, 503–522.

Bryman, A. (1988), *Quantity and Quality in Social Research* (London: Routledge).

Bryman, A. and Cramer, A. (1992), *Quantitative Data Analysis for Social Scientists* (London: Routledge).

Burns, R.B. (2000), *Introduction to Research Methods* (London: Sage Publications).

Burrell, G. and Morgan, G. (1993), *Sociological Paradigms and Organisational Analysis: Elements of the Sociology of Corporate Life* (Aldershot: Ashgate Publishing Limited).

Chandler, A.D. (1962), *Strategy and Structure: Chapters in the History of American Industrial Enterprise* (Cambridge, MA: MIT Press Books).

Chen, M.J. and MacMillan, I.C. (1992), 'No Response and Delayed Response to Competitive Moves: the Role of Competitor Dependence and Action Irreversibility', *Academy of Management Journal*, **35**, 539–570.

Chisnall, P. (1986), *Marketing Strategy*, 3rd edn (London: McGraw-Hill).

Churchill, G.A. and Peter, P.J. (1984), 'Research Design Effects on the Reliability of Rating Scales: A Meta-Analysis', *Journal of Marketing Research*, **21**, 360–375.

Cohen, L. and Holliday, M. (1982), *Statistics for Social Scientists: An Introductory Text with Computer Programs in Basic* (London: Paul Chapman Publishing Ltd.).

Cohen, L. and Manion, L. (1980), *Research Method in Education* (London: Croom-Helm).

Cramer, D. (1994), *Introducing Statistics for Social Research* (London: Routledge).

Curran, J. and Blackburn, R.B. (2001), *Researching the Small Enterprise* (London: Sage Publications).

Donaldson, L. (1996), *For Positivist Organisation Theory* (London: Sage Publications).

Douglas, J.D. (1970), *Understanding Everyday Life* (Chicago: Aldine Ltd.).

Dyson, R.G. and O'Brien, F.A. (1998), *Strategic Development* (New York: John Wiley and Sons).

Feltenstein, T. (1992), 'Strategic Planning for the 1990s: Exploiting the Inevitable', *Cornell Hotel and Restaurant Administration Quarterly*, **32**, 50–67.

Feurer, R., Chaharbaghi, K. and Wargin, J. (1995), 'Analysis of *Strategy* Formulation and Implementation at Hewlett-Packard', *Management Decision*, **33**(10), 4–16.

Foster, M.J. (1993), 'Scenario Planning for Small Businesses', *Long Range Planning*, **26**(1), 123–129.

Giddens, A. (1978), *Positivism and Sociology* (London: Heinemann/Educational Books Ltd.).

Gilbert, N. (1993), *Researching Social Life* (London: SAGE Publications Ltd.).

Gimeno, J. and Woo, C.Y. (1996), 'Hyper-competition in a Multi-Market Environment: the Role of Strategic Similarity and Multi-Market Contact in Competitive De-Escalation', *Organization Science*, **7**, 322–341.

Gorton, K. and Dool, I. (1998), *Low-cost Marketing Research* (Chichester: John Wiley).

Green, G.J.L. and Jones, E.G. (1982), 'Strategic Management Step By Step', *Long Range Planning*, **15**(3), 61–70.

Gupta, A. (1988), 'A Stakeholder Analysis Approach for Inter Organisational Systems', *Industrial Management and Data Systems*, **95**(6), 3–7.

Hambrick, D.C. and Mason, D.A. (1984), 'Upper Echelons: The Organisation as a Reflection of its Top Executives', *Academy of Management Review*, **9**(2), 193–206.

Hart, S. (1987), 'The Use of Survey in Industrial Market Research'. *Journal of Marketing Management*, **3**(1), 25–38.

Hertz, L. (1982), *In Search of a Small Business Definition* (Washington, DC: University Press of America).

Hickey, A.A. (1986), *An Introduction to Statistical Techniques for Social Research* (London: Random House Books Inc.).

Hitt, M.A., Gimeno, J. and Hosskisson, R.E. (1998), 'Current and Future Research Methods in Strategic Management', *Organizational Research Methods*, **1**, 6–44.

Hollis, M. (1994), *The Philosophy of Social Science: An* (Introduction, UK: Cambridge University Press).

Hoskisson, R.E., Hitt, M.A., Wan, W.P. and Yiu, D. (1999), 'Theory and Research in Strategic Management: Swings of a Pendulum', *Journal of Management*, **25**(3), 417–456.

Hunt, S.D. (1991), *Modern Marketing Theory* (Cincinnati: South-Western Publishing Co).

Hurley, R.E. (1999), 'Qualitative Research and the Profound Grasp of the Obvious', *Health Services Research*, **34**(5, part 2), 1119–1136.

Judd, C.M., Smith, E.L. and Kidder, L.H. (1991), *Research Methods in Social Relations, International Edition*, 6th edn (Holt; Rinehart and Winston, Inc.).

Judge, W.Q., Jr and Zeithaml, C.P. (1992), 'Institutional and Strategic Choice Perspectives on Board Involvement in the Strategic Decision Process', *Academy of Management Journal*, **35**, 766–794.

Kohn, L.S. and Dipboye, R.L. (1998), 'The Effects of Interview Structure on Recruiting Outcomes', *Journal of Applied Social Psychology*, **28**(9), 821–843.

Kudla, R.J. (1980), 'The Effects of Strategic Planning on Common Stock Returns', *Academy of Management Journal*, **23**(1), 5–20.

Langer, J. (1999), '15 Myths of Qualitative Research: It's Conventional, but is it Wisdom?' *Marketing News*, **33**(5), 13–14.

Learned, E.P., Christensen, C.R., Andrews, K. and Guth, W.D. (1969), Business Policy: Text and Cases, (Homewood, IL: Richard D. Irwin).

Linneman, R.E. (1980), *Shirt-sleeve Approach to Long Range Planning for the Smaller, Growing* (Corporations, NJ: Prentice-Hall Books).

Malhotra, N.K. (1999), *Marketing Research: An Applied Orientation*, 3rd edn (Upper Saddle River, New Jersey: Prentice-Hall Books Inc.).

Marshal, C. (1985), 'Approximate Criteria of Trustworthiness and Goodness for Qualitative Research', *Quality and Quantity*, **19**, 353–373.

May, T. (1997), *Social Research: Issues, Methods and Process*, 2nd edn (Buckingham: Open University Press).

McKiernan, P. and Morris, C. (1995), 'Strategic Planning and Financial Performance in UK SMEs: Does Formality Matter?', *British Journal of Management*, **5**, 31–41.

McNeill, P. (1990), *Research Methods* (London: Routledge).

Miller, C.C. and Cardinal, L.B. (1994), 'Strategic Planning and Firm Performance: A Synthesis of More than Two Decades', *Academy of Management Journal*, **37**, 1649–1665.

Miller, D.C. (1991), *Handbook of Research Design and Social Measurement*, 5th edn (London: SAGA Publications).

Mintzberg, H. (1994), 'The Fall and Rise of Strategic Planning', *Harvard Business Review*, **72**(1), 107–114.

Nachmias, C.F. and Nachmias, D. (1996), *Research Methods in Social Science (forth ed)* (London: Edward, Arnold).

Niv, A., Jehiel, Z. and Isaac, M. (1998), 'Environmental Scanning and Information Systems in Relation to Success in Introducing New Products', *Information and Management*, **33**(4), 201–211.

Pearce, J., Freeman, E. and Robinson, R. (1987), 'The Tenuous Link between Formal Strategic Planning and Financial Performance', *Academy of Management Review*, **12**, 658–675.

Peel, M.J. and Bridge, J. (1998), 'How Planning and Capital Budgeting Improve SME Performance', *Long Range Planning*, **31**(6), 848–856.

Phillips, P.A. and Moutinho, L. (2000), 'The Strategic Planning Index: A Tool for Measuring Strategic Planning Effectiveness', *Journal of Travel Research*, **38**(4), 369–370.

Porter, M. (1998), *On Competition* (Boston: Harvard Business School Publishing).

Remenyi, D., Williams, B., Money, A. and Swartz, E. (1998), *Doing Research in Business, and Management: An Introduction to Process and Method* (London: SAGE Publications).

Rhyne, L.C. (1986), 'The Relationship of Strategic Planning to Company Performance', *Strategic Management Journal*, **7**, 423–436.

Robson, C. (1997), *Real World Research: A Resource for Social Scientists and Practitioner-Researcher* (Oxford: Blackwell).

Root, M. (1996), *Philosophy of Social Science* (Oxford: Blackwell Publishers Inc.).

Rumelt, R.P., Schendel, D. and Teece, D.J. (1994), *Fundamental Issues in Strategy: A Research Agenda* (Boston, Mass.: Harvard Business School Publishing).

Sapsford, R. and Jupp, V. (1996), *Data Collection and Analysis* (London: Open University, SAGE Publication).

Sayer, A. (1992), *Methods in Social Science: A Realistic Approach*, 2nd edn (London: Routledge).

Schendel, D.E. and Hatten, K.J. (1972), 'Business Policy or Strategic Management: A Broader View for an Emerging Discipline', *Academy of Management Proceedings*, 99–102.

Scott, M. and Bruce, R. (1987), 'Five Stages of Growth in Small Business', *Long Range Planning*, **20**(3), June, 45–52.

Shrader, C., Taylor, L. and Dalton, D. (1984), 'Strategic Planning and Organisational Performance: A Critical Appraisal', *Journal of Management*, **10**, 149–171.

Shrader, C.B., Mulford, L. and Blackburn, V.L. (1989), 'Strategic and Operational Planning, Uncertainty and Performance in Small Firms', *Journal of Small Business Management*, **27**(4), 45–60.

Shuman, J.C. and Seeger, J.A. (1986), 'The Theory and Practice of Strategic Management in Smaller Rapid Growth Firms', *American Journal of Small Business*, **11**(1), 7–18.

Siegel, S. and Castellan, J.N., Jr (1988), *Non-parametric Statistics for the Behavioural Science* (Columbus, OH: McGraw-Hill).

Silverman, D. (1998), 'Qualitative and Quantitative' in *Core Sociological Dichotomies*, Jenks, C. (ed.) (London: Sage Publications).

Singleton, R., Jr, Straits, B.C., Straits, M.M. and McAllister, R.J. (1988), *Approaches to Social Research* (Oxford: Oxford University Press).

Small Business Services (2000), 'UK Small Business Services'. Available at www.sbs.gov.uk.

Smith, J.A. (1998), 'Strategies for Start-Ups', *Long Range Planning*, **31**(6), 857–872.

Thomas, H. (1984), 'Mapping Strategic Management Research', *Journal of General Management*, **9**(4), 52–72.

Van Maanen, J. (1983), *Qualitative Methodology* (London: Sage Publications).

Wheelen, T.L. and Hunger, J.D. (1998), 'Strategic Management and Business Policy', *Six* (Edition, NY: Addision-Wesley Publication).

Wilson, E.J. (1995), 'Research Design Effects on the Reliability of Rating Scales in Marketing: An Update on Churchill and Peter', *Advances in Customer Research*, **22**, 360–365.

Chapter 4

Data Analysis and Major Findings

Introduction

The discussion on the methodology adopted for this empirical research, was provided in Chapter 3. It has been explained that the main method of data collection in this research was the postal survey. In this chapter the data generated through postal survey will be analysed, explored and discussed further. The aim of this chapter is to present the findings from the data analysis carried out for this empirical research. Furthermore, in Chapters 5 and 6, these findings will be interpreted in relation to the research questions of the study and will be discussed with respect to the existing theories which were reviewed in the preceding chapters. In order to analyse the data and consequently discuss the results, the collected data were summarized using descriptive statistics. This type of data analysis gives a clear picture of the distribution of the data and consequently helps to select appropriate statistical tests for testing the hypotheses. In this chapter, first the firm details and demographic profile of the respondents will be explored. Second the data regarding the strategic planning activities in small and medium-sized enterprises will be analysed. Third the discussion will continue with respect to environmental analysis in the studied firms. Strategy implementation, organizational factors and firm performance will be discussed in the fourth section. Finally, the chapter will end with a conclusion and summary.

Company Details

Let's start analysis of the data with details of the studied firms and demographic profile of the respondents. Of the 508 questionnaires distributed, 132 completed questionnaires were returned from small and medium-sized enterprises. This accounted for a response rate of 27 per cent. Typically, the studied companies were operating in the high tech electronic and electrical industry. The size of the companies varied from small to medium sized based on two criteria: the number of employees and the amount of annual turnover. As it has been discussed in the sampling Section (5.8.1) that the small and medium sized companies are here defined as those which have less than 250 employees and have an annual turnover of up to £50 million. Figure 4.1 provides a summary of the number of employees groups (Mean = 2.24, Std = 1.35) in the sample firms.

As shown in Figure 4.1, 40.9 per cent (n = 54) of the companies studied have less than 50 employees. Thirty-two (24.2 per cent) employed 51–100 employees. Only 19 of the studied firms had between 101 and 150 employees, 14 (10.6 per cent)

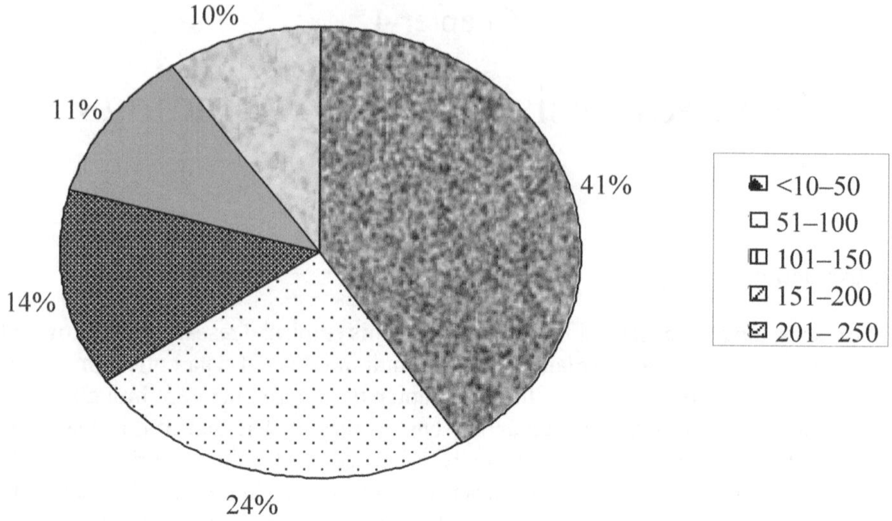

Figure 4.1 Demographic profile of respondents

companies were located in the employees group 151 to 200, and finally, 13 (9.8 per cent) companies were classified in the employees group of between 201 and 250. Regarding the companies founders, the result of the data analysis shows that the majority of the companies (n = 93, 70 per cent) were established by more than two founders, whilst only 30 per cent of the studied companies (n = 39) were established by one or two founders. This result also reflects the findings of Cooper (1973) and Berry (1998) who concluded from their empirical research that, successful small businesses were founded by a team of two to five people rather than an individual. As explained the firm size was measured by the amount of their annual turnover and the number of employees (see Figure 4.2).

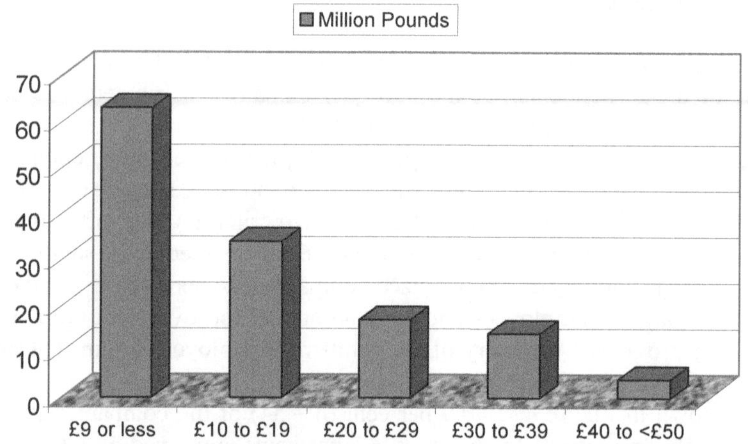

Figure 4.2 Annual turnover of studied firms

The amount of annual turnover of the studied firms (Mean = 1.95, Std. = 1.14) varied from £1.25 to £49.6 million. As illustrated in Figure 4.2, a total number of 63 (47.7 per cent) companies studied had a turnover level of up to £10 million and only 25.8 per cent (n = 34) had a turnover of up to £20 million. Some 17 companies (12.9 per cent) had an annual turnover of between £20 and £29 million. The findings also show that, 14 of the companies studied had a turnover of between £30 and £39 million for a response rate of 10.9 per cent, whilst the remainder ranged between £40 million and less than £50 million (3 per cent).

Managerial Characteristics of the Respondents

Building on the premises of strategy research, researchers argue that observable executive characteristics serve as indicators of the mental models executives use during strategy formulation and implementation. In this section the managerial and personal characteristics of the senior managers of the studied companies such as age, gender, management training, educational backgrounds, and functional background are reported. Table 4.1 summarizes the demographic profile of the respondents involved.

Table 4.1 Demographic profile of the respondents (percent)

Firm size (number of employees)	%	*Annual turnover of the firm (Million Pounds)*	%
Micro-enterprises	7	9 or less	47.7
Small-enterprises	48	10-19	25.8
Medium-enterprises	45	20-29	12.9
total	100	30-39	10.9
Age of the respondents	%	40-<50	3
30 or less to 39	29.5		
40 to 49	46.2	*Respondent's educational level*	%
50 to 59 or more	24.2	Up to A level	50.8
		Bachelor degree	22.7
Respondent's sex	%	Master degree	22.12
Male	92.4	Ph.D.	5.3
Female	7.6		
Respondent's years of work experiences	%	*Respondent's educational background*	%
9 or less	27.3	Engineering	34
10-19	47.7	Management	26
20-29	16.7	Science	11
30-39	5.3	Technology	8
		General	21

Source: Survey questionnaire

Respondents' Age

It has been argued that, the age of the senior managers is highly correlated with their total work experience, and organizational and industry tenure. For instance, it has been proposed that, older executives are more committed to the status quo than are the younger executives. Kakabadse (1999) also argues that younger does not [necessarily] mean better.

The analysis of the data show that the respondents age (Mean = 44, Std = 8) ranged from minimum 32 to maximum 65 years old. Figure 4.3 provides the classification of the respondents age groups. The respondents were categorized into three groups: group one (under 30–39 years old), group two (40–49 years old), and group three (over 50).

Thirty-nine of the respondents (29.5 per cent) reported their age to be between under 30 and 39 years old. The majority of the respondents (n = 61, 46.2 per cent) were between 40 and 49 years old and the remainder (n = 32, 24.2 per cent) reported their age as being 50 or older.

Work Experiences

As mentioned early, age is highly correlated to the work experiences of the executives. In order to examine this proposition, in this research the researchers measured the work experiences of the CEOs as well as their age. The respondents' average number of years work experience (Mean = 15.91, Std = 7.99) was 34 years. In other words, the minimum years of respondents' work experience was 8 years, while the maximum number of years work experience was 42. The total work experiences of the respondents were categorized into five groups (see Figure 4.4.).

The findings of the research show that 36 of the respondents (27.3 per cent) had less than 10 years work experience, whilst many of them (n = 63, 47.7 per cent) fall

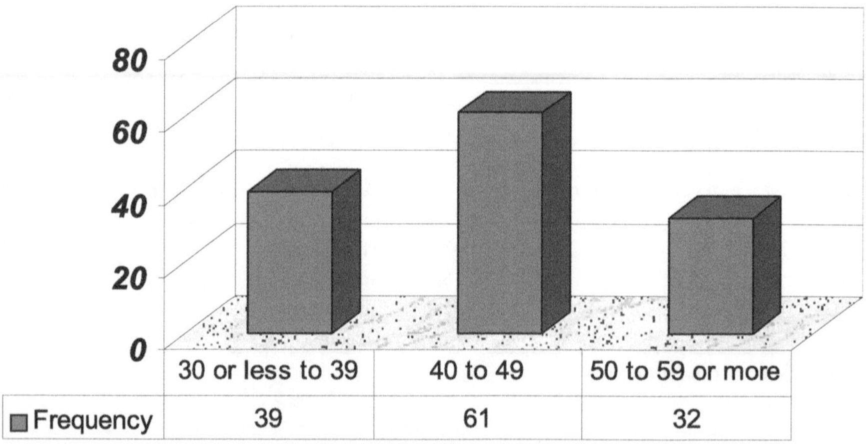

Figure 4.3 The age groups of respondents

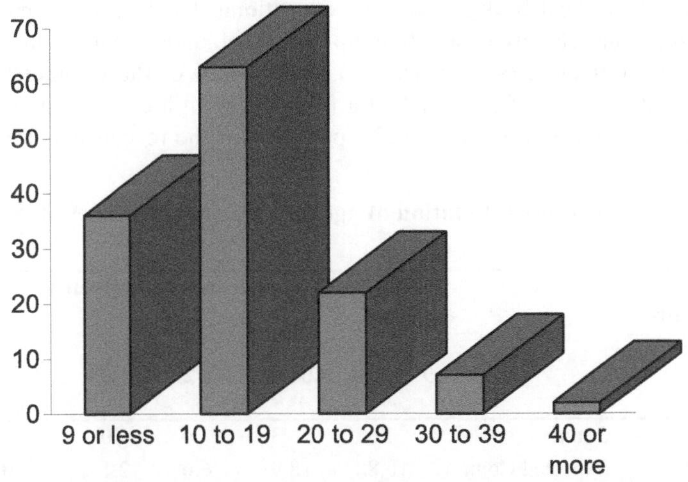

Figure 4.4 The total years of work experiences of respondents

into the category ranging from 10 to 19 years. Although 22 (16.7 per cent) of the respondents reported that, they had between 20 and 29 years experience, only seven people (5.3 per cent) reported that their work experience amounted to 30–39 years. The remainder (n = 2, 1.5 per cent), possessed 40 or more years of work experience. Therefore, in short, the findings reveal that the majority of the respondents (n = 63) had a total work experience of between 10 and 19 years and minority of them (n = 2) had a total work experiences of 40 years or more. The correlation between work experiences and the other managerial characteristics will be discussed later. Table 4.2 shows the cross tabulation between the age of the respondents and their total years of work experience.

Gender

Regarding gender, the majority of the respondents (n = 122, 92.4 per cent) were male and only 7.6 per cent of the respondents (n = 10) were female. This result confirms that, most of the top management and especially the executive positions in the electric and electronic industry were occupied by men rather than women. Perhaps this result is related to the nature of the industry.

Education

Another interesting characteristic of the CEOs is their education. Education may be considered as indicative of one's knowledge and skill base. As noted by Hitt and Tyler (1991) the executive who has one type of formal education can be expected to have developed different problem-solving skills and mental models with which to formulate strategy than an executive with a different type of formal education. In this regard the researchers decided to measure the CEOs' educational level in conjunction with their educational background. The educational level of the respondents was divided into four categories including: up to A level, undergraduate, master degree, and PhD or equivalent (see Figure 4.5). Nearly half of the respondents (n = 67, 50.8 per cent) reported that, they had a first degree in areas such as engineering, management and sciences. Thirty (22.7 per cent) of the respondents reported their

Table 4.2 The cross tabulation of age and work experiences of respondents

Age of respondents		**Work experiences of respondents**					**Total**
		9 or less	**10–19**	**20–29**	**30–39**	**40 or more**	
30 or below 39	Count	36	3	0	0	0	39
	Expected Count	10.8	18.9	6.6	2.1	0.6	39
	% of Total	**27.69**	**2.3**	**0**	**0**	**0**	**30**
40–49	Count	0	60	0	0	0	60
	Expected Count	16.61	29.07	10.15	3.23	0.92	60
	% of Total	**0**	**46.15**	**0**	**0**	**0**	**46.15**
50–59 or more	Count	0	0	22	7	2	31
	Expected Count	8.58	15.02	5.24	1.66	0.47	31
	% of Total	**0**	**0**	**16.92**	**5.38**	**1.53**	**23.84**
Total	Count	36	63	22	7	2	130
	Expected Count	36	63	22	7	2	130
	% of Total	**27.69**	**48.46**	**16.92**	**5.38**	**1.53**	**100**

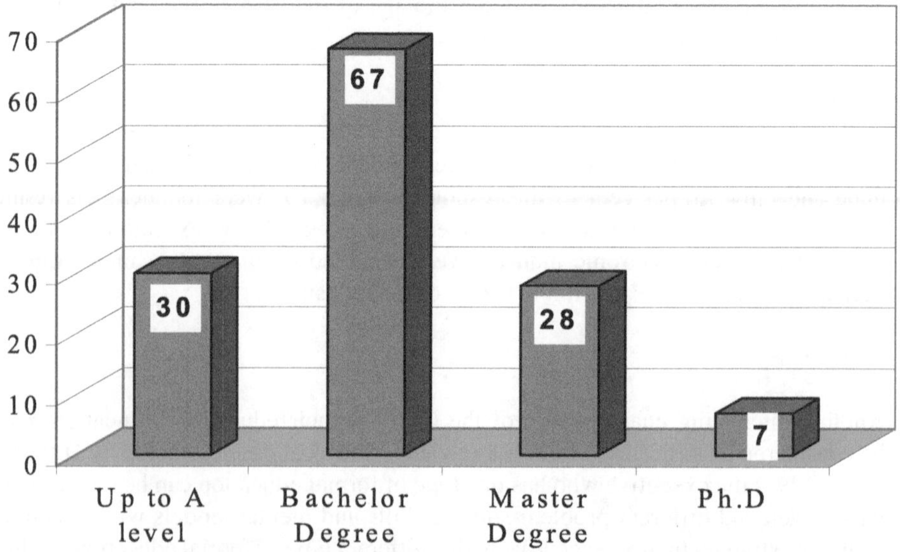

Figure 4.5 Educational level of respondents

education was up to A level, whilst 26.5 per cent (n = 35) of the respondents reported that they possessed a postgraduate degree. The post graduate category includes Master degree (n = 28, 21.2 per cent), and PhD or equivalent (n = 7, 5.3 per cent).

In order to find out about the educational background of the CEOs, they were also asked to indicate their area of study and the field in which they had graduated. The responses received were categorized into five groups. The first group, 'engineering' included mainly electronic engineering and the other engineering fields of study. The second group, 'management and business studies' included different areas such as, business administration, marketing, management, finance and accounting, human resource management, and public administration. The third group, 'science' included the respondents who graduated in a variety of pure and applied science courses such as mathematics, physics and computer sciences. The fourth group, 'technology' included information technology, industrial technology, industrial management, and technology development. Finally the last group, 'general' accommodates the respondents who did not seem to have had any formal degree from a further or higher education institute. The respondents, who had general qualifications such as diplomas, are included in this category.

From amongst these groups, the engineering group had the most frequency (n = 45, 34 per cent). In contrast, the technology group had the minimum frequency of respondents (n = 10, 7.6 per cent). One of the considerable findings of this research is that, about 21.2 per cent (28) of the respondents had not had any higher education. It has also been found that 34 of the CEOs for the response rate of 25.8 per cent reported that they had a degree in management and business studies. Figure 4.6 provides a summary of the respondents' educational background.

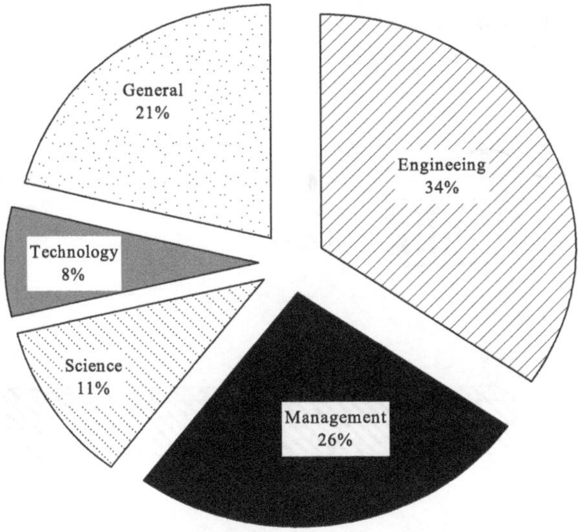

Figure 4.6 Respondents' educational background

Management Training

Regardless of the respondents' differing educational levels or background, the CEOs were asked to indicate whether or not they have had any management training. In this regard, 89 per cent of the respondents reported that, they have attended some form of management training programme, while only 11 per cent of the respondents reported that, they have not attended any management training programmes at all (see Figure 4.6). The management training programs reported here are different from those of the formal degrees offered in management. However, by checking the details of the responses provided, it was realized that, all the CEOs with a formal degree in management, answered yes to this question.

Strategic Planning Activities

In the first section of the business planning audit the respondents' perceptions of strategic planning in the studied firms were examined. Developing business plans, the firms' objectives, mission statement, the degree of formality of the strategic planning, and planning typology are some of the main issues which have been investigated and reported in this section.

The Degree of Formality Involved in Business Planning

One of the main issues in small and medium-sized enterprises is the degree of formality involved in the planning activities. In this study, 83 per cent of the business owners and operators surveyed indicated that they employed business planning techniques (see Figure 4.7).

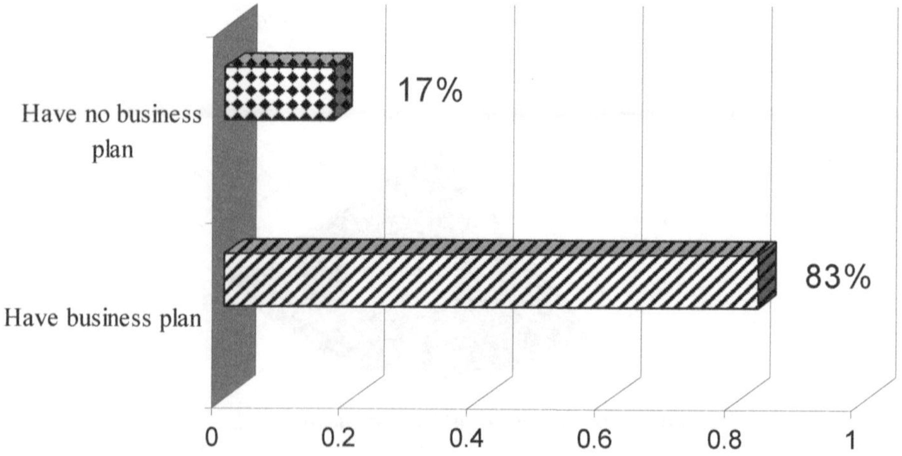

Figure 4.7 Employing business plan in the studied firms

They stated that they are implementing a business plan outlining all strategic, operation and financial plans of their companies. Consequently, the majority of the respondents indicated that they also have many of the components of a business plan, such as a corporate mission statement, marketing, financial and operational plans. The respondents believed that formal business planning is necessary for the success of the small business. In contrast, only 17 per cent of the respondents indicated that they do not employ either formal or informal business plans. Regarding the review of the business plan in the studied firms, 72 per cent of the respondents noted that the senior management of their companies meet at least monthly to deal with the issue of business planning.

Who are involved in Business Planning?

The majority of business owner managers were responsible for business planning in the studied firms. Whilst 76 per cent of respondents reported that senior managers were primarily responsible for the task of business planning in their companies, 14 per cent stated that middle managers have the responsibility of developing business plans in the studied firms. Another 6 per cent of the respondents indicated that internal strategic planning groups and committees were primarily responsible for business planning and 2 per cent indicated external professionals, such as consultants or colleagues not employed by their company, as being primarily responsible for business planning. The remaining 2 per cent stated that a combination of individuals, both internal and external to the company, oversee the business planning process for their companies.

The Degree of Involvement of the Studied Firms in Planning Activities

Respondents were asked to indicate whether or not their companies were employing specific indicators and elements of the formal business planning and also to indicate the extent to which their firms place emphasis on the specific indicators in developing their strategic plans. These indicators include mission statement, trend analysis, competitor analysis, long term plans, annual goals, short term plans, and ongoing evaluation. Figure 4.8 illustrates the categories of the studied firms in terms of their involvement in planning activities.

No planning Varying degrees of strategic planning were observed among the sample. If a company did not engage in any of the strategic planning indicators, that company was categorized as a non-planner. Only 17 per cent of the respondents indicated that they employ none of the seven business planning techniques. In these firms, no planning activities were reported. Accordingly, no mission and objectives either short term or long term have been developed.

Informal financial planning if a company employed up to two of the techniques, such as short-term objectives, then it was categorized as being an informal financial planner. Data analysis shows that 21 per cent of the studied firms employed financial planning. In this group, respondents rated formal financial planning as being an essential activity. CEOs stress the importance of tight financial controls and performance. It has also been found that, the firms develop short-term (up to one

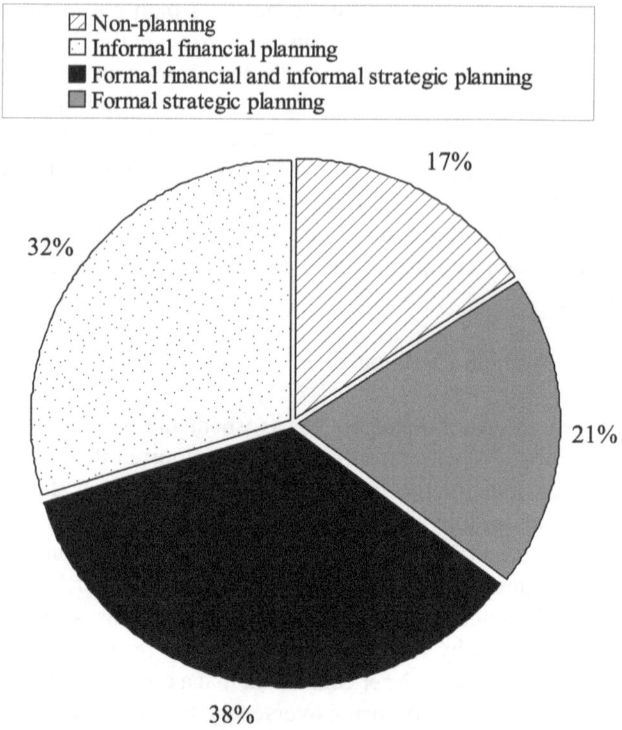

Figure 4.8 Classification of the studied firms in terms of their involvement in planning activities

year) to medium-term (up to two years) financial objectives. The firms in this group were not engaged in strategic planning at all.

Formal financial and informal strategic planning if a company incorporated three or four of the mentioned techniques, then the company was categorized as being a formal financial and informal strategic planner. It has been found that 38 per cent of the studied firms were involved in formal financial and informal strategic planning. Respondents in this group, believed in the importance of informal strategic planning. While financial planning and performance were tightly controlled and monitored. The firms that have had a mission statement and long-term financial objectives specified a two to five years planning horizon. In this group of the studied firms, mission statement, objectives and business strategies are not formalized in a business plan. However, their business plan has been clearly communicated and known throughout the firm.

Formal strategic planning Finally, if a company has been engaged in five or more of the seven strategic planning indicators, then that company was categorized as being a formal strategic planner. Data analysis shows that 32 per cent of the studied firms reported practicing five or more of the business planning techniques, therefore, these firms were categorized as being formal strategic planners. In this group management stressed the importance of a formal and explicit process of strategy formulation, written mission statement and stating long term objectives over a two to five years planning horizon. Formal and written strategic plans were produced and reviewed on a six monthly or annual basis. In these firms, the formal strategic business plans are developed reflecting management perception and belief that significant benefit will arise for the company.

Developing Objectives and Mission Statement in the Studied SMEs

The respondents were asked to indicate whether or not in their firm they have either stated business objectives or a mission statement. If so, what are those objectives? The results showed that, the majority of the firms (n = 104, 78 per cent) have a formal mission statement, while only (n = 25) 19 per cent of the respondents reported that, they do not have a formal mission statement. Two per cent of the respondents (n = 3) did not answer the question at all (see Figure 4.9). The findings of this research supports the results of the previous studies. For instance, in David's (1989) survey of the Business Week 1000, only 41 per cent of the firms indicated that, they had mission statements.

Purposes of Mission Statement

In order to explore why SMEs have a mission statement, it would be useful to compare the result of this study with the result of a similar study in large firms. Baetz and Bart's (1996) work on developing mission statement in 135 large Canadian organizations showed that, mission statements have been used by 86 per cent of the

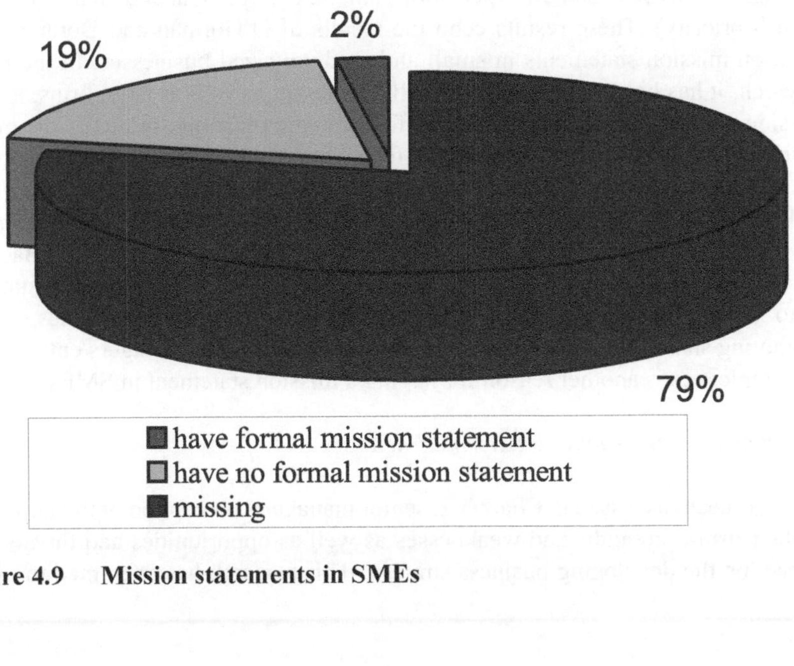

Figure 4.9 Mission statements in SMEs

firms. They reported that, the main reasons for having a mission statement in large firms were:

1. to guide the strategic planning system;
2. to define the organization's scope of business operations/activities;
3. to provide a common purpose/direction transcending individual and department needs;
4. to promote a sense of shared expectations among all levels of employees, thereby building a strong corporate culture (i.e. shared value); and finally,
5. to guide leadership style" Baetz and Bart (1996, 528).

In the present study the respondents were specifically asked to indicate the purpose of developing a mission statement within their firms. In this regard, the data analysis shows that, the mission statements were being used for different reasons. The purposes of having a mission statement based on the respondent's stated priority are as follow:

- developing and planning business strategies
- increasing profit and growth rate
- customer satisfaction
- and promoting a sense of shared expectations among entrepreneur and all employees.

The list of the purposes for having mission statements according to the respondents own priority shows that, the firms choose to have a mission statement in order to develop and plan their business strategies (first priority), to increase profit and growth (second priority); to increase the customers satisfaction (third priority), and to promote a sense of shared expectations among entrepreneur and all the employees (fourth priority). These results echo the results of O'Gorman and Doran's (1999) work on mission statements in small and medium sized businesses. In the present research, it has been found that, in small businesses as well as large firms, a formal mission statement is an important tool for strategic planning. In SMEs the mission statement is more related to strategy formulation rather than implementation of business strategies. Also, SMEs use mission statement for increasing their profit and growth within the industry. Increasing customer satisfaction is another reason for developing mission statement in SMEs. While based on the results of Baetz and Bart (1996) study, in large firms, the second priority for having a mission statement is to define the organization's scope of business operations/activities. Finally, promoting shared thinking and expectation amongst owner managers/entrepreneurs and employees is another reason for having a mission statement in SMEs.

Significance of Internal and External Factors

As it has been discussed in Chapter 2, senior managers' perception of the importance of their firms' strengths and weaknesses as well as opportunities and threats could impact on the developing business strategy. This research has attempted to explore the perceptions of the SMEs managers' perception of the above four factors. The respondents were asked to indicate the significance of each of the firm's internal strengths, internal weaknesses, and external opportunities and threats in developing business strategies. According to the data analysis, the respondents believed that external opportunities (Mean = 4.32, Std = 1.73) are significant factors in developing business strategies. In contrast, the respondents considered the external threats (Mean = 1.98, Std = 1.32) as being less of a significant factor in developing business strategies. Regarding the internal factors, the respondents gave the priority to the internal strengths ((Mean = 4.18, Std = 0.95), rather than internal weaknesses (Mean = 3.72, Std = 1.14) in developing business strategies. Generally speaking, it could be said that, in the studies of SMEs the strategists give the priority to the external opportunities and internal strengths when developing business strategies. The details of these findings will be discussed in the next chapter.

Environmental Analysis in Small and Medium-sized Enterprises

Importance of the External Environmental Factors

As discussed in Chapters 2 and 3, in strategy research the external and task environment have been considered as key factors in developing business strategies. In order to investigate the importance of external factors in formulating business strategies in SMEs, in this research, the respondents were asked to indicate to what extent internal and external environment factors affect their firm's strategy. A five-scale Likert scale was applied for these questions in this section. As for the reliability of the data, by calculating alpha (α) coefficient, it was found that there was internal consistency between the responses provided in each group (see Table 4.3).

Table 4.3 Importance of environmental factors in the firm's decision-making process

Environmental factors	Alpha* α	Percentage	Mean	Std. Deviation
Technological changes	0.83	34%	3.84	1.03
Competitors	0.79	23%	3.76	1.07
Economic Trends	0.68	20%	3.55	1.12
Social and cultural trends	0.76	12%	3.01	1.15
Political & legal developments	0.62	11%	2.82	1.15

*Internal consistency within each group

Regarding the external factors, the importance of economical trends, socio-cultural trends, competitors, technology and political factors in strategic management have also been investigated. As illustrated in Table 4.4 regarding the effect of technological changes (Mean = 3.84, Std. *D* = 1.03) on the firm's strategy, only one of the respondents (n = 1, 0.76 per cent) rated the effect as poor. While, many of

Table 4.4 Importance of environmental factors in strategic management

	Technological Changes	Competitors	Economical Trends	Social & Cultural Trends	Political Factors
Poor	N=1 (.76%)	N=6 (4.58%)	N=7 (5.34%)	N=12 (9.16%)	N=16 (12.21%)
Below average	N=16 (12.21%)	N=7 (5.34%)	N=17 (12.98%)	N=34 (25.95%)	N=40 (30.53%)
Average	N=27 (20.61%)	N=36 (27.48%)	N=31 (23.66%)	N=41 (31.30%)	N=37 (28.24%)
Above average	N=46 (35.11%)	N=45 (34.35%)	N=49 (37.40%)	N=29 (22.14%)	N=27 (20.61%)
Outstanding	N=41 (31.30%)	N=37 (28.24%)	N=27 (20.61%)	N=15 (11.45%)	N=11 (8.40%)
Total	N=131 (100.00%)	N=131 (100.00%)	N=131 (100.00%)	N=131 (100.00%)	N=131 (100.00%)

the respondents (n = 41, 31.30 per cent) rated the effect of technological change on developing firm's strategy as outstanding. 35.1 % of the respondents also rated the importance of the technological changes above average. Generally speaking, technological changes have been considered as the strongest factor which influences the formulation of business strategies in the studied firms. In contrast, political factors have been considered as the weakest factor in influencing the formulation of the business strategies in the studied firms. The respondents rated the importance of the political and legal developments factors (Mean = 2.82, Std. D = 1.15) as poor and below the average (n = 56, 42.47 per cent).

While 11 of the respondents rated technological changes as outstanding, in comparison, the importance of competitors (Mean = 3.76, Std. = 1.07) has been rated as being in second priority After the technological factors (poor and below average 9.92 per cent, average 27.48 per cent, above average and outstanding 62.59 per cent). The importance of economical trends (Mean = 3.55, Std. = 1.12) has been rated as third priority (poor and below average 18.32 per cent, average 23.66 per cent, above average and outstanding 58.01 per cent). It is interesting to note that, the respondents rated the importance of social and cultural factors as the fourth level of priority (Mean = 3.01, Std. = 1.15) (see Figure 4.10).

The Five Competition Forces of Strategy

Apart from assessing the general environmental factors on the process of strategy formulation in the studied companies, the effects of the factors within the industry have also been investigated. To do this, Porter's five-force model (Porter, 1980) has been applied.

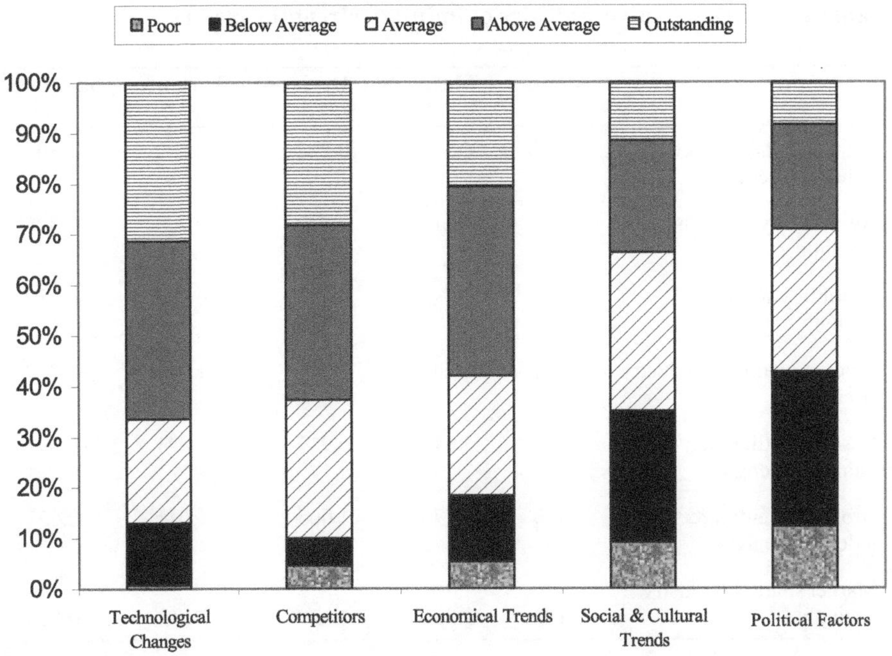

Figure 4.10 Importance of environmental factors in strategic management

The results of the analysis show that, five external forces including the bargaining power of customers (Mean = 3.71, Std. = 0.88), bargaining power of suppliers (Mean = 3.09, Std. = 0.91), rivalry among existing firms (Mean = 3.73, Std. = 0.99), threat of new entrants (Mean = 3.12, Std. = 0.95) and finally, threat of substitute products (Mean = 3.32, Std. = 1.12) tend to influence the strategy formulation in the electrical and electronic industry. Accordingly, the respondents were asked to rank the above factors based on their perceived importance on the firm's strategy formulation process. It has been found that the bargaining power of customers (62.8 per cent) seemed to be regarded as the most important factor. Rivalry amongst existing firms (62.1 per cent) followed closely as the second most important factor and the threat of substitute new products (40.7 per cent) formed the third priority. In contrast, the threat of new entrants (28.1 per cent) and the bargaining power of suppliers (25 per cent) did not seem to influence strongly the formulation of strategy in the targeted firms.

Industry Strength Factors

In this research the factors relating to industry strengths have been studied using seven indicators including potential growth, market share, financial stability, resource usage, productivity, capacity usage, flexibility and finally adaptability. These indicators were measured using ordinal scale from not important to essential. As it has been illustrated in Table 4.5, financial stability (Mean = 4.356, Std. = 0.782)

Table 4.5 Descriptive statistics of industry strengths factors

	Number	Mean	Std. Deviation	Variance	Skewness
Financial stability & industry strength	132	4.356	0.782	0.612	-1.304
Adaptability & industry strength	128	4.218	0.85	0.723	-0.827
Flexibility & industry strength	128	3.96	0.873	0.762	-0.789
Product quality & industry strength	128	3.89	1.117	1.247	-0.779
Resource utilization & industry strength	128	3.843	0.917	0.841	-0.491
Growth potential & industry strength	130	3.776	1.005	1.011	-0.651
Market share & industry strength	129	3.565	1.029	1.06	-0.528

is perceived as the most important factor in determining industry strengths in the studied firms. In contrast, market share (Mean = 3.565, Std. = 1.029) was reported as the weakest factor in determining industry strengths. It seems that, the turbulent environment of the industry and the changing expectations of the customers in the electronic industry, pushes the firms to be more adaptable and flexible in developing business strategies.

The importance of each factor in determining industry strengths were measured using the Likert scale. Regarding the financial stability of the firms, 106 respondents (87.9 per cent) believed that, financial indicators are very important and essential in determining industry strength. In contrast, only a few of respondents (n = 3, 2.3 per cent) considered financial indicators as not important or of limited importance in determining industry strengths. The respondents considered the adaptability (n = 103, 78 per cent for very important and essential) and flexibility (n = 87, 65.9 per cent very important and essential) of the firm's strategies with customers' expectations as a factor determining the industry's strengths but in second priority. The flexibility of the firm in terms of coping with unexpected changes in the marketplace, managerial style, and technology usage have been considered as an essential factor in the firm performance. Respondents prioritized the other factors in determining industry strengths including: quality of products and services (n = 81, 61 per cent very important and essential) as third priority, resources usage like HR and financial resources (n = 79, 59 per cent very important and essential) as fourth priority, growth potential (n = 75, 56 per cent very important and essential) as fifth priority, and market share (n = 71, 53 per cent very important and essential) as the sixth priority.

Environmental Analysis and Firm Size

In the second part of the questionnaire the aim was to examine the respondents' perception of environmental scanning as the first step towards formulating a strategic management process in SMEs. The respondents were asked to indicate whether or not they were engaged in formal or informal environmental scanning in their organizations. Whilst the majority of the respondents (n = 125, 94 per cent) indicated that, they were generally involved in environmental scanning for the purpose of formulating their firm's business strategies, only 118 firms (89 per cent) claimed to use formal environmental analysis. Accordingly, the respondents were asked to rate the importance of formal or informal environmental scanning within their organizations. The responses were varied in terms of the size of organizations. Table 4.6 shows the variation in the managerial perception of the CEOs of the importance of environmental analysis within the studied firms. Some 3 per cent of the firms considered environmental analysis as not an important factor in the firm's strategy formulation. In contrast, some 51 per cent of the respondents described the environmental analysis as a very important and essential factor in their firms' strategic management process. The findings seem to indicate that the perception concerning the importance of environmental analysis seems to increase, as firms get bigger.

Almost all managers in medium sized enterprises (n = 40 out of 59) felt that, environmental analysis is important and therefore it forms an essential factor in developing their business strategy. In contrast, only one micro-enterprise CEO (n = 1 out 8) rated environmental analysis as a very important factor. Simultaneously, a slightly lower proportion of the smaller enterprises than the medium sized ones (n = 26 out of 68) felt that environmental analysis must be considered as a very important factor in developing business strategies.

Table 4.6 Environmental analysis by firm size

	Size of organization by number of employees			
Extent of importance of environmental analysis	*Micro enterprises*	*Small enterprises*	*Medium enterprises*	*Total*
Not important	3 (2.27%)	1 (0.70%)	0 (0.00%)	2.97%
Limited important	2 (1.53%)	16 (12.12%)	0 (0.00%)	13.65%
Important	2 (1.53%)	38 (28.78%)	3 (2.27%)	32.58%
Very Important	1 (0.70%)	21 (16.11%)	12 (9.09%)	25.81%
Essential	0 (0.00%)	5 (3.78%)	28 (21.21%)	24.99%
Total	**8**	**81**	**43**	**132 (100%)**

Strategy Implementation in SMEs

Effective strategy implementation is an important part of the strategic management process in the organization. According to the researches in the field of strategic management there are some elements which help strategists to implement the business strategies successfully. In this research an attempt has been made to identify these elements in small and medium-sized enterprises and explore the senior managers perception of their importance in SMEs. Some of these elements included organizational structure, human resources, quality of leadership, costing programmes and flexibility of business plans. Table 4.7 illustrates the descriptive statistics of the strategy implementation variables.

In this section the respondents' perception of the importance of these elements have been explored.

Table 4.7 Descriptive statistics of the strategy implementation variables

Variables	N	Mean	Std. Deviation
Organizational structure	130	3.90	1.041
Organizational employees	130	3.58	1.263
Costing programs	128	3.91	.959
Standard operating procedures	129	3.70	1.020
Flexible and adaptable business plans	130	3.95	1.081
Quality of leadership	131	4.14	1.135
Lower managers involvement in implementation of strategy	131	3.56	1.272

Organizational Structure

The respondents were asked to indicate the extent of the importance of organizational structure for the implementation of strategy. The data analysis shows that the majority of respondents (Mean = 3.90, Std = 1.04) believed that the business strategy should be associated with the type of organizational structure. Employing one-sample T test ($t(129) = 42.370$, $P < 0.01$) it has been found that SMEs managers perceive organizational structure to be a significant factor in developing the business strategies (see Table 4.8). In other words, the respondents believed that if the firm's structure and strategy are not matched, in practice such a strategy could not be implemented effectively.

Employees

Human resource is an important variable in strategy implementation. No strategic plan will be implemented without highly skilled and motivated employees. The

Table 4.8 One-sample test on strategy implementation variables

			Sig.	Mean
organisational structure	42.730	129	.000	3.90
organisational employees	32.294	129	.000	3.58
costing programs	46.069	127	.000	3.91
standard operating procedures	41.168	128	.000	3.70
flexible and adaptable business plai	41.638	129	.000	3.95
quality of leadership	41.715	130	.000	4.14
lower managers involvement in strategy implementation	32.088	130	.000	3.56

respondents believed (Mean = 3.58, Std = 1.263) that the firm's employees are significantly important in implementing business strategies. Data analysis (t (129) = 32.294, $P < 0.01$) shows that in small and medium enterprises, employees are considered to be the main factor in implementing strategy effectively. The respondents put more emphasis on trained and skilled human resources for strategy implementation. Accordingly, it was observed that the firms, especially within the high tech industry, invest in people. The details of the human resources and their importance in strategy implementation will be discussed in the next chapter. In summary, recently human resources has been considered as a strategic asset in organizations.

Costing Programmes and Standard Operating Procedures

In order to implement the strategy, it should be defined in the format of the programmes. Accordingly, each programme should contain the standard operating procedures. It is clear that the financing and budgeting of programmes can put them into action. In this regard, the respondents in the studied firms perceived costing programmes as an important factor in implementing business strategies. They strongly believed (Mean = 3.91, Std = 0.959) that without costing no strategic plan will be implemented. Accordingly, they believed (Mean = 3.70, Std = 1.020) that the firm should develop standard operating procedures to implement their programmes and strategy.

Flexibility of Business Plans

The respondents were asked to indicate whether they agree or disagree with the association between the flexibility and adaptability of business plans and their implementation in action. In general the respondents believed (Mean = 3.95, Std = 1.081) that successful business plans are flexible and adaptable to the organizational culture and unpredictable circumstances. They emphasized that rigid business plans cannot cope with the turbulent environment and consequently would be difficult to implement effectively.

Quality of Leadership

Finally, the quality of leadership and type of management has been considered as another variable in implementing strategy successfully. The respondents were asked to indicate the importance of the quality of leadership in implementing strategy. Data analysis shows that the SMEs managers believed that (Mean = 4.14, Std = 1.135) the quality of leadership and management style significantly ($t(130) = 41.715$, $P < 0.01$) influence the implementation of the business strategies in small and medium-sized enterprises.

Strategic Management and Organizational Factors

The respondents were asked to show whether or not a systematic approach to strategic management has been established within their firms. The data analysis shows that the majority (n = 96, 74 per cent) of the SMEs' managers believed that a systematic approach to strategic management had been established within their firms. In the next section the respondents were asked to rate the impact of establishing a systematic approach to strategic management on these organizational factors.

Generally speaking, it has been found that establishing a systematic approach to strategic management positively impacts on the organizational factors (see Table 4.9). The details of the data analysis are as follows.

Table 4.9 Impact of strategic management approach on organizational factors*

Variable	*d.f*	*t-statistics*	*P-value*
Adapting with environmental changes	130	36.659	P<0.01
Operational decision making	128	34.903	P<0.05
Developing business plans	128	39.782	P<0.01
Implementing business plans	124	40.943	P<0.01
Quality of product or services	131	18.695	P<0.05
Solving organizational problems	129	19.860	P<0.01
Employees satisfaction	129	39.590	P<0.05
Changing organizational culture	126	18.804	P<0.01
Reducing organizational conflict	128	21.138	P<0.05
Firm's profitability	130	39.661	P<0.01
Achieving organizational objectives	128	39.774	P<0.01
Organizational effectiveness	128	38.873	P<0.01

* : Mean Importance Rating 3
: Mean Importance Rating < 3

Adaptability to Environmental Changes

The respondents were asked to rate how important establishing a systematic approach to strategic management, within the studied firms, was to their ability to adapt to environmental changes. The result of T test ($t(130) = 36.659$, $P < 0.01$) shows that there was a significant association between establishing a systematic approach to strategic management and the firm's adaptability to the environmental changes. The firms, which employed strategic management tools, were more adaptable to environmental changes such as changes in the technological domain.

Developing and Implementing Business Plans

The respondents believed that establishing a strategic management approach helps senior managers to develop an effective business plan. It has also been found that in order to implement a business plan successfully there is a need to establish a strategic management approach. In this research, the findings of the data analysis illustrates the significant impact of establishing a strategic management approach on developing ($t\ (128) = 39.782$, $P < 0.01$), and implementing business plans ($t\ (124) = 40.943$, $P < 0.01$) in the studied firms.

Operational Decision-Making

The respondents were asked to indicate whether or not employing strategic management tools impacts on the operational decision-making process. Using T test, the result of data analysis reveals that, establishing a strategic management approach, significantly ($t(128) = 34.903 P < 0.05$) impacts on the operational decision making in the studied firms. This finding will be discussed in the next chapter.

Employees' Satisfaction and Organizational Culture

Based on the findings from the data analysis, it became apparent that the respondents believe that, a strategic management approach significantly impacts on employees' satisfaction ($t(129) = 39.590$, $P < 0.05$), and the changing organizational culture ($t(126) = 18.804$, $P < 0.01$). In other words, the employees satisfaction in the firms which have employed strategic management tools seems to be higher than the firms which have not employed such decision making tools. Probably, involving the employees in the process of decision making as an example of a strategic management technique will increase their participation in implementing the plans and consequently leads to their organizational satisfaction.

Organizational Conflict and Problem Solving

The result of data analysis shows a significant association between establishing a strategic management approach within the studied firms and solving organizational problems. For instance, the respondents believed that, using a strategic management process in SMEs significantly helps in solving organizational problems (t(129)

$= 19.860$, $P < 0.01$), and reducing organizational conflict ($t(128) = 21.138$, $P < 0.05$).

Overall Firm's Objectives and Performance

Initially an attempt has been made to answer the question whether or not establishing a systematic approach to strategy impacts on the overall firm performance. Accordingly, by using the two-sample T test it was discovered that, the respondents believed employing strategic management procedures in the studied firms significantly impacts on the quality of product or services ($t(131) = 18.69$, $P < 0.05$), achieving organizational objectives ($t(128) = 39.774$, $P < 0.01$), firm profitability ($t(130) = 39.661$, $P < 0.01$), and overall organizational effectiveness ($t(128) = 38.873$, $P < 0.01$). The measurement of the firm performance will be explained in the next section and the details of the strategy and firm performance will also be discussed in the next chapter.

Firm Performance Measurement

Performance measures are a common control mechanism. They communicate desired outcomes or behaviour to employees and are used to evaluate the degree of success in achieving goals. It is generally believed that the best performance measures are those linked to a firm's strategy (Kaplan and Norton, 1992; Nanni, Dixon and Vollmann, 1992; Langfield-Smith, 1997). In order to measure the organizational performance at corporate level, a methodology has been developed by Quezada et al. (1999). This methodology, which is based on the Buzzell and Gale (1987) work, considers the internal and external analysis as well as monitoring the process of the results of the strategy as being supported by the use of performance indicators. The questions that usually arise when attempting to define the indicators to be used is, 'do the factors have an impact on producing a sustainable profit and how can they be quantified?' An important investigation to answer these questions was carried out in a programme called Profit Impact of Market Strategies (PIMS). This methodology considers the 30 most important factors found by PIMS study, although a reduced number of them is selected to be used in each company according to its particular characteristics. They are calculated for the past three years for two reasons: (a) to analyse their trend and (b) PIMS specifies that three years is the minimum number to obtain valid conclusions. A partial list of them is:

- Net sales.
- Sales index: net sales in relation to a reference value of 100.
- Capital intensity: investment divided by added value.
- (Added value = net sales − cost of purchases)
- Productivity: added value per employee.
- Relative market share: market participation in relation to three main competitors.
- Market growth.

- Frequency of innovation: sales of products with less than three years in the market.
- Vertical integration: added value divided by sales.
- Direction of the change of the previous indicators

These performance indicators are calculated at a company level – to obtain an overall picture of the situation of the company – and at an SBU level in order to obtain an evaluation of the present situation of each SBU as well as its perspectives. As it can be seen, the indicators are easily obtained from the Balance Sheet and the Income Statement. A simple questionnaire is used to obtain those data not contained in the financial statements. It should be noted that the methodology looks at what the customer wants in order to formulate a strategy that is consistent with the scale of values of the owner. The performance indicators have the objective of evaluating whether the strategy is making the company achieve the goal defined.

In addition to the above-discussed methodology, some other methodologies were employed to measure the firm performance in SMEs. For instance Stewart (2002) in his recent study has defined the small business success by the extent to which the firm exhibits a number of indicators of business growth and success. A total of five indicators were incorporated to measure small business success: 1) increasing staff, 2) expanding clientele, 3) international growth, 4) establishing new sites and, 5) acquiring businesses. All of the small business success indicators were weighted equally.

As noted earlier, this study relies on perceptual measures of the firm's performance. It has benefited from the former methodologies for measuring the firm performance in small and medium-sized enterprises. In order to measure the firm's performance respondents were asked to indicate using a five-point scale, ranging from 1 = very unimportant to 5 = very important, the degree of importance they attached to each of financial and non-financial performance indicators. The employed performance indicators were as follows:

- Net sales.
- Profitability
- Market growth.
- Increasing product quality
- Productivity
- Innovation and IT
- Increasing number of employees
- Entering to international markets

This method has been widely used in previous studies (Beal, 2000). The respondents were further asked to indicate the extent of their satisfaction with their firm's performance along each of the performance indicators. In order to analyse the data and determine the specification of the firms in terms of their performance, the firms that responded to the survey were ranked into three categories based on their performance namely, high, moderate, and low performance. This method has already been used largely in similar studies (for example, O'Gorman and Doran, 1999; Chan and Foster, 2001). Of 132 firms involved in the survey, 52 (39 per cent) were ranked in the top performing quartile (high performance), 41 (31 per cent) in moderate and 39 (30 per cent) were ranked in the lowest performing quartile (low performance). In some cases the firms with moderate performance were excluded and consequently compared with the percentage of the high-performer and low-performer firms in terms of the research questions.

Summary and Conclusion

In this chapter the data collected through postal questionnaire was analysed. Descriptive statistical techniques such as mean, standard deviation, and statistical graphs such as bar chart, pie chart were employed to get a clear picture of the data. Using statistical tests for normality, the collected data were categorized into two groups consisting of the data which was distributed normally and the data which did not distribute normally. Accordingly, based on the distribution of the data and the level of the measurement of the data, statistical techniques for data analysis and testing the hypotheses namely parametric and non-parametric methods were selected.

References

Baetz, M.C. and Bart, C.K. (1996), 'Developing Mission Statements which Work', *Long Range Planning*, **29**(4), 526–533.

Beal, R.M. (2000), 'Competing Effectively: Environmental Scanning, Competitive Strategy, and Organisational Performance in Small Manufacturing Firms', *Journal of Small Business Management*, **38**(1), 27–47.

Berry, M. (1998), 'Strategic Planning in Small High Tech Companies', *Long Range Planning*, **31**(3), 455–466.

Buzzell, R.D. and Gale, B.T. (1987), The P.I.M.S. Principles: Linking Strategy to Performance, (The First Press, New York).

Chan, S.Y. and Foster, J.M. (2001), 'Strategy Formulation in Small Business: the Hong Kong Experiences', *International Small Business Journal*, April/June.

Cooper, R.G. (1973), 'Technical Entrepreneurship: what do we Know?' *R&D Management*, **3**(2), 59–64.

David, F. (1989), 'How Companies Define their Mission', *Long Range Planning*, **22**(2), 90–97.

Hitt, M.A. and Tyler, B.B. (1991), 'Strategic Decision Models: Integrating Different Perspectives', *Strategic Management Journal*, **12**, 327–351.

Kakabadse, A. (1999), 'Younger Does Not Mean Better', *The British Journal of Administrative Management, Orpington*, January/February, 9–11.

Kaplan, R.S. and Norton, D.P. (1992), 'The Balanced Scorecard: Measures that Drive Performance', *Harvard Business Review* (January/February), 71–79.

Langfield-Smith, K. (1997), 'Management Control Systems and Strategy: A Critical Review', *Accounting, Organizations and Society*, **22**(2), 207–252.

Nanni, A.J., Jr, Dixon, J.R. and Vollmann, T.E. (1992), 'Integrated Performance Measurement: Management Accounting to Support the New Manufacturing Realities', *Journal of Management Accounting Research*, **4**(Fall), 1–19.

O'Gorman, C. and Doran, R. (1999), 'Mission Statements in Small and Medium Sized Businesses', *Journal of Small Business Management*, **37**(4), 59–66.

Porter, M. (1980), *Competitive Strategy* (New York: Free Press). Quezada, L.E., Córdova, F.M., Widmer, S. and O'Brien, C. (1999), 'A Methodology for Formulating a Business Strategy in Manufacturing Firms', *International Journal of Production Economics*, **60–61**(20), 87–94.

Stewart, K.S. (2002), 'Formal Business Planning and Small Business Success: A Survey of Small Businesses with an International Focus', *Journal of American Academy of Business*, **2**(1), 42–46.

Chapter 5

Strategic Entrepreneurship

Introduction

Strategic management has its roots in the efforts of early policy scholars to develop a means of cross-disciplinary integration for the purposes of increased efficiency (Teece, 1992; Hitt et al., 2002). But today, speed and action are the core elements of the rapidly changing environment. The past decade of organizational research has moved from an investigation of the organization as a static entity to an investigation of organizations as dynamic entities, much of it focused on strategy, and its formulation and implementation (Wortman, 1994; Chan and Foster, 2001). Strategic management has shifted much of its interest from static industry models and efficient markets to more dynamic models of change and flexibility (Hoskisson, 2000; Hitt et al., 2002; Johnson, Scholes and Whittington, 2005). With increasing interest in speed and action, the new economy is an entrepreneurial economy. Therefore, all organizations, regardless of their size and age, must be entrepreneurial to effectively compete and survive. This chapter considers strategy development issues addressing the role of entrepreneurs as the ultimate decision maker in entrepreneurial firms.

Considering the objectives of the study, this chapter provides the discussion of the findings of the research, related to the main propositions, in two separate but interlinked sections. In the first section the findings of the research on CEOs' perception of the importance of strategic management processes within the studied firms will be discussed. This section explores and examines the association between the establishment of a strategic management approach and selected organizational factors. The second section of the chapter explores the role of senior managers in strategic management within the entrepreneurial firms studied. In this section the relationships between managerial characteristics and strategy formulation and implementation within the studied firms will be discussed. Finally, the chapter ends with analysis of resource capabilities and innovation in entrepreneurial firms.

Entrepreneur as Strategist

It has been discussed (Burns, 2007) that 'entrepreneurs use innovation to exploit or create change and opportunity for the purpose of making profit. They do this by shifting economic resources from an area of lower productivity into an area of higher productivity and greater yield, accepting a high degree of risk and uncertainty in doing so' (Burns, 2007, 11).

As discussed earlier, in large organizations, the Board of Directors, top management team and chief executive officers (CEOs) play the role of strategic managers. In multi-business firms, strategic business unit (SBU) managers act as strategists. While in small businesses, the business-owner manager and managers who, organize and manage the business are the ultimate strategists. Business-owner managers make all strategic, as well as operational, decisions in the firm. They are simultaneously involved in all three levels of strategic decision-making processes within the firm, that is corporate, business and functional. Any manager in either a large or small firm can be an entrepreneur. Entrepreneurs can exist within both large and small firms. It is important to make it clear that, entrepreneurs are defined by their actions, not by the size of firm they happen to work within. Some managers do own the firms they manage and these make up the majority of small and medium sized firms. They are called business-owner managers. Business-owner managers significantly control the operations of their firm on a day to day basis. However, business owner-managers may not necessarily not be entrepreneurs. Many managers of small and medium-sized enterprises are employed by the firms they work for. Both business-owner managers and employed managers might be entrepreneurs, depending on the way they act (Burns, 2007). Entrepreneurs develop the vision and mission of the business in an innovative way. They formulate and implement the business strategies of the firm by bridging strategic management processes and innovation.

Characteristics of Successful Entrepreneurs

A great deal of research has been carried out in identifying the characteristics of successful entrepreneurs. Business-owner entrepreneurs have certain typical character traits, although the mix and emphasis of these characteristics will be different for each individual. Successful entrepreneurs are the strategists who are well motivated, flexible, creative and risk takers (Zimmerer and Scarborough, 2002). They are proactive leaders and use strategic planning and organization in their decision-making process. Successful entrepreneurs are skilled managers with previous experiences in the business. They are self-motivated individuals who begin the business on their own. Often successful entrepreneurs are also self-financed. According to Burns (2007) entrepreneurs have the following character traits:

- Opportunistic
- Innovative
- Self-confident
- Proactive and decisive with high energy
- Self-motivated
- Vision and flair
- Willingness to take greater risks and live with even greater uncertainty

According to Analoui and Karami (2003) some of the characteristics of successful entrepreneurs are as follows:

- Highly motivated individual
- Flexible and innovative

- Risk taker
- Proactive leader
- Good planning and organizing skills
- Previous experience
- Technical knowledge
- Hard worker
- Self-starter
- Personal financial resource

Entrepreneurs are very excited and enthused about their businesses. They are highly self-motivated, amounting almost to a driving urge to succeed in their economic goals. Successful entrepreneurs are extremely self-motivated and enthusiastic. Highly motivated individuals believe in themselves and their ability to develop the business – and they transmit that enthusiasm to others. The ability to spot opportunities and to innovate is possibly the most important distinguishing feature of entrepreneurs (Burns, 2007). Innovation is the prime tool entrepreneurs use to create or exploit opportunity. Successful entrepreneurs use innovative manners in dealing with organizational issues. They are flexible, listen to their customers and adapt to meet those needs. Burns (2007) argues that entrepreneurs are willing to take far greater risks and live with far greater uncertainty. Successful entrepreneurs are risk takers but they are not gamblers. Successful entrepreneurs are aware and accept that their decisions may have positive or negative outcomes. To succeed, entrepreneurs need to have a clear vision of what they want to achieve. Successful entrepreneurs are proactive leaders. They like challenge and enjoy competing with others. They do not wait for the future with ideal conditions to react. Successful entrepreneurs inspire other people to help them achieve their goals. They also know how to monitor and supervise people to ensure that their instructions are carried out properly. Entrepreneurs develop a system for managing their time and following up on important items. Because entrepreneurs often juggle many tasks – including sales, marketing, production and paying bills – they must be flexible and able to tolerate some degree of chaos. Prior experience in starting a business is one of the top characteristics shared by successful entrepreneurs. Successful and experienced entrepreneurs have a better understanding of the marketplace. They also have good business sense and make decisions based on a realistic appraisal of their business and the marketplace.

Research shows that the successful entrepreneur, along side with their technical skills, have a managerial and an educated background (Hitt et al., 2002). Successful entrepreneurs have managerial and technical knowledge of their business. Entrepreneurs generally work long hours and take responsibility for the hundreds of details involved in managing their business. Successful entrepreneurs are thoroughly committed to their idea, which keeps them focused even when things do go wrong. Entrepreneurs are self-motivated people who begin projects on their own. They don't wait for anybody's approval or for somebody else to motivate them. They start developing their businesses based on their own vision and instincts. Successful entrepreneurs consider the impact of the business on their personal life. They explain the changes that the new business will bring – such as long hours or extensive travel – and develop a plan that family and friends can live with.

Nature of Strategic Planning in Entrepreneurial SMEs

It has been discussed by Hitt et al. (2002) that there are three traditional approaches to strategic management – competitive forces, strategic conflict and the resource based view. Two additional approaches have recently been introduced: structured chaos and dynamic capabilities. The intersection of entrepreneurship and strategic management is evident and logical. Meyer and Heppard (2000) believe that it is time to move beyond the 'intersection' and 'integration' conversation. They offer an alternative view – that of an interface. The entrepreneurship-strategic management interface establishes boundaries for the fields working together. Entrepreneurship is about creation and strategic management is about the process with which to achieve above-average performance via competitive advantage. In developing the conceptual framework of the research, the question, whether or not strategic management is important in SMEs, has been developed.

As discussed in the literature review, proponents of strategic management in SMEs consider a strategic management approach as an important factor for increasing firm performance. They (Scott and Bruce, 1987; Berry, 1998) concluded that, the strategic management approach employed will evolve and become more formal and sophisticated over the life cycle of the business. In contrast, other writers (Shuman, Shaw and Sussman, 1985; Curran, 1996) believe that, small businesses, because of their size, nature of activities, and entrepreneurship, cannot benefit from a strategic management approach, which focuses on formal strategy formulation and implementation. They emphasized on informal planning in SMEs.

In this research as it has been discussed in Chapter 4, that CEO's of high tech SMEs considered a strategic approach as an effective factor in increasing firm performance. The respondents were asked to indicate whether or not a systematic approach has been developed within their company. The data analysis shows that, the majority of the studied firms ($n = 96$, % 74) have established a strategic management system in their organizations. Therefore, significant proportions of SMEs regard strategic management as important. But, there was a significant association ($\gamma = 0.456$, $p < 0.01$) between the establishment of a strategic management approach within the firm and the life cycle of the firms. As the firms have grown, the strategic management processes used have become formal and explicit. Generally speaking, SMEs do employ strategic management procedures, however, the majority of SMEs tend to rely on informal methods of strategic management.

Regarding the strategy formulation, it has been found that, strategic planning activities tended to be primarily concerned with the short term and are operationally orientated. These findings are very close to the findings of Berry (1998), regarding the strategic planning in high tech firms, who reported that, small high tech firms do employ strategic management.

In the next section the nature of the strategic management approach on organizational variables will be discussed. Strategy, its formulation or creation and implementation are recognized as key aspects of the management of large organizations (Ansoff, 1984). As noted in the literature review, small and medium-sized enterprises are urged to perform business, strategic, and succession planning for their survival (Ward, 1988; Bridge and Peel, 1999; Chan and Foster, 2001). However, most of the research on SMEs business planning focuses on succession planning rather than on business or strategic planning (Handler, 1994; Upton and Heck, 1997). The question that has been raised is, whether or not CEOs in studied firms employ strategic planning processes. Consequently if they do so, what is the nature of such strategic planning activity in small and medium-sized enterprises? Some authors are sceptical of the existence of clearly visible strategic planning in many small business settings (Curran, 1996). In practice, some small businessmen may simply keep doing what they have done of late, assume market conditions will continue much as before and hope for the best. The sceptics may see this as an absence of strategy.

Despite some research into the relative success of pursuing active policies of formal strategic planning or strategy formulation (Armstrong, 1982) there has been relatively little study of the situation in small businesses. The available research suggests that while SMEs should perform strategic and business planning, most do not (Brown, 1995; Rue and Ibrahim, 1996). Greenwald and Associates (1993), in a national survey of 614 small businesses, found that 58 per cent of those businesses had no written business plan. In a 1997 a survey of 3,033 small businesses (Andersen and Mutal, 1997) it was discovered that 69 per cent had no written strategic plan. In this study, referring to the descriptive analysis of the data (Chapter 6), it has been found that, the majority (83 per cent) of the studied firms employ planning activities. The nature of those employed planning activities varied from basic financial planning to formal strategic planning. This result supports the findings of Rue and Ibrahim (1996) who noted that SMEs engage in more planning than previously thought, with over half of their sample reporting written long-range plans, and 97 per cent reporting some specific plans related to growth. Ward (1997) also concludes that SMEs may not plan if the founder is fixated on a previously successful strategy.

Apart from these two researches, the findings of this study are very similar to the finding of the recent study (Berry, 1998) that reported that, successful SMEs do employ strategic planning. The results of this research also confirm the findings of Goodwin and Hodgett (1991) who concluded that, strategic planning brings major benefits to the companies that use it. However, many medium size companies confuse it with long-term budgeting and miss out on its benefits. Goodwin and Hodgett's (1991) study, which examined the planning practices of 300 medium size companies in Australia, revealed that over 86 per cent of all the responding companies do prepare a strategic plan.

Their study, attempted to identify the type of planning activities, and planning characteristics employed by the studied firms. Based on the findings of the study (see Chapter 4), the studied small and medium-sized enterprises can be categorized in to four groups (see Table 5.1) in terms of employing strategic planning. First the firms which, are not involved in planning activities (17 per cent). In these firms, there are no planning activities reported, accordingly there are no mission or objectives, either short term or long term, developed. Second, the firms which employ financial planning (21 per cent). In this group, respondents rated formal financial planning as an essential activity. The CEOs stressed the importance of tight financial controls and performance. It also has been found that, the firms develop short-term (up to one year) to medium-term (up to two years) financial objectives.

Table 5.1 Planning levels and characteristics of the studied firms

Planning level	Characteristics
Non planning (17%)	**Planning Characteristics:** No mission statement No long term objectives Less stress on short term objectives No formal or informal business plan **Firm size**: less than 10 employees **Top management** is not experienced but technically qualified
Financial planning (21%)	**Planning Characteristics:** Emphasis on short to medium term 1 up to 2 years financial objectives Stress on financial controls Strategic planning is not important Review the financial performance every one to three months **Firm size**: Less than 100 employees **Top management:** may have some experiences but technically qualified, in some cases management training
Formal financial and informal strategic planning (38%)	**Planning Characteristics:** Emphasis on long term (2 to 5 years) financial objectives Stress on importance of strategic planning Informal mission statement Informal strategic objectives **Firm size**: 100 to 200 employees **Top management:** have previous general management experiences, technically qualified, have had management training,
Formal strategic planning (32%)	**Planning Characteristics:** Emphasis on long term objectives in relation to products or markets Written mission statement Stress on importance of formal strategic planning Reviewing strategic plans every six months or one year **Firm size**: 200 to 250 employees **Top management:** have wide range of previous general management experiences, Multi-disciplinary (marketing, technology, financial, strategic) management team

The firms in this group were not engaged in strategic planning. Third group includes formal financial and informal strategic planners (38 per cent). Respondents in this group, believed in the importance of informal strategic planning. While financial planning and performance are tightly controlled and monitored. The firms have had a mission statement and long-term financial objectives specified over a two to five years planning horizon. In this group of the studied firms, mission statement, objectives and business strategies are not formalized in a business plan but are clearly communicated and known throughout the firms. Finally, the fourth group of firm can be categorized as formal strategic planners (32 per cent). In this group management stressed the importance of formal and explicit strategy formulation process, written mission statement and long term objectives over a two to five years planning horizon. A formal and written strategic plan was produced and reviewed on a six monthly or annual basis. In these firms, formal strategic business plans are developed reflecting the management perception that significant benefit will arise for the company. The relationship between employing a strategic management approach and some of the selected organizational factors will be discussed in the next sections.

Strategic Management Approach and Organizational Factors

In order to see the impact of a strategic management approach on organizational variables within the studied firms, the respondents were asked to rate its impact on the research variables such as adapting with environmental changes, operational decision making, developing and implementing business plans, and so on. The results of the T-test have been illustrated in Table 5.2.

It has been discussed that, the success of SMEs within globalization depends in large part on the senior managers' awareness of the environment (Miles and Snow,

Table 5.2 Impact of strategic management approach on organizational factors*

Variable	t-statistics	P-value	Association
Adapting with environmental changes	36.659	P<0.01	Significant
Operational decision making	34.903	P<0.05	Significant
Developing business plans	39.782	P<0.01	Significant
Implementing business plans	40.943	P<0.01	Significant
Quality of product or services	18.695	P<0.05	Significant
Solving organizational problems	19.860	P<0.01	Significant
Employees satisfaction	39.590	P<0.05	Significant
Changing organizational culture	18.804	P<0.01	Significant
Reducing organizational conflict	21.138	P<0.05	Significant
Firm's profitability	39.661	P<0.01	Significant
Achieving organizational objectives	39.774	P<0.01	Significant
Organizational effectiveness	38.873	P<0.01	significant

* : Mean Importance Rating 3
: Mean Importance Rating < 3
(Scale: 1 = Low; 3 = Average; 5 = High)

1978; Roy and Dugal, 1999; Beal, 2000). Strategy reflects the firm's short- and long-term responses to the challenges and opportunities posed by the business environment. Companies execute strategies to attract customers and deal effectively with a myriad of environmental concerns, such as competitors, suppliers, and scarce resources. Data analysis shows that, the impact that the strategic management approach has on how a firm adapts to environmental changes is significantly important ($t\ (130) = 36.659$, $P < 0.01$). Companies which establish a strategic management approach, are more adaptable to the environmental factors such as technological changes.

Using environmental analysis as a basic strategic activity, the firms can recognize their strengths and weaknesses, alongside the opportunities and threats of the industry, in order to choose the proper strategies. Furthermore, it has been found that the firms are proactive to the environmental changes, when they use innovative lens for establishing strategic management. This finding supports the strategy lenses model developed by Johnson, Scholes and Whittington (2005) who discuss that there are many different views on how strategy should be understood, developed and implemented in organizations. They used strategy lenses for explaining three different ways of looking at the issue of strategy development for an organization. These are including:

- Strategy as design
- Strategy as experience
- Strategy as ideas

The design lens views strategy development, as the deliberate positioning of the organization through a rational, analytic, structured and directive process. The experience lens views strategy development as the outcome of individual and collective experience of individuals influenced by organizational culture. While, the ideas lens sees strategy as the emergence of order and innovation from the variety and diversity which exist in and around an organization.

Strategic decision-making is an important part of managing the direction of an organization and measuring its success (Waring, 2001). The recent works focus on the development of the strategic decision making as a management tool, and explores various analytical techniques to measure the performance of an organization. The development of such a model requires a more effective use of the strategic management approach in small businesses. In this research, the result of data analysis reveals that, establishing a strategic management approach, significantly ($t(128) = 34.903$ $P < 0.05$) impacted on the operational decision making in the studied firms.

Regarding the developing and implementation of business plans, it has been discussed that, enterprise strategy provides an accepted theoretical framework for integrating the moral responsibilities of organizations into their strategy formulation and implementation processes (Stead, 2000). Recently, the concept of an integrated strategy, developed by Breene and Supron (see Copacino, 1999), has gained attention. Integrated strategy draws on the collection of analytic frameworks described above, while also emphasizing both strategic positioning and superior execution capabilities. Most significantly, integrated strategy has created a doctrine or set of principles to guide the processes of strategy formulation and implementation.

Some recent researches (Flores and Saxena, 2000; Hoskisson, 2000) reveal some major shortcomings in the way managers are approaching strategy formulation and implementation. In this research, the findings of the data analysis illustrates a significant impact on establishing a strategic management approach for developing business plans ($t(128) = 39.782$, $P < 0.01$), and implementing business plans ($t(124) = 40.943$, $P < 0.01$) in the studied firms. These findings are similar to the findings of Copacino (1999) who stated that, senior managers widely recognize the importance of strategic management nowadays, and no wonder, if they are to cope with the sweeping forces of change, then institutions must fashion strategic planning into a powerful tool. They must use organizational resources and build new competencies, all in a way that capitalizes on emerging opportunities and contends with competitive threats. Generally speaking, we are witness to emphasis now being placed on the importance of developing strategic orientation, as well as simple strategic planning, by chief executive officers (CEOs) and top management teams in the organizations. For instance, Peter Duncan Vice-President of the Centre for Simplified Strategic Planning, Inc. in his recent work (Duncan, 2001) indicates that:

> "In time of great changes, great vision and plans are needed. So how do we create great vision and plans to soar to new heights? It all comes down to having a concept-an idea that a business can pursue. By some means, you identify a real need in the market not a whim or wish, but something that will deliver real value (where the customer's perception of return is greater than their cost). And from that simple concept, you build a vision of what you need to put in place to deliver that market need better than anyone else" (Duncan, 2001).

The other interesting finding of this research is the significant impact of the establishment of a strategic management approach on the internal environmental variables of the studied firms. For instance, CEOs believed that, using strategic management processes in SMEs significantly helps in solving organizational problems ($t(129) = 19.860$, $P < 0.01$), and reducing organizational conflict ($t(128) = 21.138$, $P < 0.05$). Strategy as a unified plan (Mintzberg, 1994) integrates all of the parts of the firm together and links the subsections of the firm to each other effectively. Based on the findings of the data analysis, the respondents believe that, a strategic management approach significantly impacts on employees' satisfaction ($t(129) = 39.590$, $P < 0.05$), and changing organizational culture ($t(126) = 18.804$, $P < 0.01$). These findings support the findings of Ahls (2001). He concludes that, just as a vision and strategy are important to a company as a whole, they are essential to a change effort. By definition, change represents something different from what employees are accustomed to; therefore, a clear, well-communicated vision and a path to achieve the change are needed. Asking employees to change must be paired with giving them the tools to achieve it and removing all obstacles. Careful strategic planning will ensure that all aspects of the firm have been accounted for and that unexpected roadblocks will be avoided or minimized (Ahls, 2001).

Finally, the impact of employing strategic management on firm performance is the subject that has been investigated in this research. The findings of the data analysis (see Chapter 6) support the significant impact of a strategic management approach on the overall firm performance. In this regard CEOs believed that, employing strategic management procedures in the studied firms significantly impacted on the quality of their product or services ($t(131) = 18.69$, $P < 0.05$), achieving organizational objectives ($t(128) = 39.774$, $P < 0.01$), firm profitability ($t(130) = 39.661$, $P < 0.01$), and overall organizational effectiveness ($t(128) = 38.873$, $P < 0.01$). Generally speaking, these findings are similar to the findings of previous researches (for example Handler, 1994; Berry, 1998; Chan and Foster, 2001). They concluded that, the success of SMEs depends in large part on the formulation and implementation of strategy.

Business-owner Entrepreneurs and Strategic Planning

Strategy and organizational researchers seem to vary in the extent to which they adopt an adaptive or inertial view of strategic change, although the two perspectives can be viewed as poles on a continuum (Astrachan and Kolenko, 1994; Anderson, 1997; Bennett, Ketchen and Schultz, 1998). Those who argue for the predominance of strategic adaptation emphasize the role that managers play in monitoring environmental changes and modifying organizational strategy to better match environmental contingencies (Barry, 1998; Analoui, 2000). Past researches have typically not empirically examined organizational effectiveness as a function of the combined effects of organizational performance and managerial characteristics. More importantly, it has been argued (Analoui, 2000) that managerial characteristics interact with organizational performance to create a context through which strategic changes become particularly likely.

This section discusses the findings of the data, which was analysed in Chapter 4, on managerial characteristics of the business-owner managers, and strategy, which refers to the strategic management process in SMEs. As was discussed in the literature (Chapter 2), in previous researches it was suggested that, when undertaking strategic planning, companies should form planning groups to oversee the process. In this study, respondents were asked: who or what group are involved in preparing the strategic business plans? The responses are summarized in Table 5.3. While forming strategic planning groups has frequently been adopted by large companies (Goodwin and Hodgett, 1991; Curran, 1996; Copacino, 1999), in the current research there was

Table 5.3 Senior managers' involvement in strategic planning

Groups	Percentage
Senior managers	76
Middle managers	14
Strategic planning groups (Committees)	6
Consultants	2
Other	2

little evidence that small and medium size companies in the UK frequently form such groups (2 per cent).

As can be seen, few SMEs create formal planning groups or committees to prepare the strategic business plans. In addition, there was little support given to the suggestion that consultants are frequently used (2 per cent). The use of consultants for preparing strategic plans in the studied firms appears to be very limited. In contrast, it is interesting that the involvement of the senior management group in accepting responsibility for the process is strong. The majority of the respondents (76 per cent) reported that, senior managers or top management are involved in preparing strategic plans in the studied firms.

There was, however, little evidence of middle management being the initiators of the strategic planning process (14 per cent). It is concluded that, in the UK small and medium size companies, senior management are mainly involve in preparing strategic business plans. This finding recalls the work of Goodwin and Hodgett (1991) who conclude from an empirical research in Australia that, senior managers are those who drive the process of strategic management and if changes to current practices are to be encouraged, it is this group that should be targeted rather than middle management.

Managerial Characteristics and Strategy Development

Some researchers suggest that a high level of management quality and managerial characteristics, measured in terms of capabilities, skills and expertise, age and education is more common among successful than unsuccessful firms (Hambrick and Mason, 1984; Leonidou, Katsikeas and Piercy, 1998; Analoui, 2000). In this section the role of senior managers in the strategic management processes within small and medium-sized enterprises will be explored. Consequently, the findings of this study in managerial and firm characteristics and their relationship to the firm performance are discussed. Some of the managerial and firm-characteristics examined are: age, educational level and background, and strategic awareness of the managers in small and medium-sized enterprises.

Age

Age is expected to be inversely related to risk taking and to the value placed on risk. Younger CEOs may pursue risky strategies (Hambrick and Mason, 1984). Studies by Child (1974) and Norburn and Birley (1988) indicate that younger CEOs show superior performance. Younger managers are also expected to be better educated and have more current technical knowledge (Bantel and Jackson, 1989). As flexibility decreases, rigidity and resistance to change increase, and risk-taking propensity are expected to decrease with age (Wiersema and Bantel, 1992). The age of managers has been proposed as a predictor of differences between firms in terms of performance in general and developing business strategies in particular. In order to examine this relationship first it has been assumed that younger managers have a more complete knowledge of the strategic orientation required for the development of the strategies of the company, than do the older senior managers.

As discussed in Chapter 6, there was no significant correlation between the age of respondents and pursuing a strategic orientation in the firms ($\gamma = 0.70$: $p > 0.05$). In other words, the firms which pursue a strategic orientation are run by either younger or older managers. As it is shown in Table 5.4 the result of the ANOVA F-test also, $F(41,91) = 2.180$; ($p > 0.05$) confirms that, having strategic orientation by the firms was not statistically different among the firms being run by younger managers and those firms that were being run by older managers. So the null hypothesis that the firms run by younger managers have more strategic orientation in developing business strategies is accepted with an F-value of 2.180 ($p = 0.129$).

A managers' age has also been perceived as closely associated with the manager's level of risk tolerance (Roux, 1987). In other words, younger managers are more likely to accept risk than older managers. So the risk acceptance behaviour of the managers could have an impact on the development of more aggressive strategies in the firm. The discussion here is, whether or not there is any significant relationship between the age of senior managers and pursuing risky and innovative strategies in SMEs? One study investigating the impact of this variable on export expansion, however, produced no significant results, while another study confirmed the positive relationship between age and risk tolerance (Gomez-Mejia, 1988; Berry, 1998). Younger managers were also assumed to pursue more risky strategies than older managers. As discussed in Chapter 6, a significant correlation ($\gamma = 0.81$: $p < 0.01$) has been found between the age of CEOs and the pursuit of more risky and innovative strategies in the studied firms.

In addition, using one-way analysis of variance, it has been found that, the firms run by young senior managers would be more likely to pursue risky and innovative strategies than firms with older managers would. Therefore, the result of ANOVA

Table 5.4 ANOVA table for age of respondents

Source of Variation	*Sum of Squares*	*d.f*	*Mean Square*	*F-value*	*P-value*
Having strategic orientation					
Between groups	28.571	41	2.012	2.180	0.129
Within groups	113.088	91	1.245		
Total	141.659	132			
Risk tolerance					
Between groups	34.623	32	3.563	3.417	0.004
Within groups	128.962	99	2.987		
Total	163.585	131			
Performance					
Between groups	38.194	33	1.157	0.768	0.804
Within groups	147.685	98	1.507		
Total	185.879	131			

(see Table 5.4) F-value 3.417 ($P = 0.004$) confirms the significant relationship between variables.

Many international business scholars regard innovative and risky orientation as an important factor in the initiation of strategy development (Jones, 1982; Knight, 1993). In this context, managers in SMEs are expected to be more innovative, creative, and willing to break away from the existing norms and patterns of behaviour within the company, compared with their counterparts in large firms. This result supports the findings of previous research (Cavusgil, 1982; Dichtl et al., 1990) which concluded that young managers are more likely to influence export activity and select risky strategies in the stages of internationalization.

It has been posed that the firm performance is related to the age of the CEOs. It has been assumed that, the firms that are run by younger managers are more successful than those firms that are run by older managers. The correlation analysis of the data show that, there were no significant correlation ($\gamma = 0.37 p > 0.5$) between age of the managers and performance of the studied firms. Firm performance is not associated to the age of the senior manager. Using analysis of variance technique (see Table 5.4) the above hypothesis has been rejected $F(33,98) = 0.768$ ($p = 0.804$). It is notable that, accordingly, the above hypothesis was not strongly validated by the previous empirical researches (Leonidou, Katsikeas and Piercy, 1998; Kakabadse, 1999). The findings of this research support the findings of the recent research in managerial age and performance (Kakabadse, 1999; Chan and Foster, 2001). Kakabadse (1999) concluded that:

Indeed, it is the older manager who makes the most of his or her people, and who fosters continuous, effective performance. Younger managers are seen as ambitious and more concerned with the immediate. The challenge of working in today's flatter organizations demands resilience and wisdom – characteristics more often associated with the experienced manager. Many employers, however, are ignoring the value of older managers. Separately, research shows that quality of management, communication, clarity of vision and ability to relate within a team and across the organization are no different according to gender.

Generally speaking, it is concluded that, younger senior managers do not have a more complete knowledge of the strategic orientation for developing the strategies of the company than older senior managers. But the firms run by younger senior managers would be more likely to pursue risky strategies than firms with older managers. Younger senior managers are more inclined to develop novel and innovative strategies than older managers. Finally, the firm performance is not significantly related to the age of the CEOs.

Working Experiences

The professional experiences of the managers, in terms of previous occupations, technical expertise, or product knowledge, have been associated with firm performance. This is particularly important when professional experiences were attained in a strategy setting, through involvement in hi-tech SMEs. This was based on the assumption that, senior managers with managerial work experiences place more weight on formal strategy development than those senior managers who lack managerial work experiences. The data analysis shows that, there is a strong and significant correlation ($\gamma = 0.76$; $p < 0.1$) between the professional expertise of the CEOs and emphasis on formal strategy development in SMEs. This result has been confirmed by ANOVA result ($F(5,126) = 3.68$; $p < 0.01$) which has been shown in Table 5.5. In other words, CEOs with professional expertise and managerial work experiences put more emphasis on formal strategy development than the CEOs without such work experiences. This result supports the findings of previous studies which concluded that, such managerial work experience exposes the managers to information and contacts relating to foreign markets and the development of business strategies (Reid, 1983), enriches managerial expertise and increases the firm's aggressiveness and performance in overseas markets (da Rocha, Carl and da Cunha, 1990).

Table 5.5 ANOVA table for CEOs' experiences and education

	Parametric Test		Non-Parametric Test	
	ANOVA		Kruskal-Wallis Test	
		Formal Strategic Planning		
	F-Value	Sig. Level	-Value	Asymp. Sig.
V.I	3.681	P<0.01		
V.II	0.266	P<0.05		
V.III			5.488	P<0.05
		Firm Performance		
	F-Value	Sig. Level	-Value	Asymp. Sig.
V.I	2.892	P<0.05		
V.II	1.221	P>0.05		
V.III			6.302	P>0.05

V.I. Respondents' professional years of experiences
V.II. Educational background of the respondents (Management and Business Studies)
V.III. Educational level of the respondents

Regarding the work experiences of the CEOs and firm performance, it has been assumed that, there is a significant association between variables. Running correlation analysis it has been found that the managerial work experiences of the managers within the industry significantly ($\gamma = 0.67$; $p < 0.05$) impacts on the firm performance. This result has been confirmed by ANOVA result ($F(4,127) = 2.892$; $p < 0.05$). This result is very similar to the results of previous researches (Chan and Foster, 2001). Schell (1996) in answer to the question, what is the number one determinant of the entrepreneur's success?, they explain that,

> "The number one determinant of your success is you. The entrepreneur. The chief enchilada. The big kahuna. It's fact that, the decisions you made and the directions you take place you light years ahead of whatever the number two determinant is" Schell (1996, 7).

By and large, it can be conclude that, senior managers with managerial work experiences place more weight on formal strategy development than those senior managers who lack of managerial work experiences. The firms that are run by managers with long work experience are more successful than the firms, that are run by managers who lack or who have short work experience.

Education

Both the level of formal education and the type of education (business or non-business) provide us with some measure of an individual's knowledge and skill base (Hambrick and Mason, 1984; Hitt and Tyler, 1991). CEOs with higher levels of education and with business degrees are expected to generate a wider range of creative solutions when faced with complex problems. Level of education has been linked to firm performance (Norburn and Birley, 1988), degree of firm innovation (Bantel and Jackson, 1989), and change in corporate strategy (Wiersema and Bantel, 1992).

The levels of formal education attained by managers and their educational background have been suggested as factors affecting the strategy development process. Some scholars have hypothesized that better educated decision makers are more likely to be open-minded, interested in foreign affairs, and willing to objectively evaluate the benefits accruing from international business (Garnier, 1982). Others have claimed that higher-level education is vital for success in overseas operations, since it enhances management knowledge and capabilities (Schlegelmilch and Ross, 1987). This managerial factor has received particular empirical attention in the extant literature. In this research it has been found that, companies whose senior managers have management educational backgrounds are more inclined to develop strategic plans than those managers have not had such an educational background. The hypotheses validated by using statistical analysis by ANOVA result ($F(1,129) = 0.266$; $p < 0.05$). It has also been found that a significant correlation ($\gamma = 0.81$; $p < 0.01$) exists between managers' educational background and emphasis on strategy development in the studied firms. Where the firms were run by senior managers without a management educational background, longer strategic plans are unlikely to be initiated within the firm. It also has been found that, senior managers with a management educational background place more weight on opportunities and less weight on threats than those managers have not had such an educational background in small businesses.

It has been hypothesized that, there is a significant relationship between the educational level of the managers and firm performance in SMEs. In this regard the analysis of the data show that, there was no significant difference ($= 6.302$; $p > 0.05$) between firms which were run by more and less educated managers in terms of performance. This finding is very similar to the findings of Koh (1991) and Chan and Foster (2001). One explanation would be the relation between the age and education level of respondents. As discussed in the data analysis chapter, older managers are likely to have less education. While the younger managers are likely to have more education. In other words, managers with less industry experience are younger and, very likely, better educated. They are therefore more knowledgeable and prepared to break away from their immediate circle to find appropriate information. In contrast, the managers with less education are older.

The findings in this section confirms the findings of the relationship between age and firm performance. The discussion in this section could be summarized as, managers with a management educational background put more emphasis on developing strategic plans in small businesses; and firm performance in small businesses is not significantly related to the educational level of managers.

Strategic Awareness of the Managers

Burns (2007) argues that a prerequisite to all creative processes is the generation of awareness of different ideas and ways of doing things through reading and travelling widely, and talking with different people with different views about the world. In an entrepreneurial firms' context, this is to be placed in the context of environmental scanning and strategy development. It may be important to develop managers' awareness of how what they do can matter at the strategic level. Particularly in fast-changing conditions successful firms may be those that have developed the dynamic capabilities to continually readjust the required competences. In effect their competences become that of learning and development. Therefore, the strategic awareness becomes more important in developing strategy in entrepreneurial firms. The awareness of strategic issues is not necessarily an analytical process; rather, managers get a 'gut feeling' based on their previous experiences or received wisdom (Johnson, Scholes and Whittington, 2005). They argue that this awareness incubates as various stimuli that help to build up a picture of the extent to which circumstances deviate from what is normally to be expected, perhaps in terms of internal performance measures such as profit performance or perhaps as a reaction to the quality of products and services. Strategic awareness may result in creativity. It reduces blocks to individual creativity in spotting opportunities and developing strategy. Von Oech (1998) identified 10 blocks to individual creativity. These include:

- The belief that there is only one solution to a problem
- The fallacy that logic is important in creativity
- The tendency to be practical
- The tendency to follow established rules
- Avoiding ambiguity in viewing a problem
- The tendency to assign blame for failure
- The unwillingness to recognize the creative power of play
- The tendency to think too narrowly and with too much focus
- The unwillingness to think unconventionally because of the fear of appearing foolish
- The lack of belief that you can be creative.

Increasing strategic awareness may result in the realization that they have these blocks and then dismantling them. In this research it has been assumed that, the strategic awareness of the managers is significantly correlated to determining the strategic orientation of the company. As discussed in Chapter 4, it has been found that, 74 per cent of the studied firms reported that a strategic management system had been established in their firms. So the association between managers' awareness of the importance of strategic management and establishing such a system was targeted in this section. Using the t-test results (see Table 5.6) it has been found that, the environmental awareness of the managers in SMEs is significantly (t-statistics = 35.873, p-value < 0.00) important. The respondents considered the external opportunities as extremely important (t-statistics = 23.515, p-value < 0.00) while they considered the external threats below average (t-statistics = 54.423, p-value > 0.05). Therefore, the association between the strategic awareness of the managers and establishing a strategic management system within the studied firms was significant.

It is notable that, where a strategic management system had been established in the firm, those CEOs considered environmental awareness as an important factor. So, the strategic awareness of the senior managers significantly impacts upon the establishment of a systematic approach to strategic management within those firms. The other assumption that has been made is the association between the strategic awareness of the managers and strategic planning. The data analysis in Chapter 4 shows that, the strategic awareness of the CEOs plays an important role in the formulation of the business strategies ($\gamma = -0.79$; $p < 0.01$). Where the CEO exhibits a distinct lack of strategic awareness, they do not emphasis on formal strategic planning. Further analysis using T-test ($t(131) = 42.534$, $P < 0.01$) confirms this result. This finding is similar to the findings of previous researches (Chan and Foster, 2001). Finally, it is contended that CEOs ought to be assisted (trained) to develop a wider awareness of the importance of the environment and market in which their firms operate. Therefore, providing the necessary flexibility within their

Table 5.6 Strategic awareness of respondents, results of t-test*

Variable	d.f	t-statistics	Mean difference	P-value
Establishing strategic management system				
Environmental awareness of the managers	131	28.352	3.41	0.003
Formal strategic planning				
External opportunities	130	35.873	3.22	0.001
External threats	131	42.534	3.14	0.003
Internal strengths	129	23.515	4.32	0.000
Internal weaknesses	131	54.423	1.98	0.095
Management training	128	31.523	4.18	0.000
	129	43.456	3.72	0.002
	131	19.423	4.19	0.000

* : Mean Importance Rating 3
: Mean Importance Rating < 3
(Scale: 1 = Not Important; 3 = Important; 5 = Extremely Important)

strategic organizational decision-making processes will enable prompt and proactive responses to changes in the environment.

Managing Resource Capabilities

As it has been discussed earlier, the resources-based view (RBV) of the firm is traceable to early classic management treatises. The basic insights of the resource-based view of the firm are well known. The resource based view of the firm argues that the firm is best viewed as a bundle of resources or factors of production that management must deploy systematically to add value (Boxall, 19,960). Perhaps the significance of the resource-based view of the firm was recognized when Wernerfelt's work (1984) 'A Resources-based View of the Firm' was selected as the best 1994 paper published in the *Strategic Management Journal*. Chandler (1977); Nelson and Winter (1982), Barney (1986), Teece (1988, 1989) and Teece, Pisano and Shuen (1994) contributed to this theory with their remarkable work. The RBV emerged as 'an important new conceptualization in the field of strategic management' and is 'one of the most important redirections of the strategic research in this decade' (Zajac, 1995, p. 169).

The central promise of RBV addresses the fundamental question of why firms are different and how firms achieve and sustain competitive advantage. Extending the original work, researchers have attempted to explain more specifically how differences in firms' resources realize superior firm performance. Barney (1986) presents a more concrete and comprehensive framework to identify the needed characteristics of firm resources in order to generate a sustainable competitive advantage. Johnson et al (2005) consider such resources as unique resources. Four criteria are proposed to assess the economic implications of the unique resources:

- Value
- Rareness
- Inimitability
- Substitutability

Analoui and Karami (2003) argue that value refers to the extent to which the firm's combination of resources fits with the external environment so that the firm is able to exploit opportunities and/or neutralize threats in the competitive environment. While, rareness refers to the physical or perceived physical rareness of the resources in the factor markets. Inimitability is the continuation of imperfect factor markets via information asymmetry such that resources cannot be obtained or recreated by other firms without a cost disadvantage. Finally, the framework also considers whether the organizations are substitutable by competitors. It has been argued that the firms can rely on unique resources for the development and implementation of their business strategies (Karami et al., 2004; Johnson et al. (2005).

Another extension strand of the resource-based view of the firm is the theory of dynamic capabilities. Teece, Pisano and Shuen (1994) define dynamic capabilities as the firm's ability to integrate, build, and reconfigure internal and external competences to address rapidly changing environments. Dynamic capabilities thus reflect an organization's ability to achieve new and innovative forms of competitive advantage given path dependencies and market positions (Chan and Foster, 2001). Dynamic capabilities theory suggests that firms can accumulate knowledge, expertise, and skills through organizational learning to overcome the inherent constraints. There is an expanding stream of literature focusing on corporate learning and organizational modes that facilitate such learning. The studies (Hagedoorn and Schakenraad, 1990) view inter-firm collaboration as a vehicle for organizational learning, and moreover view knowledge accumulation and internalization via organizational learning as the motives, process and outcomes of strategic technical alliance.

According to resource-based theory, a firm accumulates its own resource capability over time and this accumulation process is path-dependent. Any technological innovation requires new or specific resources which focal firm may lack and can not develop with cost efficiency in competitive time. Small and medium-sized enterprises are more unlikely to have the broad range of skills, assets and capabilities necessary for innovation. In these instances, inter-firm technological cooperation seems to be an efficient solution for gaining complementary resources. Teece (1992, 22) argues that 'to be successful, innovating organizations must form linkages, upstream and downstream, lateral and horizontal.'

In this research the nature and forms of the resources of the firms and their relationship with the firms performance have been investigated. As discussed earlier a hypotheses has been proposed that there are significant differences between high and low performance firms in terms of mobilization and usage of the resources. Data analysis illustrates that both independent-sample t test and Mann-Whitney U test are used to examine the differences in firms' resource capabilities between two group of firms. The results are presented in Table 5.7.

Parametric test and non-parametric test illustrate a big difference in ρ value significance for firm size and inter firm collaboration variables in the studied firms. Due to the skew distribution of the variables, this study adopts the results from Mann-Whitney U test and keeps the results of the independent-sample t test for comparison. The results in Table 5.7 show that the firm size of high performance firms is significantly larger than low performance firms. It also illustrates that high performance SMEs are most likely to have inter firm collaboration with the other firms. In other words, firm size and inter firm collaboration are essential elements for firms success. The findings in this study show that firm size is the significant factor that impacts on a firm's propensity to cooperate among the examined resource factors. It has been found that there is a significant relationship between firm size and the level of inter-firm cooperation within the studied firms. As firm size grows it is more likely to establish partnerships with other firms. Cooperating with partner firms would require specific capabilities and complementary resources in order to meet their partners' requirement. Firm size determines to a higher extent what level of resource capability a firm may hold. This finding supports the result of other researches. For example, Hagedoorn and Schakenraad (1990) stress that in general larger firms have been found to be more likely to engage in alliance relationships than smaller firms. In explaining the positive effect of firm size on cooperation, Hagedoorn and Schakenraad (1990, 300) state that 'size of firms partly reflects

Table 5.7 The differences between high and low performance firms in terms of their capabilities

Variable	T test			U test	
	Mean	S.D.	Sig. (2-tailed)	Median	Exact Sig. (2-tailed)
Business manager's managerial experience					
High performance firms	6.89	5.18		7	
Low performance firms	8.45	5.48	.612	8	.572
Firm age					
High performance firms	6.98	7.50		5	
Low performance firms	6.20	5.24	.118	4	.211
Firm size					
High performance firms	5.27	1.47		4.642	
Low performance firms	3.74	1.57	.001	3.4	.001
Research & Development					
High performance firms	.38	.31		0.19	
Low performance firms	.46	.57	.047	0.41	.053
Inter-firm collaboration					
High performance firms	.88	.96		0.085	
Low performance firms	.17	.30	.001	0.060	.001

their degree of diversification which broadens their basis for potential cooperation with other firms, forging alliances takes substantial administrative, organizational and monitoring support (and) the support of a staff for these particular activities is usually only available to large firms.'

Innovation

The current literature on managing innovation as a part of entrepreneurial management contains at its heart a contradiction. A number of authors have argued that entrepreneurial management to facilitate innovation requires a different kind of organization (Hitt et al. l, 2002). It has been discussed that (March, 1991) organizations must trade off gains in average performance through exploration against the reduction in variance in returns gained through exploitation.

Entrepreneurial firms require a flexible structure enabling them to cooperate with the other firms. In the previous section it has been discussed that as firm size grows, it is more likely be involved in inter firm cooperation in order to develop and use its potential capabilities. Theoretically, according to resource-based theory, inter-firm technological cooperation is a mechanism by which firms use external technology and information to develop innovation capabilities dynamically. Now the question is, to what extent does involvement in inter – firm cooperation may result in innovation? Is there a significant difference in innovation performance between high performance and low entrepreneurial firms? And how inter-firm technological cooperation improves firms' innovation performance?

In this research, innovation performances, has been measured by multiple indicators namely developing new product or service, filed patent and granted patent. It has been found that the firm size moderates the relationship between inter firm cooperation and innovation performance in new product, filed patent and granted patent. The data analysis illustrates that entrepreneurial SMEs that have a larger employment size, coupled with engaging in cooperation, have perform better in introducing new products and creating technology patents. Again to examine whether there are differences in innovation between high and low performance firms, independent-sample t-test is employed. The results are presented in Table 5.8.

The results in Table 5.8 show that high performance firms have significantly better innovation performance than low performance firms. In other words, high performance SMEs develop and bring more new products and services to the market than low performance SMEs. They spend more financial resources on research and development than the low performance firms do. High performance firms have more

Table 5.8 The differences between high and low performance SMEs in terms of innovation

Variable	T test		
	Mean	**S.D.**	**Sig. (2-tailed)**
New product/service			
High performance firms	6.84	5.28	
Low performance firms	5.01	4.11	P< 0.00
R & D investment			
High performance firms	6.20	6.30	
Low performance firms	3.21	4.14	P< 0.00
Granted patent			
High performance firms	4.58	6.12	
Low performance firms	2.39	3.67	P< 0.00

granted patents than low performance firms. Globally, new product intensity in high performance firms is significantly larger than in low performance firms. This result may suggest that the firms which been involved in inter firm cooperation have a stronger capability for carrying out radical innovation than the SMEs without any inter firm cooperation experiences.

It can be conclude that in entrepreneurial firms, specifically those operating in the high tech sector, it is not a firm's choice whether it should undertake technological innovation or not, the firm's survival and growth depends on its innovativeness against its competitors. However, it is a firm's choice to decide its innovation strategy, go-it-alone or cooperation. Empirical research on cooperative activities can provide systematic analysis results to help firms' decision making. Empirical research into inter-firm cooperation in both resource theory and transaction cost theory framework still lags behind and leaves many aspects unclear. Furthermore, the analysis of innovation performance can be conducted by comparing the innovation performance that is supposed to have been affected by cooperation strategy to the innovation performance before adopting the cooperation strategy. This longitudinal empirical research is expected to give a better understanding of the innovation performance on adopting a cooperation strategy.

Summary and Conclusion

The chapter is divided into two separate but interrelated sections. In the first section CEO's perception of the importance of strategic management in SMEs is explored. A significant proportion of the studied SMEs regarded strategic management as important. In the second section the role of senior managers in the strategic management processes within the studied firms is investigated. It has been found that the CEOs of the successful SMEs perceive employing a strategic management process as an important factor in running the business. A significant proportion of the studied SMEs regard strategic management as important. It also has been found that the firms, which employ strategic management techniques, whether formal or informal, exhibit more enhanced levels of success in the formulation and implementation of business strategies than those firms which do not employ such procedures.

The second objective of this chapter was to explore the role of senior managers in the strategic management processes within small and medium enterprises. In this regard, it has been found that there is a significant relationship between senior managers' age, work experience, educational background and strategy formulation in SMEs. It has been found that the environmental awareness of the managers in SMEs is significantly important. Particularly, the strategic awareness of the senior managers in SMEs significantly impacts upon firm performance. Where a strategic management system has been established in a firm, those CEOs considered environmental awareness as an important factor. So, the strategic awareness of the senior managers significantly impacts upon the establishment of a systematic approach to strategic management within those firms.

Is has been concluded that high performance SMEs are most likely to have inter-firm collaboration. In other words, firm size and inter-firm collaboration are essential elements for a firms' success. Consequently, high performance firms have significantly better innovation performance than low performance firms. In other words, high performance firms develop and bring more new products and services to the market than low performance firms.

References

Ahls, B. (2001), 'Organizational Behaviour: A Model for Cultural Change', *Industrial Management*, **43**(4), 6–9.

Analoui, F. (2000), 'Identification of Clusters of Managerial Skills for Increased *Effectiveness: the Case of Steel Industry in Iran*', *International Journal of Training and Development*, **4**(3), 217–234.

Analoui, F. and Karami, A. (2003), *Strategic Management in Small and Medium Enterprises* (London: Thomson Learning).

Andersen, A. and Mutual, A. (1997), *American Family Business Survey* (Houston, Tex.: Family Business Center).

Anderson, W.R. (1997), 'The Future of Human Resources: Forging Ahead or Falling behind'? *Human Resource Management*, **6**(1), 17–22.

Ansoff, H.I. (1984), *Implanting Strategic Management* (Upper Saddle River, NJ: Prentice-Hall Books).

Armstrong, J.S. (1982), 'The Value of Formal Planning for Strategic Decisions', *Strategic Management Journal*, **3**, 100–111.

Astrachan, J.H. and Kolenko, T.A. (1994), 'A Neglected Factor Explaining Family Business Success: Human Resource Practices', *Family Business Review*, 7(3), 251–262.

Bantel, K.A. and Jackson, S.E. (1989), 'Top Management and Innovations in Banking: Does the Composition of the Top Management Team Make a Difference?' *Strategic Management Journal*, **10**, 107–124.

Barney, J.B. (1986), 'Strategic Factor Markets: Expectations, Luck, and Business Strategy', *Management Science*, **12**(10), 1211–1241.

Barry, B.W. (1998), A Beginner's Guide to Strategic Planning, *The Futurist*, Washington, **32**(3), 33–36.

Beal, M.R. (2000), 'Competing Effectively: Environmental Scanning, Competitive Strategy, and Organizational Performance in Small Manufacturing Firms', *Journal of Small Business Management*, **37**(1), 27–47.

Bennett, N., Ketchen, D.J., Jr and Schultz, E.B. (1998), 'An Examination of Factors Associated with the Integration of Human Resource Management and Strategic Decision Making', *Human Resource Management*, **37**(1), 3–16.

Berg, S.V., Duncan, J. and Friedman, F. (1982), *Joint Venture Strategies and Corporate Innovation* (Cambridge, Mass.: Oelgeschlager).

Berry, M. (1998), 'Strategic Planning in Small High Tech Companies', *Long Range Planning*, **31**(3), 455–466.

Boxall, P. (1996), 'The Strategic HRM Debate and the Resource-Based View of the Firm', *Human Resource Management Journal*, **6**(3), 59–75.

Bridge, J. and Peel, M.J. (1999), 'Research Note: A Study of Computer Usage and Strategic Planning in the SME Sector', *International Small Business Journal*, **17**(4), 82–87.

Brown, R. (1995) Family Business: Rethinking Strategic Planning, paper presented at the 40th Annual International Council on Small Business, Sydney, Australia, June.

Burns, P. (2007), *Entrepreneurship and Small Business*, 2nd edn (Basingstoke, Hampshire: Palgrave Macmillan Books).

Cavusgil, S.T. (1982), 'Some Observations on the Relevance of Critical Variables for Internationalisation Stages', 'In' in *Export Management: An International.* Czinkota, M.R. and Tesar, G. (eds.) (Context/N.Y.: Praeger Publishing), 276–285.

Chan, S.Y. and Foster, J.M. (2001), 'Strategy Formulation in Small Business: the Hong Kong Experiences', *International Small Business Journal*, April/June.

Chandler, A.D. (1977), *The Visible Hand: the Managerial Revolution in American Business* (Cambridge: Belknap/Harvard University Press).

Child, J. (1974), 'Managerial and Organizational Factors Associated With Company Performance – Part 1', *Journal of Management Studies*, **11**, 13–27.

Copacino, W.C. (1999), 'A New Direction in Strategic Planning', *Logistic Management and Distribution Report*, **38**(10), 36.

Curran, J. (1996), 'Small Business Strategy' in *The Concise International Encyclopaedia of Business and Management, London: International Thomson Business Press*. Warner, M. (ed.), 4510–4520.

da Rocha, A., Carl, H.C. and da Cunha, C.E. (1990), 'Aggressive and Passive Exporters: A Study in the Brazilian Furniture Industry', *International Marketing Review*, 7(5), 6–15.

Dicthl, E., Koglmayr, H.G. and Muller, S. (1990), 'International Orientation as a Precondition for Export Success', *Journal of International Business Studies*, **21**(1), 23–40.

Duncan, J.P. (2001), 'Simple Planning', *Executive Excellence*, **18**(8), 10.

Eisenhardt, K.M. and Schoonhoven, C.B. (1996), 'Resource-based View of Strategic Alliance Formation: Strategic and Social Effects in Entrepreneurial Firms', *Organization Science*, **7**, 136–150.

Flores, L.G. and Saxena, N. (2000), 'Energizing Strategic Planning', *Banking Strategies*, **76**(1), 6–12.

Fusfeld, H. and Haklisch, C. (1985), 'Cooperative R&D for Competitors', *Harvard Business Review*, **63**, 60–76.

Garnier, G. (1982), 'Comparative Export Behaviour of Small Canadian Firms in the Printing and Electrical Industries' in *Export Management: An International Context*. Czinkota, M.R. and Tesar, G. (eds.) (New York: Praeger Publishing), 113–131.

Gomez-Mejia, L.R. (1988), 'The Role of Human Resources Strategy in Export Performance: A Longitudinal Study', *Strategic Management Journal*, **9**, 493–505.

Goodwin, D.R. and Hodgett, R.A., '(1991) Strategic Planning in Medium Size Companies', *Australian Accountant*, **61**(2), 71–83.

Greenwald and Associates (1993), *Major Findings of the Family Business Survey* (Springfield, Mass: Massachusetts Mutual Life Insurance Company).

Hagedoorn, J. and Schakenraad, J. (1990), 'Technology Cooperation, Strategic Alliances, and their Motives: Brother, Can you Spare a Dime, or do you Have a Light?', *Paper for SMS Conference, Stockholm, September, 24-27, 1990.*

Hambrick, D.C. and Mason, P.A. (1984), 'Upper Echelons: The Organisation as a Reflection of its Top Managers', *Academy of Management Review*, **9**, 193–206.

Handler, W.C. (1994), 'Succession in Family Business: A Review of the Research', *Family Business Review*, **7**(2), 133–158.

Hitt, M.A., Ireland, R.D., Camp, S.M. and Sexton, D.L. (2002), *Strategic Entrepreneurship Creating a New Mindset* (Oxford: Blackwell Publishing).

Hitt, M.A. and Tyler, B.B. (1991), 'Strategic Decision Models: Integrating Different Perspectives', *Strategic Management Journal*, **12**, 327–351.

Hoskisson, R.E. (2000), 'Strategy in Emerging Economics', *Academy of Management Journal*, **43**(3), 249–268.

Johnson, G., Scholes, K. and Whittington, R. (2005), *Exploring Corporate Strategy*, 7th edn (Harlow, Essex: Prentice-Hall).

Jones, W.D. (1982), 'Characteristics of Planning in Small Firms', *Journal of Small Business Management*, **20**(3), 15–19.

Kakabadse, A. (1999), 'Younger Does Not Mean Better', *The British Journal of Administrative Management*, January/February.

Karami, A., Analoui, F., Cusworth, J. (2004) Strategic human resource management and resource-based approach: the evidence from the British manufacturing industry, *Management Research News*, **27**(6), 50–68.

Knight, R.A. (1993), 'Planning: the Key to Family Owned Business Survival', *Management Accounting*, **74**, 33–34.

Koh, A. C. (1991) Relationships Among Organizational Characteristics, Marketing Strategy and Export Performance, *International Marketing Review*, **8**(3), 46–60.

Leonidou, L.C., Katsikeas, C.S. and Piercy, N.F. (1998), 'Identifying Managerial Influences on Exporting: past Research and Future Directions', *Journal of International Marketing*, **6**(2), 74–102.

March, J.G. (1991), 'Exploration and Exploitation in Organizational Learning', *Organization Science*, **2**(1), 71–87.

Meyer, G.D. and Heppard, K.A. (2000), *Entrepreneurship as Strategy: Competing on the Entrepreneurial Edge* (Thousand Oaks, Calif.: Sage).

Miles, R.E. and Snow, C. (1978), *Organisational Strategy, Structure and Process* (New York: McGraw-Hill).

Mintzberg, H. (1994), *The Rise and Fall of Strategic* (Planning, N.Y.: The Free Press).

Nelson, R.R. and Winter, S.G. (1982), *An Evolutionary Theory of Economic Change* (Cambridge, Mass.: Harvard University Press).

Norburn, D. and Birley, S. (1988), 'The Top Management Team and Corporate Performance', *Strategic Management Journal*, **9**, 225–237.

Reid, S.D. (1983), 'Firm Internationalisation, Transaction Costs and Strategic Choice', *Journal of International Business Studies*, **2**, 44–56.

Riedle, K. (1989), 'Demand for R&D Activities and the Trade off between In-House and External Research: a Viewpoint from Industry with Reference to Large Companies', *Technovation*, **9**, 213–225.

Roux, E. (1987), 'Managers' Attitudes toward Risk among Determinants of Export Entry of Small- and Medium-Sized Firms' in *Managing Export Entry and Expansion*, Rosson, P.J. and Reid, S.D. (eds.) (Westport CT: Praeger Publishing), 95–110.

Roy, H.M. and Dugal, S.S. (1999), 'The Effect of Technological Environment and Competitive Strategy on Licensing Decisions', *American Business Review*, **17**(2), 112–118.

Rue, L.W. and Ibrahim, N.A. (1996), 'The Status of Planning in Smaller Family Owned Businesses', *Family Business Review*, **9**(1), 29–43.

Schell, J. (1996), *The Entrepreneur Magazine Small Business Answer Book* (Chichester: John Wiley & Sons Inc.).

Schlegelmilch, B.B. and Ross, A.G. (1987), 'The Influence of Managerial Characteristics on Different Measures of Export Success', *Journal of Marketing Management*, **3**(2), 145–158.

Shuman, J.C., Shaw, J.J. and Sussman, G. (1985), 'Strategic Planning in Smaller Rapid Growth Companies', *Long Range Planning*, **18**(6), 48–53.

Stead, J.G. (2000) Eco-enterprise Strategy: Standing for Sustainability, *Journal of Business Ethics*, **24**,(4), 313–330.

Teece, D., Pisano, G. and Shuen, A. (1994), 'Dynamic Capabilities and Strategic Management', *Working Paper*. Center for Research in Management, University of California, Berkeley.

Teece, D.J. (1988), 'Technological Change and the Nature of the Firm' in *Technical Change and Economic Theory*. Dosi, G., Freeman, C., Nelson, R., Silverberg, G. and Soete, L. (eds.) (London: Frances Pinter).

Teece, D.J. (1992), 'Competition, Cooperation, and Innovation Organizational Arrangements for Regimes of Rapid Technological Progress', *Journal of Economic Behavior and Organization*, **18**, 1–25.

Upton, N. and Heck, R.K.Z. (1997), '*The Family* Business Dimension of Entrepreneurship, in', *Entrepreneurship*, ed. D.L. Sexton and R.A. Smilor. Chicago, IL.: Upstart Publishing, 243–266.

Von Oech, F. (1998), *A Whack on the Side of the Head* (New York: Warner Books).

Ward, J.L. (1988), 'The Special Role of Strategic Planning for Family Business', *Family Business Review*, **1**(2), 105–117.

Ward, J. L. (1997) 'Growing the Family Business: Special Challenges and Best Practices', *Family Business Review*, **10**(4), 323–337.

Waring, S. (2001) 'The Right Decision', *Australian CPA*, **71**(8), 81–89.

Wernerfelt, B. (1984), 'A Resource-Based View of the Firm', *Strategic Management Journal*, **5**, 171–180.

Wiersema, M.F. and Bantel, K.A. (1992), 'Top Management Team Demography and Corporate Strategic Change', *Academy of Management Journal*, **35**, 91–121.

Wortman, M.S. (1994), 'Theoretical Foundations for Family-Owned Business: A Conceptual and Research-Based Paradigm', *Family Business Review*, **7**(1), 3–27.

Zajac, E. (1995), SMJ 1994 Best Paper Prize to Birger Wernerfelt. *Strategic Management Journal*, **16**(3), 169–170.

Zimmerer, T.W. and Scarborough, N.M. (2002), *Essentials of Entrepreneurship and Small Business Management*, 3rd edn (Upper Saddle River: Prentice-Hall).

Chapter 6

Crafting Strategy and Environmental Context

Introduction

The main purpose of this chapter is to discuss strategy formulation in the *SME* sector. The chapter reveals some findings on the existence and nature of environmental analysis in the formulation of business strategies in the firms studied. It also covers the discussion of the effective factors associated with the formulation and implementation of strategy in the studied firms. It is useful to start by reviewing the concept of strategy. The strategy of a firm forms a comprehensive master plan stating how the firm will achieve its mission and objectives. It maximizes competitive advantages and at the same time, minimizes competitive disadvantages (Wheelen and Hunger, 1998). The typical business firm usually considers three linked and interdependent levels of strategy consisting of corporate strategy, business strategy and functional strategy. Corporate strategy, essentially and simply is deciding what businesses the organization should be in, and how the overall group of activities should be structured and managed (Thompson, 1996). It is also argued that, corporate strategy describes a company's overall direction in terms of its general attitude toward growth and the management of its various business and product lines (Wheelen and Hunger, 1998).

The second level of strategy is business strategy which is concerned with creating and maintaining a competitive advantage in each and every area of the business. It can be achieved through any one function, or a combination of several (Thompson, 1996). Business strategy usually occurs at the business unit or product level and it emphasizes the importance of the competitive position of a corporations products or services in the specific industry or market segment served by that business unit (Wheelen and Hunger, 1998). Figure 6.1 illustrates three levels of strategy.

Accordingly, the third level of strategy is functional strategy. Functional strategy is concerned with functional areas of the firm such as, marketing, financial, human resource, and research and development. It is the approach taken by a functional area to achieve corporate and business unit objectives and strategies by maximizing resource productivity (Wheelen and Hunger, 1998). It is critical that these functional strategies are designed and managed in a coordinated way, such that they interrelate with each other and at the same time, collectively allow the competitive strategies to be implemented properly (Thompson, 1996). In most cases, small and medium-sized enterprises use all three levels of strategy simultaneously. Functional strategies

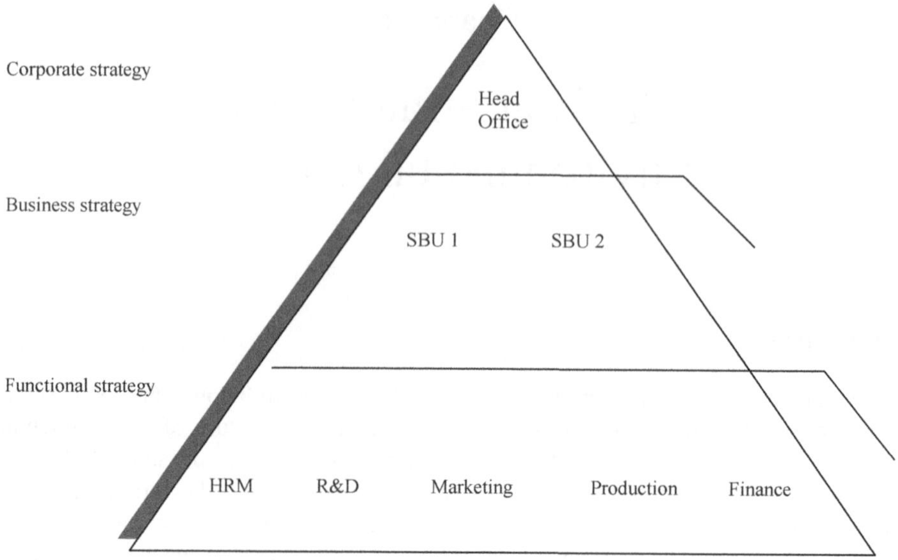

Figure 6.1 Strategy levels

support business strategies, which, in turn, support the corporate strategy. Lets start with discussion on the main elements of corporate strategy.

Elements of Corporate Strategy

As discussed earlier, corporate strategy explains the nature of the activities of the organization and its philosophy for existing in an industry. In practice, adding value through buying and selling businesses has been one form of corporate strategy. This has been explained in different ways. For example, Porter (1998) terms this as portfolio management. He identifies three main concepts of corporate strategy: restructuring, sharing activities, and transferring skills. Restructuring occurs when businesses are acquired with the specific intent of achieving value by active intervention and improvement. Sharing activities is a value activity that is based on the component businesses using the same processes or systems. And transferring skills is managing ongoing interrelationships between the businesses (McGee, Thomas and Wilson, 2005).

Johnson et al. (2005) argue that corporate strategy should answer four key questions as follows:

- What is the overall rationale of the corporate parent in terms of how it envisages itself enhancing the value created by the business units for its shareholders/stakeholders?
- What is the logic of the mix of business units in the corporate portfolio and how does this make sense in terms of the corporate rational?

- Whether the extent and type of diversity of the corporation are sensible given the corporate rationale and logic of the portfolio.
- Whether the nature of corporate control of subsidiaries is appropriate in terms of the corporate rationale, the logic of the portfolio, and the extent of diversity.

According to Johnson et al. (2005) corporate strategy, describes a corporation's overall direction in terms of its general philosophy towards growth and the management of its various business units. It answers the question: what business are we in? Corporate strategy helps to:

- Establishing investment priorities and steering resources into the most attractive business units
- Initiating actions to improve the combined performance of business units
- Improving synergy between related business units to increase performance
- Making decisions re diversification.

Based on Collis and Montgomery's (1997) framework for corporate strategy, an effective corporate strategy consists of five elements vision, goals and objectives, resources, structure, system and process, and corporate advantages that together as a system lead to a corporate advantage that creates economic value. Now let's discuss these elements in some detail.

Vision and Mission Statement

It has been said that 'if you don't know where you are going, any road can take you there' (Collis and Montgomery, 1997). A clear vision defines the rules for acting incrementally and opportunistically. It is better to distinguish between the terms vision and mission. Some people like to consider vision and mission as two different concepts: a mission statement describes what the organization is now; a vision statement describes what the organization would like to become (Campbell and Yeung, 1991). A manager facing an unexpected situation can take a decision after asking himself the question 'will such an action further the company's vision?' Vision statements often embody the core values of the founding entrepreneur, and say something about the inspiration behind the company that would not be obvious from a reading of its business plans (Bowman and Faulkner, 1997).

Strategic vision is where all acquisitions begin. Management vision of the acquisition is shared with suppliers, customers, lenders and employees as a framework for planning, discussion, decisions and reactions to change (Sirower, 1997). Sirower argued that the vision must be clear to large constituent groups and adaptable to many unknown circumstances. In addition the vision must be a continuous guide to the actual operating plans of the company. If vision does not translate into real actions, it can provoke damaging reactions from competitors (Wit and Meyer, 1998). Bowman and Faulkner indicated that 'a vision is an image of a better future, however defined; it is a state to which the company aspires, and therefore can at least logically be achieved. What happens when Komatsu succeed in encircling Caterpillar? Clearly a new vision needs to be adopted if the company is not to sink beneath the competitive waves, enthusiastically telling stories of past triumphs. For an ongoing sense of purpose, the mission statement is needed' (Bowman and Faulkner, 1997, 181).

Goals and Objectives of the Firm

If the vision describes what the corporation wishes to become in many years' time, an effective corporate strategy must also have a set of shorter-term goals and objectives such as to sustain a 40 per cent equity ratio. Objectives refer to specific short and medium-term quantitative targets. On the other hand goals refer to qualitative intentions to be achieved during the same time, such as to improve new product development capabilities or become a global organization (Collis and Montgomery, 1997).

Bowman and Faulkner have argued that the process of setting objectives for the corporation, and subsequently for the business unit, is the process of translating the corporations strategies into specific and, if possible, measurable objectives, the achievement of which will signal that the corporation's adapted strategies are working successfully (Bowman and Faulkner, 1997). They argued that objectives are frequently, but not always, financial. They need not even be measurable, but obviously it helps the monitoring process if they are measurable

Resources and Capabilities

The most important of the three elements of corporate strategy are the available corporate resources. Based on the new resource-based view of the firm, resources are defined as the set of assets and capabilities, both tangible and intangible, which, when competitively superior, scarce, and appropriable, have the potential to create value from diversification (Collis, 1996).

Commonly referred to as core competencies, the term resources actually covers a broad range of assets that can contribute to the competitive advantage of many different businesses. Resources are the critical building blocks of strategy. They determine not what a firm wants to do, but what it can do. Resources are inputs into a firm's production process such as capital equipment, the skills of individual employees, patents, finance, and talent managers. The main resources of the firm, on which corporate strategy rests, include the assets, skills and capabilities of the firm. From another point of view the resources of the firms can be classified into, tangible and intangible resources.

The different types of tangible resources consists of; financial, physical, human, and organizational resources. In contrast, the three types of intangible resources include, technological resources, the resources for innovation and company reputation. Within the term 'technological resources' are contained the stock of technology such as patents, trade marks, copyright, and trademarks. Tangible and intangible resources are a critical part of the pathway to the development of competitive advantage.

Resources strategic value is increased when they are integrated or combined. Before choosing any strategy, the firm must evaluate the strengths and weaknesses of its resources. Choosing an effective strategy is dependent on the firms resources.

Resources determine the range of market opportunities that are appropriate for a firm and so have a major impact on firm scope. The most valuable resources are those that enable a firm to compete successfully in more than one market (Collis and Montgomery, 1997). The capacity of the firm to perform a task or activity is called its 'capability'. Capabilities are the unique combination of the firm's information-based tangible or intangible resources and are what the firm is able to do as a result of teams of resources working together. Hitt and Ireland have argued that capabilities represent the firm's capacity to deploy resources that have been purposely integrated to achieve a desired end state. The glue that binds the organization together. Capabilities emerge over time through complex interactions between and among tangible and intangible resources. They are based on developing, carrying, and exchanging information and knowledge through the firm's human capital. Thus, the firm's knowledge base is embedded in and reflected by its capabilities. It is a key source of advantage in the new competitive landscape (Hitt and Ireland, 2000).

Businesses

The value intrinsic in a firm's resources will only be realized if the corporation diversifies in to the appropriate business – the second element of corporate strategy framework. Every effective corporate strategy must involve related business, not necessarily related in the similarity of their products, but in the sense that all draw, and directly benefit from, these resources (Collis, 1996). Competition is at the core of the success or failure of the business. As Porter has discussed, competition determines the appropriateness of a firm's activities that can contribute to its performance, such as innovations, a cohesive culture, or good implementation. Competitive strategy is the search for a favourable competitive position in an industry, the fundamental arena in which competition occurs (Porter, 1985).

The business side of the corporate strategy framework refers to the industries in which a firm operates, as well as to the competitive strategy is adopts in each. Industry choice is critical to the long-term success of a corporate strategy. It has repeatedly been demonstrated that the best predictor of firm performance is the profitability of the industries in which it competes (Rumelt, 1991). The set of industries in which a firm operates also influences the extent to which it will be able to share resources across its business. The notion of relatedness may be used as a surrogate for a firm's ability to create synergy among its businesses.

The particular competitive strategy a firm pursues in each industry also has an impact on corporate performance. While it may be unusual to find a corporation that pursues exactly the same source of competitive advantage in every one of its businesses, it is important to recognize that a corporations resources are often only valuable when applied to similar generic strategies (Collis and Montgomery, 1997).

As mentioned earlier, the first fundamental determination of a firm's profitability is industry attractiveness. In any industry, whether it is domestic or international, or produces a product or a services, the role of competition is embodied in five competitive forces: the entry of new competitors, the threat from substitutes, the bargaining power of buyers, the bargaining power of suppliers, and the rivalry among the existing competitors. The collective strength of these five competitive forces determines the ability of firms in any industry to earn, on average, rates of return on investment, in excess of the cost of capital. The strength of the five forces varies from industry to industry, and can change as an industry evolves. The five forces determine industry profitability, because they influence the price, costs, and the required investment of the firm in an industry. The strength of each of the five competitive forces is a function of industry structure (Porter, 1985). The five-force framework allows the firm to see through the complexity and pinpoint those factors that are critical to competition in its industry as well as to identify these strategic innovations that would most improve the industry's profitability. It directs manager's creative energies toward those aspects of industry structure that are most important to long-run profitability. Finally the framework aims, in the process, to raise the odds of discovering a desirable strategic innovation (Wit and Meyer, 1998).

Structure, System and Processes

The third element of the corporate strategy framework is the organizational structure, systems and processes that the corporation has in place to manage its various businesses. Collis argued that the organizational design must solve the twin problems of any corporate office – maintaining control of delegated decision making within individual business units, and providing coherence to the entire corporation by deploying valuable resources throughout the businesses (Collis, 1996).

In providing coherence to the corporation, the corporation must mobilize its valuable resources within the various businesses. The structure, systems and process of a firm determine how the organization controls and coordinates the activities of its various business units and staff functions. Collis and Montgomery argued that structure refers to the way the corporation is divided into discrete units. It describes the formal organization chart that delineates the allocation of authority inside the corporation hierarchy.

Systems are the set of formal policies and routines that govern organizational behaviour. They are the set of rules that define how tasks, from strategic planning to personnel evaluation, are to be fulfilled. Processes describe the informal elements of an organization's activities (Collis and Montgomery, 1997). Matching the structure to the strategy is a fundamental task of company strategists. Each of the organizational structures has advantages and disadvantages that strategists must consider when choosing an organization form. In the case of choosing an effective organizational structure Pearce and Robinson have argued that since the structural design ties together the key activities and resources of the firm, it must be closely aligned with the demands of the firm strategy (1991). Chandler, based on his researches, observed a common sequence of evolution in strategy and structure among American firms (Chandler, 1962). Most of firms began as simple functional units operating at a single site and within a single industry. The initial growth strategy of such firms was value expansion, which created a need for an administrative office to manage the increased volume. The next growth strategy was geographic expansion, which required multiple field units, performing in different locations. Administrative problems with regard to standardization, specialization, and inter unit coordination gave rise to the need for geographic units and for a central administrative unit to oversee them. Vertical integration was usually the next growth strategy. Firms remained within the same industry but perform additional functions. Problems associated with the flow of information and materials among the various functions led to the functional organization, in which staff personnel developed forecasts and schedules that facilitated overall coordination. The final growth strategy was product diversification.

In establishing a firm's infrastructure, corporate managers have a wide array of organizational mechanisms at their disposal, from the formal boxes in an organization chart to the more subtle element of corporate culture and style (Rumelt, 1991; Pearce, and Robinson, 1991). Because every corporate a firm's degree of diversification from its core business affected its choice of structure. Strategy is different, there is no one optimal set of structure, systems, and processes (Collis and Montgomery, 1997). Successful corporate strategies can, therefore, look very different. There in not one right corporate strategy for all companies to adopt, but rather a fundamental logic for all managers to follow when building and deploying a set of valuable and competitively superior resources into a limited set of businesses with the appropriate organizational design.

Business Level Strategy

Business level strategy refers to the way strategic managers devise a plan of action to use a company's resources and distinctive competencies to gain a competitive advantage over competitors in the market place. Business level strategy focuses on developing a firm-specific business model that will allow the firm to gain a competitive advantage. Business level strategy deals with decisions and actions pertaining to each business unit in order to make each unit more competitive in its market-place. It answers the question: How does the firm compete? As has been discussed in Chapter 2, the firm should identify its unique resources that can be the basis for competitive advantages. Hill and Jones (2004) argue that defining the firm's business is the first step in developing a business strategy. The process of business definition entails making decisions about three main key factors:

- Customers' needs, or what is to be satisfied
- Customer groups, or who is to be satisfied
- And distinctive competencies, or how customers' needs are to be satisfied.

In developing a business strategy and business model, strategists use one of the four generic business strategies: cost leadership strategy, differentiation strategy, focus differentiation and focus cost leadership. Business-level strategy: an integrated and coordinated set of commitments and actions the firm uses to gain a competitive advantage by exploiting core competencies in specific product markets. Business-level strategies are intended to create differences between the firm's position relative to those of its rivals. To position itself, the firm must decide whether it intends to perform activities differently or to perform different activities as compared with its rivals. There are many factors influencing business strategy (Johnson, Scholes and Whittington, 2005). Some of those important factors are as follows:

- The nature of the competitive environment, stable, mature or fast changing?
- What is specially valued by customers?
- Does the firm have competencies which allow it to deliver the desired competitive strategy?
- Does the firm have a sustainable competitive advantage or might competitors quickly be able to imitate, or improve on them?
- Are there constraints placed upon the choice of competitive strategy? For example, stakeholder expectations.

When choosing an effective business strategy two aspects of the competitive environment have to be considered. First, the source of competitive advantage: differentiation or low cost, and second, the competitive scope of the target customer: broad target, narrow target. As has been discussed earlier, each of these strategies can be applied in particular circumstances. Table 6.1. Illustrates commonly required skills and resources and also common organizational requirements.

Table 6.1 Generic business strategies

Generic Strategy	Commonly Required Skills & Resources	Common Organizational Requirements
Cost leadership	• Sustained capital investment & access to capital • Process engineering skills • Intense supervision of labor • Products designed for ease in manufacturing • Low cost distribution system	• Tight cost control • Frequent detailed control reports • Structured Firm and responsibilities • Incentives based on meeting strict quantitative targets
Differentiation	• Strong marketing abilities • Product engineering • Creative flair • Strong capability in basic research • Reputation for quality or technological leadership • Long tradition in the industry or unique combination of skills drawn from other businesses • Strong cooperation from channels	• Strong coordination among functions in R&D, product development, and marketing • Subjective measurement and incentives instead of quantitative measures • Amenities to attract highly skilled labor, scientists, or creative people
Focus	• Combination of the above • Policies directed at the particular strategic target	• Combination of the above • Policies directed at the particular strategic target

Effective Strategy Formulation and Implementation Process in SMEs

It has been argued that strategy is the outcome of a formal planning process and that the ultimate decision makers play the most important role in this process. This approach suggests that a firm's strategy is the result of a highly structured plan. Johnson et all (2007) termed this as design lens. Hill and Jones (2004) developed a model of the strategic planning process. They argue that the formal strategic planning process has five main steps. These steps are as follows:

1. Select the corporate mission.
2. Analyse the organization's external environment.
3. Analyse the internal environment of the firm.
4. Select strategy that build on the organization's strengths and correct its weaknesses.
5. Implement the strategy.

In Chapter 2 the task of developing a mission, analysing the external and internal environment of the firm and selecting an appropriate strategy, which is referred to as, strategy formulation, was discussed. In contrast, strategy implementation involves putting that strategy into action. Recently, the formal strategic planning model have been criticized. Hill and Jones (2004) have summarized the main reasons for criticizing formal planning process as follows:

- The unpredictability of the real world
- The role that lower managers can play in the strategic management process, and,
- The fact that many successful strategies are often the result of serendipity, not rational strategizing.

Amongst those who criticized formal strategic planning, Mintzberg's model is widely cited in the literature. His model of strategy development provides a more comprehensive view of strategy. According to his model, the firm's realized strategy is the product of whatever planned and/or intended strategies, are actually put into action and of any unplanned, or emergent strategies (Hill and Jones, 2004). Herzberg maintains that emergent strategies are often successful and may be more appropriate than intended strategies.

Apart from nature of the strategy whether formal of informal, this research targets the factors, which are associated with effective strategy formulation and implementation in entrepreneurial firms. These include mission and objectives, formal or informal strategic planning techniques, firm size, factors determining industry strength and competitive advantages of the firm, human resources involvement in strategy development, and firm performance.

Strategic Planning Tools

This section discusses the employment of some of the activities in strategy formulation and implementation within the studied firms. The respondents were asked to rate the degree of emphasis for each of the following indicators: mission statements, trend analysis, competitor analysis, long range plans, annual goals, short term action plans, ongoing evaluation, standard operation procedures (SOP), flexibility and adaptability of plans and finally, the importance of employees in strategy implementation. Summary statistics for the variables shows that, respondents placed the most emphasis on annual goals, followed by long-term goals, the mission statement, and action plans. Trend analysis and competitor analysis received the two lowest results from the respondents. The respondents considered standard operation procedures, flexibility of the plans, and human resources as important factors in implementing business strategies. The variability of the means, standard deviations, and correlations among these variables suggests that more discussion is required. So the next sections of the chapter provide the details of findings and discussion on the studied variables.

Developing Mission Statement and Objectives in SMEs

The contents of the mission statements in large and small firms have been analysed using different approaches. Table 6.2 illustrates a sample of studies in identifying and analysing the components of mission statements. Perhaps the research done by Pearce and David (1987) was the first attempt to empirically study the content of mission statements. They found the specification of target customers and markets as the highest in terms of frequency, and the identification of the firm's desired public image as the lowest frequency.

Baetz and Bart (1996) in their study of mission statements in 135 Canadian firms developed a number of categories for analysing the statements using the Ground Theory approach. Concerning the content of the analysed mission statements, they indicated that,

> the typical mission statement contained: essentially only one financial objectives (e.g. to enhance profitability and long-term value), or none at all; one or two non-financial objectives (e.g. to provide a challenging work environment); one value/belief/philosophy statements (e.g. to be a responsible company); the organisation's definition of success (e.g. meet or exceed customer's expectations); the organisation's number one priority; a definition of the organisation's strategy (i.e. a definition of specific products, specific markets and two bases for competing) and reference to one stakeholder (typically the customer) (p. 528).

Accordingly, O'Gorman and Doran (1999) in their recent study found that, the mission statement in SMEs put more emphasis on concern for survival, product or services, and their customers. Their finding is similar to the findings of Pearce and David (1987); O'Gorman and Doran (1999) also found that, the least important

Table 6.2 Components of mission statements identified by empirical researches

Researcher(s)	Relevant Country	Identified components
Pearce and David (1987)	USA	• The specification of target customers and markets • Principal products and /or services • The geographic domain • Core technologies used • Growth, survival and profitability • Company philosophy •
Klemm et al (1991)	UK	• Long term purpose of the organization reflecting deeply held corporate views • Long term strategic objectives outlining desired direction and performance in broad term • Objectives in the form of quantified planning targets over a specific period • Scope and activities of the company in terms of industry and geographical spread
Baetz and Bart (1996)	Canada	• Financial objectives • Nun-financial objectives • Firm's value, belief, and philosophy • Organization's definition of success • Definition of organization's strategy • Customers
O'Gorman and Doran (1999)	Ireland	• Concern for survival • Product and or services • Concern for customers • Geographic domain • Company philosophy • Concern for quality • Self-concept • Public image •
Karami and Analoui, 2003	UK	• Profitability • Customer satisfaction • Product/service quality • Public image

components of mission statements in SMEs are customer/market, concern for suppliers and core technology.

In comparison with the previous researches, in this research it has been decided to identify the components of the firms' mission statement based on the CEOs' priority. This method is very similar to the research methods used by previous researchers (for example Rarick and Vitton, 1995; O'Gorman and Doran, 1999; Bart, 2000). Thus, the respondents were asked to list the components of the mission statements of their firms. An analysis of the data (see Chapter 4) shows that, the firms emphasized on 'long term profit, survival and growth' as the first priority in their mission statements (74 per cent). Similarly, the same result has been reported by Baetz and Bart (1996) for 'financial objectives' (46 per cent); and O'Gorman and Doran (1999) for 'concern for survival' (72 per cent).

The results of this research show that, the respondents have emphasized on 'concern for supplier' as their last priority (9 per cent). Based on the analysis of the data, generally, a typical mission statement in SME contained: long term profit, survival and growth; customer satisfaction; core technology; market; company philosophy and values; product and services quality; public image; geographic domain; Self concept; and concern for suppliers. The 'customer satisfaction' component, which was the third most frequent (64 per cent) in O'Gorman and Doran's (1999) study, was the second most frequent component (67 per cent) in this study. More especially, the 'core technology' component which was the fourth most frequent in the Pearce and David (1987) study in the USA, and not a part of O'Gorman and Doran's (1999) study in Ireland, was the third most frequent in the current study.

Perhaps the technology intensive nature of the electronic industry could be considered as an important factor in this case. On the other hand, the data analysis shows that, the three least important components of the mission statements were geographic domain, self-concept, and finally concern for suppliers.

Mission Statements and Firm Performance

It has been argued that, one of the reasons for the lack of consistent guidelines concerning the development of mission statements is that researchers have not attempted-or have not been able-to empirically link their recommendations to performance (Ireland and Hitt, 1992; Bart, 2000). Pearce and David (1987) were among the first to demonstrate that a relationship existed between selected mission statement components and one measure of performance, that is to say, 'high versus low' performing Fortune 500 companies. Pearce and David found that:

- higher performing firms have a comparatively more comprehensive mission statement;
- corporate philosophy, self-concept, and public image are especially important components to include in mission statements.

In addition they argue that, their findings provide a realistic portrayal of the components used in corporate mission statements. Two years later, David (1989) performed a content analysis on the mission statements of 75 Business Week 1000 firms and tried to find a link between mission statements and firm performance. He measured the firm performance in terms of gross earnings, return on investment (ROI), and earnings per share (Eps). The results of the study showed that, there was no significant relation between mission statement and firm performance. Similarly, Klemm, Sanderson and Luffman (1991) in their study of 59 top companies from the *Times* 1,000 that had mission statements found no significant differences in performance (measured in terms of employee turnover and profits). In contrast, there have been several successful attempts at linking mission statements to firm performance. For instance, Baetz and Bart (1996) found a significant correlation between selected mission content items (that is financial objectives, values, purpose business strategy and length) and such performance measures as return on sales, return on assets, percentage change in sales and percentage change in profits. More recently, O'Gorman and Doran (1999) investigated the relationship between mission statement and firm performance in Irish SMEs. They reported that, '...high-growth SMEs do not have more comprehensive mission statements (ones that exhibit more of the eight components) than low-growth SMEs.... this study suggests that including "company philosophy", "self-concept," or "public image" in a mission statement does not improve a firm's performance. Neither are "more comprehensive" or "high content" mission statements more likely to be correlated with high performance' (O'Gorman and Doran, 1999, 64).

In this study, the CEOs perceptions of importance of having formal mission statements on the firm performance were examined. The majority of respondents ($n = 89$, 67 per cent) considered a written and formal mission statement as an essential factor in increasing firm performance. While only 3 per cent of respondents ($n = 4$) believed that, having a mission statement is not important in developing firm strategies and achieving its objectives. In order to analyse the impact of mission statement on firm performance all of the firms that responded to our survey were ranked into two categories based on their performance namely, high performance and low performance. This method has already been used extensively in similar researches (for example Campbell, Devine and Young, 1990; Smith, 1998; O'Gorman and Doran, 1999). Consequently a percentage of the high-performer and low-performer firms, were compared for each of the 10 components of their mission and objectives (see, Table 6.3).

It has been concluded that, high performance firms put more emphasis on long term profit, survival and growth (91 per cent), customer satisfaction (82 per cent), core technology (76 per cent) and geographic domain (69 per cent). In comparison, low performance firms put more emphasis on long term profit, survival and growth (83 per cent), core technology (73 per cent), and product and service quality (64 per cent). Both low and high performance firms have put less emphasis on concern for suppliers (High performance 17 per cent, and Low performance 12 per cent). The results of this study support the findings of O'Gorman and Doran's (1999) work indicating that, high performance firms do not have more comprehensive mission statements than low performance firms. In comparison with the previous researches in this research it has been found that, respondents emphasized on one additional component in the firm's mission statements namely, core technology. Perhaps, because of the dynamic nature of the electronic industry, the firms have targeted developing technology. Apart from comparison analysis, an attempt has been made to study the association between having a mission statement and the research variables. Using the t-test results it has been found that, there is a significant association (t-statistics = 28.342, p-value < 0.00) between having a formal mission statement and firm performance in the studied firms. This result confirms the significant ($\gamma = 0.69$, $p < 0.01$) correlation between firm performance and developing a mission statement (see Chapter 4). In other words, successful SMEs, tend to have formal mission

Table 6.3 A comparison of mission statements in high and low performance SMEs

Components	Total firms†	High performance firms††	Low performance firms†††
Long term profit, survival and growth	74	91	83
Customer satisfaction	67	82	61
Core technology	63	76	73
Product and services quality	52	51	64
Company philosophy and values	48	42	46
Market	47	39	34
Public image	32	28	22
Geographic domain	21	69	52
Self concept	17	47	33
Concern for suppliers	9	17	12

† The percentage of the total of the firms, which included component in their mission statements.
†† The percentage of the high performance firms, which included component in their mission statements.
††† The percentage of the low performance firms, which included component in their mission statements.

statements. As noted already, one of the most notable findings of this research is the difference between professionally run SMEs and family run SMEs in terms of developing formal mission statements. The analysis of the data, reveals that, professionally run SMEs are more inclined to have formal and written mission statements, and long run business plans than do family firms (t-statistics = 34.561, p-value < 0.00). In contrast, family run small businesses are more inclined to have an informal mission statement. It also has been found that, when increasing in size, the studied firms then insisted on developing a formal mission statement (t-statistics = 23.512, p-value < 0.01). These findings are very close to the findings of Smith (1998) and O'Gorman and Doran (1999).

Industry and Environment Analysis in SMEs

The discussion in this section covers the findings on the existence and nature of environmental analysis when developing business strategies in small and medium-sized enterprises. Environmental scanning is considered to be the first element of the strategic management process in the organizations. Businesses use information to develop strategies that address opportunities and threats, and allow them to gain or maintain a competitive edge. Previous researches have shown that more and more large multinational corporations have adopted a formal process for collecting and analysing information on the external environment (Inkpen, 2000; Ma, 2000; McEvily and McCabe, 2000). However, there is a big debate about gathering and analysing the information from the external environment by SMEs. For instance, research into the personality characteristics of entrepreneurs has found that many have the attitude that the owner or manager knows the market in which the business competes and does not need information gathered in a more systematic approach (McKenna, 1996). However, it may be equally important for small businesses to have the capabilities to assess the external business environment properly. Therefore, the question which has been raised in the conceptual framework of the research, is related to the importance of environmental analysis as a basic part of the strategic management process in small businesses. In this section, the findings of the data analysis on the importance and impact of environmental scanning on research variables such as firm size and firm performance are discussed.

As discussed in Chapter 2, an organization's overall business strategy is related to the sophistication, scope and intensity of its environmental scanning (Choo, 1999). An organization that follows a particular strategy, such as product differentiation, cost leadership or focus strategy, or adopts a certain strategic stance, such as prospector, analyser or Defender, is likely to operate a scanning mode that provides the required information and information processing capabilities to pursue its desired strategy. Now the question has been raised, whether or not SMEs can benefit from establishing a formal scanning system. The results of the data analysis show that, significant correlations exist between an increased emphasis on environmental analysis and effective strategy formulation in the studied firms. Further analysis (see Table 6.4) confirms that, a scanning system is necessary for the formulation and planning of business strategies ($t\ (129) = 31.226$; $P < 0.01$); increasing profit ($t\ (130) = 28.152$; $P < 0.05$); and growth rate ($t\ (124) = 26.251$; $P < 0.01$) of the firm, and developing the firm's adaptability to unexpected environmental changes in a turbulent marketplace ($t\ (128) = 21.821$, $P < 0.01$). It also has been found that, practitioners and SMEs' senior managers (strategists) perceive environmental scanning as an important dynamic ($t\ (127) = 29.852$, $P < 0.05$) system, which should be particularly sustained and controlled within the firms. It was discovered that, planning and implementing environmental scanning is a strategic activity in SMEs. Thus, in order to apply a strategic management system in the firm and benefit from it, it is particularly important to consider the environmental scanning activity as a base for strategic management.

Supporting the findings of the statistical analysis of the data, through analysis of the results of the interviews, it has been found that, environmental analysis is considered to be a strategic activity in the studied firms. It was learnt that, managing directors believe that their awareness of the environment plays a significant role in the strategy formulation process. For instance, one of the managing directors of a medium-sized enterprise indicated that:

> ....It is a golden opportunity to take the blinkers off and to look at external factors in the business in order to assess the impact of these environmental factors on your business in particular and to view your firm as part of an interconnected business ecosystem.

Another manager has made a similar point:

Table 6.4 Importance of environmental analysis, results of t-test*

Variable	d.f	t-statistics	P-value
Importance of establishing formal environmental scanning system in:			
Developing effective business strategies	129	31.226	0.001
Increasing profit	130	28.152	0.048
Growth rate	124	26.251	0.002
Firms adaptability with unexpected environmental changes	128	21.821	0.003
Firm performance	131	23.282	0.002
Managerial perception of importance of variables in environmental scanning:			
Personal sources	130	25.002	0.017
Formal and external sources	130	24.103	0.082
Quality of sources	128	31.453	0.013
Manager's background	131	38.257	0.022
Dynamic environmental analysis	127	29.852	0.040

* is rejected for $P < 0.05$
(Scale: 1 = Not Important; 3 = Important; 5 = Extremely Important)

> ....We worry about things nowadays that we never used to worry about before. Think about the technological changes in the industry. Now we worry about it. Environmental issues like technology are important external factors that influence firm strategy.

Regarding the source of information it has been found that, although managers scan with a wide range of sources, they prefer live information from personal sources ($t(130) = 25.002$, $P < 0.05$), rather than formal and external sources ($t(130) = 24.103$, $P > 0.05$) when seeking information about market-related environmental sectors. This finding is similar to the findings of Choo (1999). There is some evidence to indicate that source selection for scanning is influenced by the perceived quality of the source ($t(128) = 31.453$, $P < 0.05$). Generally speaking, it has been found that, managers in the studied firms perceive environmental analysis as an important factor in the formulation and implementation of business strategies. However, they intended to rely on informal rather than formal and systematic methods of gathering and analysing the information.

Environmental Scanning and Firm Size

Basically, organizations scan the environment in order to understand external forces of change so that they can develop effective responses that could secure or improve their market positions in the future (Orser, 2000; Wolff, 2000). As summarized in the literature review (Chapter 2) the extent of an organization's ability to adapt to its Outside environment mainly depends on knowing and interpreting the external changes that are taking place (Berry, 1998). Considering the blind spots of the previous researches (Apfelthaler, 2000; Downs, 2000; Pelham, 2000), it has been assumed that there is a significant relationship between firm size and establishing formal environmental analysis in developing business strategies within small and medium-sized enterprises.

As discussed earlier, it has been found that, by increasing the size of the firms, in terms of the number of employees, there was more emphasis on formal environmental scanning systems. Supporting this result Spearman-rank order correlation analysis (see Table 6.5) shows that, a strong and significant correlation ($\gamma = 0.71$, $p < 0.01$) exists between environmental analysis and firm size.

Managers from medium, rather than small and micro firms, believe that the firm should analyse external factors before formulating business strategies. It was also discovered that, correlation between managers' strategic awareness and firm size was positive and significant ($\gamma = 0.68$, $p < 0.01$). These findings are very similar to the findings of Pelham (2000) and Apfelthaler (2000). Apart from correlation analysis, in order to examine the relationship between environmental analysis and firm size one-way analysis of variance technique has been employed. To investigate the relationships among firm size and having formal environmental analysis several measurement proxies were calculated. Firm size was represented by three categories (micro, small, and medium) that accounted for both annual turnover and number of employees (see Chapter 4). The hypotheses validated by using statistical analysis by ANOVA result ($F(2,128) = 0.281$; $p < 0.05$). As a result, by increasing firm size, emphasis on having formal environmental analysis in developing business strategies is increased. Managers of medium enterprises put more emphasis on environmental analysis than did the managers of small and micro enterprises. The findings of this research is supported by the findings of Smith (1998); Lundvall (2000), and Wolff (2000).

Table 6.5 The result of correlation analysis on environmental scanning

Variables	Mean	S.D.	γ-value	P-value
Managers' strategic awareness	3.66	1.11	0.58	P < 0.01
Technological changes	3.84	1.03	0.32	P > 0.05
Strategies of competitors	3.76	1.07	0.01	P > 0.05
Economical trends	3.55	1.12	0.17	P > 0.05
Social and cultural trends	3.01	1.15	0.38	P > 0.05
Political and legal developments	2.82	1.15	0.23	P > 0.05
Firm size	2.27	0.56	0.71	P < 0.01
Performance	3.73	1.39	0.82	P < 0.01

Priority of External Factors within the Industry

Theoretically, through environmental analysis, the key economic, political, social, and technological trends can be correlated and identified with opportunities, strengths, and threats and weaknesses in order to determine the necessary strategies for the future development of the firm. Senior managers cannot build an effective strategic plan if they do not know where the firm has been or where it is likely to go. Generally speaking, this result has been confirmed by findings regarding managerial perception of the impact of environmental factors changing on the firm's strategy formulation and implementation (see Table 6.6).

Table 6.6 Impacts of environmental factors on developing strategy within studied firms, results of t-test*

Variable	d.f	t-statistics	Mean difference	P-value
Economic trends	128	27.531	3.21	0.020
Changes' on competitors' business strategies	130	32.539	3.32	0.017
Technological changes	127	39.762	4.27	0.001
Political and legal factors	129	27.328	2.12	0.182
Social and cultural trends	131	54.423	1.98	0.095

* : Mean Importance Rating 3
: Mean Importance Rating < 3
(Scale: 1 = Not Important; 3 = Important; 5 = Extremely Important)

The results of the T-test analysis reveals that, technological environmental changes significantly ($t(127) = 39.762$, $P < 0.01$) impacts upon strategy development within the studied firms. It also has been found that, economic trends ($t(128) = 27.531$, $P < 0.05$) and changes in competitors' business strategies ($t(130) = 32.539$, $P < 0.05$) significantly influence the developing strategy within the studied firms.

In contrast, respondents did not consider political and legal factors ($t(129) = 27.328$, $P > 0.05$) or social and cultural trends ($t(131) = 54.423$, $P > 0.05$) as important factors, which could impact on strategy development within the studied firms. This finding suggests that, the strategists in the electrical and electronic industry, in their decision-making, should consider the technological changes more than other environmental factors. In this regard it has been assumed that, environmental factors such a technology significantly impacts upon strategy development in small and medium-sized enterprises. The respondents were asked to indicate to what extent internal and external environment factors affect their firm's strategy. The findings show that the respondents ranked the degree of impact of environmental factors on their firm's decision-making process as follows. First priority: technological changes; second priority: competitors; third priority: economic trends; fourth priority: social and cultural trends; and finally fifth priority: political and legal developments. In other words, 91 per cent of the respondents believed that, technological changes in the environment impacts on the strategy decision-making process within their organizations. In contrast, political and legal developments (45 per cent) seem to affect the strategic decision making process far less than the other factors. Subsequently, the impact of the strategies employed by their competitors; economic trends; and social and cultural trends were 83 per cent, 64 per cent, and 57 per cent respectively.

Further analysis of the data show that the respondents indicated that factors such as financial stability, flexibility and adaptability with environmental changes in technology, increasing market share, and growth were classed as strengths within the industry. More importantly, they considered resource utilization, and especially efficient human resources utilization, as another indicator of industry strengths. It is important to note that, the changes in the electrical and electronic industries market in terms of products and technology are very fast. So the findings of the research are suggesting that the firms, in order to improve their threats and weaknesses, and use the opportunities in the market, and increase their strengths, need to be flexible in adapting to the technological changes in the market. They should also use their internal resources effectively.

Environmental Scanning and Firm Performance in SME Sector

As discussed in Chapter 2, a question has been raised in the debate that, whether or not environmental scanning impacts on firm performance (Bourgeois, 1980; Chaganti, Chaganti and Mahajan, 1989; Venkatraman and Prescott, 1990; Lang, Calatone and Gudmundson, 1997). Superior firm performance is a major objective of all the stakeholders of a firm. Strategists and strategic management scholars generally agree that both large and small firms that align their competitive strategies with the requirements of their environment outperform firms that do not (Chaganti, Chaganti and Mahajan, 1989; Venkatraman and Prescott, 1990). Based on the conceptual framework of the research it has been hypothesized that, there is a significant relationship between firm performance and having environmental scanning in small businesses.

In this study, we examined CEOs perceptions of the importance of having environmental scanning on the firm's performance. It has been found that, the majority of respondents considered a scanning system as an essential factor in increasing the firm's performance ($n = 111$, 83.37 per cent). As discussed in Chapter 4, through the correlation analysis, it discovered that there was a very strong and significant relationship between a firm's performance and having a scanning system ($\gamma = 0.82$, $p < 0.01$) in the studied firms. Regarding the frequency of environmental scanning, it has been found that, high performance firms seem to put more emphasis (Mean = 3.824, SD = 1.05) on a high frequency and coordinated scanning system. Successful SMEs stress the importance of environmental analysis in the development of corporate strategy. In comparison, low performance firms tend to place less emphasis (Mean = 2.472, SD = 0.71) on the need for a high frequency of environmental scanning. The result of ANOVA ($F(1,128) = 0.328$; $p < 0.05$) confirms that, this difference is significant (see Table 6.7). In other words, there is a significant difference between high performance and low performance firms in terms of the frequency of environmental scanning.

Table 6.7 ANOVA results on environmental scanning and firm performance

Factors	Low Performance Firms		High Performance Firms		F-value	P-Value
	Mean	S.D.	Mean	S.D.		
Having Formal Scanning System	2.126	0.81	4.273	1.32	0.427	$P < 0.05$
Scanning Frequency	2.472	0.71	3.874	1.05	0.328	$P < 0.05$
Informal and personal resources	3.371	1.17	3.462	1.29	0.081	$P > 0.05$
Formal and external resources	2.957	0.98	3.683	1.27	0.219	$P > 0.05$

One reason for this is managers' involvement in daily operations. CEOs of small and medium-sized enterprises, constrained by their involvement in their firms' daily operations, may not have time for frequent scanning of their external environments. Consequently, environmental scanning may be relatively infrequent. Relatively infrequent scanning should be reflected in low mean values in the frequency-of-scanning indexes. Generally, having an environmental scanning system significantly impacts upon the firm performance $F(1,129) = 0.427$, $P < 0.05$. As discussed already, in comparison with high performance firms (Mean = 4.273, SD = 1.32), low performance firms put less emphasis (Mean = 2.126, SD = 0.81) on having environmental scanning. The impact of this difference could be seen in firm performance. Not surprisingly, environmental scanning in high performance firms becomes increasingly sophisticated and forms a formal and explicit activity within the studied firms. Thus, scanning of the environmental sectors that arguably have the most impact on firm performance and the formulation and implementation of competitive strategy occurs relatively infrequently in low performance SMEs.

Strategic Planning: Formal or Informal?

There is a growing body of literature examining the effects of formal strategic planning in the small firms (Robinson, Pearce and , 1984; Shrader et al., 1989). There are also numerous field studies examining the effects of various forms of strategic and operational planning activities on a variety of financial performance measures for both large and small firms (Robinson, Pearce and , 1984; Schwenk and Shrader, 1993). Researchers who have undertaken these studies, especially those of small firms, have drawn conflicting conclusions: some claim that formal strategic planning provides structure for decision making, helping small business managers take a long-term view, and, in general, benefits small firms; others conclude that formal strategic planning has no potential pay off for small firms because it is a heady, high-level, conceptual activity suited solely to large firms and therefore has no effect on the financial performance of small firms.

It has been discussed that, in the world of the small business, strategy may be much less formal in its nature (Chan and Foster, 2001). At the extreme the small owner-managed business may have an implicit rather than an explicitly stated strategy (US, see, for example Robinson, Pearce and , 1984; Aram and Cowen, 1990, or Europe, see, for example Bridge and Peel, 1999). In this research an attempt has been made to discover the form of the strategic planning techniques formal or informal, employed in the studied firms. Data analysis (see Chapter 4) shows that a number of significant correlations exist between employing formal strategy and business life cycle, competition and firm size in the studied firms.

In connection with employing formal strategic management in the studied firms, the first variable, which has been analysed, is business life cycle. Academics and practitioners generally agree that the firms' life cycle concept is a crucial factor in the successful management of a firm's strategic management effort (Kotler, 1997). By identifying the stage that the firm is in, or may be headed toward, companies can formulate better business plans and more effective strategies and tactics. For instance it has been discussed that, the stage of the product life cycle has a definite impact on the decision to choose technology and R&D strategies (Roy and Dugal, 1999). The studied firms in the growth stages of their life cycle, were found to have significant differences in developing business plans. Table 6.8 illustrates the results of T-test of comparing means of formal strategic planning and the other variables. It has been found that (t (128) = 24.354$P < 0.01$) the strategic management process within SMEs becomes increasingly formal and explicit over the life cycle of the firm. More strategic management techniques which result in a written strategic plan and involve formal strategic review sessions on a six monthly or annual basis are likely to be apparent in SMEs which have grown successfully through the early stages of their life cycle.

Table 6.8 Formal strategic planning in SMEs, results of t-test*

Variable	d.f	t-statistics	P-value
Firm's turnover	128	34.452	P<0.05
Number of employees	130	35.269	P<0.01
Firm size	129	28.342	P<0.01
Firms' established date (age)	130	45.231	P<0.05
Stage of the firms (life-cycle)	128	24.354	P<0.01
Competition	131	28.247	P<0.01
Environmental turbulence	127	36.253	P<0.05
Manager's educational background	130	25.348	P<0.05
Export activities	130	45.571	P<0.01

* is rejected for P < 0.05
(Scale: 1 = Not Important; 3 = Important; 5 = Extremely Important)

During the firm's infancy, the purpose of planning is likely to be that of securing external control. In later life cycle stages, however, the business plan will be developed where the CEOs perceive benefits will arise for the firm in terms of internal control. Apart from business life cycle, a number of significant relationships have been found between firm growth indicators such as firm's turnover ($t(128) = 34.452$ $P < 0.05$), number of employees ($t(130) = 35.269$ $P < 0.01$), firm size ($t(129) = 28.342$ $P < 0.01$), and importance of formal strategic planning in the studied firms. Generally speaking, as the size of firms grows, the CEOs' perception of the importance of strategic planning to the future success of the business increases. The findings support the theses (Aram and Cowen, 1990; Berry, 1998) that, during the early stages of the firm's life strategic management activities such as developing written business plans, and long term objectives, are unnecessary in terms of enhancing firm performance. More details of the relationships between firm size and strategy will be discussed in the next section. The last finding regarding the formal or informal strategic planning is that, as SMEs extend operations into globalization, they tend to undertake more strategic management activities. For instance it has been found that there is a significant relationship between formal strategic planning and competition ($t(131) = 28.247$ $P < 0.01$), increasing complexity ($t(127) = 36.253$ $P < 0.05$), and export activities ($t(130) = 45.571$ $P < 0.01$). Therefore, it can be conclude that, the firms which are engaged in a high level of competition and export activities tend to undertake more formal strategic management activities. This finding supports the findings of Cavusgil (1982); da Rocha, Carl and da Cunha (1990), Dicthl, Koglmayr and Muller (1990) regarding SMEs involvement in an export context.

Does the Size of the Firm Matter?

An important question that, by and large, has remained under discussion is whether the size of the firm influences whether or not they employ strategic management activities. As it has been reviewed in the literature there are pros and cons to this issue. For instance, Ghobadian and O'Regan (2000) in their recent research, empirically examined the relationship between the size of small and medium sized manufacturing organizations (SMEs with up to 250 employees) and their culture, leadership and strategic planning. They concluded that, size does not have a significant influence on leadership, organizational culture or the strategic planning processes.

In contrast, some of the writers believe that there is a significant association between firm size and employing strategic planning (Berry, 1998; Smith, 1998; Gartner and Bhat, 2000; Analoui and Karami, 2003). For instance, Berry (1998) concluded that, strategic planning is important to SMEs long term growth and development. Urata and Kawai (2000) reported that, SMEs regard well-developed plans, infrastructure, and industrial agglomeration, as important elements. As statistically discussed in the previous sections, the size of the firm was significantly correlated to environmental scanning The result of analysis shows that, medium sized enterprises were more involved in environmental scanning than small or micro firms.

It also has been found that, there was a significant association between firm size and planning level in the studied firms. The firms with less than 10 employees were not engaged in any planning activities. This group of firms has been categorized as non-planners. In the second level, the firms with between 10 and 100 employees, engaged in financial planning, while, the firms with between 100 and 200 employees, were engaged in formal financial and informal strategic planning. Finally, firms that had between 200 and 250 employees were involved in strategic planning. Therefore, it can be conclude that, as the size of the firm grows, their involvement in planning increases.

The other variable in connection with firm size that has been analysed is developing mission and objectives. It has been found that, there is a significant association between firm size and having a formal and written mission statement and objectives. For instance, the firms with less than 10 employees have not had any mission statement or long-term objectives. In contrast, the firms with 200 up to 250 employees have emphasized on written mission statement and long-term objectives in relation to the firm's products or market. Accordingly, the association between firm size and formal strategic planning was significant.

Regarding the firm performance, the result of this research confirms a weak association between firm performance and firm size. In other words, there is no significant difference between the studied firms in terms of their size. Since a significant statistical relationship was noted between firm size and some strategic activities, therefore, analysis of firm size and business plan data indicated that larger firms were more likely to engage in strategic planning. It can be concluded that, as the size of the firm increases they undertake more formal strategic management processes.

Strategy Development and Human Resources Involvement

In the conceptual framework of the study, it has been hypothesized that, there is a positive association between CEOs perceptions of the importance of human resources and their involvement in the process of strategy formulation and implementation in the studied firms. The purpose of this section is to identify the nature and impact of human resource capabilities and their involvement in formulation and implementation of business strategies on the firm's performance. In this regard, as discussed in the literature, the resource-based approach of the firm has been used. Boxall (1996) argues that by defining firms as unique bundles of resources, the resource-based perspective emphasized the inevitable imperfection of factor markets. The HR capability of the firm is a considerable resource that determines the competitive advantages of the firm. Wright et al. (1998) also define the skilled work force as the HR capabilities. Accordingly, Analoui (1999) defines managerial skills namely, task related, people-related and self-development analytical categories as HR capabilities of the firm. In the light of a resource-based view of the firm, it has been assumed that, HR capabilities including skilled human resources, innovative human resources, human resource effectiveness, HR commitment, and training competent HR are all factors that determine the competitive advantages of the firm. The hypothesized relationships have been tested among variables using non-parametric statistical techniques namely Spearman rank order correlation analysis and Kruskal-Wallis test (see Chapter 4). These analytical techniques allowed the researcher to identify the relative magnitudes of the relation between HR capabilities, HR involvement in strategy and firm performance. Supported by the results of previous works by Lahteenmaki, Storey and Vanhala (1998) it is stated that the hypothesis is mainly concerned with the answer to the question: do or do not CEOs perceive HR capabilities as factors for determining competitive advantage of the firm? And if they do, to what extent does this factor have impact on a company's performance? The finding of the research shows that, the majority of respondents rated HR capabilities as a key resource (n = 94, 71.2 per cent as very important and essential) within the organization. Thus, confirming the previous researches (Dyer and Reeves, 1995; Analoui and Karami, 2003), it has been found that, putting the firm's resources, more especially its human resources, into best use could be related to the CEOs' perception of the importance of HR as a key resource of the firm.

Accordingly, it has been assumed that if CEOs perceive HR as key resources they will put more emphasis on increasing the HR capabilities. Consequently, increasing HR capabilities will lead to increased firm performance. To test this, the CEOs were asked to rate the effects of the HR capabilities on the firm's performance. The results (see Chapter 4) confirm that, the majority of CEOs believe that human resource capabilities namely, skilled work force (n = 91, 69 per cent); innovative human resource (n = 78, 59 per cent); effective human resources (n = 102, 78 per cent); HR commitment (n = 82, 62 per cent); and training competent employees (n = 108, 81 per cent) have a high impact on increasing the firm's performance.

In order to verify this result statistically and to see whether or not any relationship exists between the HR capabilities and a firm's performance, the Kruskal-Wallis test was used (Non-parametric ANOVA). It was been found that there is a significant relationship between the HR capabilities and the performance of the firms. Data analysis revealed the following results of Chi-square test on firm performance and each of the HR capability indicators, including skilled human resources ($\chi^2 = 234.115$: d.f. = 16: $p < 0.01$), innovative human resources ($\chi^2 = 201.732$: d.f. = 16: $p < 0.05$), effective human resources ($\chi^2 = 119.272$: d.f. = 18: $p < 0.01$), training competent HR ($\chi^2 = 172.233$: d.f. = 16: $p < 0.01$) and HR commitment ($\chi^2 = 166.152$: d.f. = 16: $p < 0.01$) (see Table 6.10). Therefore, supporting the findings of previous researches (Wright et al., 1998; Rangone, 1999) this result led the researcher to conclude that, increasing HR capabilities will impact on increasing firm performance. Additionally, this result shows that, human resources capabilities have been considered as key competitive advantages of the firm so as to enable the generation of organizational effectiveness, and the high performance of the firm. Thus, any investment in increasing human resource capabilities must be considered as a strategic and crucial factor, which in turn will increase the firm's performance. It can be therefore concluded that, increasing HR competencies and capabilities will lead to a firm's success in achieving its goals and objectives in a competitive landscape. This will take place when the CEOs of the firms perceive HR as a key resource of the firm and act accordingly.

An increasing number of studies have attempted to assess the HR involvement in the process of formulating strategy (Golden and Ramanujam, 1985; Buller, 1988; Huselid, 1995; Martell and Carroll, 1995; Anderson, 1997; Wright et al., 1998). Indeed, numerous writers (for example, Bennett et al., 1998; Wright et al., 1998;

Analoui, 1999) have called for an increase in the extent to which HR are involved in the strategic management of the firm, yet very little data exists to confirm the effectiveness of it. Anderson (1997) has argued that HR specialists, in order to help management realize the full value from the HR function in support of business objectives, could use two fundamental and specific processes.

The first is linking people strategies to the company's strategic management process. The second is developing an HR strategy to support the corporation strategies (Anderson, 1997). As Wright et al. (1998) argue, although many researchers (for example, Schuler, 1992; Truss and Gratton, 1994; Brockbank, 1997) have called for the increased involvement of HR in strategic management, very little research has been carried out to examine the consequences of such HR involvement in the process of developing and implementation of business strategies. For instance, Bennett et al. (1998) in their study, argue that there is a negative relationship between HR involvement and HR effectiveness. In contrast, Wright et al. (1998) in their recent study found a strong correlation between HR involvement and HR effectiveness. In other words, they pointed to the fact that 'managers highly value the HR function when the HR executives are heavily involved in strategic decision making' (Wright et al. (1998, 24). To examine this thesis in the UK small and medium-sized enterprises (SMEs), in this study the CEOs were asked to rate the level of HR involvement in strategy within their firms. The analysis of the data show that, human resources are more involved in strategy activities in high performance firms rather than in low performance firms (see Table 6.9).

Table 6.9 HR involvement in strategic activities within high and low performance firms

Factors	Low Performance Firms*	High Performance Firms**
Strategy formulation	42	94
Long range planning	39	82
Strategic Decision-making	28	78
Developing HR systems	44	91

* The percentage of the low performance firms which shows the level of HR involvement in strategy.
** The percentage of the high performance firms which shows the level of HR involvement in strategy.

For instance in the high performance firms human resources were highly involved in strategy formulation (94 per cent), long range planning (82 per cent), strategic decision-making (78 per cent), and developing HR systems (91 per cent). The result reveals that, the contribution of the human resources in the development and implementation of strategies is very much related to the firm's CEOs' perception of HR as an important factor in a firm's performance. As shown in Table 6.10, using Kruskal-Wallis analysis of variance a significant relationship was found between firm performance and HR involvement in strategy.

Table 6.10 Results of Kruskal-Wallis test on HR capabilities, involvement in strategy, and firm performance

Measured Variables	χ2 Value	d.f	Significant (2-sided)
Firm Performance V.			
a) HR Capabilities			
Skilled HR	234.115	16	P<0.01
Innovative HR	201.732	16	P<0.05
Effective HR	119.272	18	P<0.01
Training Competent HR	172.233	16	P<0.01
HR Commitment	166.152	16	P<0.01
b) HR Involvement in Strategy	171.912	17	P<0.01
Long Range Planning	227.830	16	P<0.01
Strategic Decision Making	246.121	16	P<0.01
Developing HR systems			

The result of the test between firm performance and HR involvement in LRP ($\chi^2 = 171.912$: d.f. $= 17$: $p < 0.01$), HR involvement strategic decision-making ($\chi^2 = 227.830$: d.f. $= 16$: $p < 0.01$), and developing HR systems ($\chi^2 = 246.121$: d.f. $= 16$: $p < 0.01$) were significant. A positive and significant relationship between HR involvement and firm performance in general ($\gamma = 0.70$: $p < 0.01$) has also been found. Generally speaking, supporting Astarachan and Kolenko (1994) and Wright et al. (1998) theses, the results indicate that, human resources are more involved in the formulation and implementation of the business strategy in those firms where, their CEOs' perceive HR as a key source of competitive advantage. Human resources as a factor for creating knowledge, play an important role in increasing a firm's performance and its competitiveness. In other words, there is a positive association between a CEOs perceptions of the importance of human resources, and their involvement in the process of strategy formulation and implementation. So human resources are more involved in the strategic activities including: long range planning, revising HR systems, and developing HR systems, in high performance firms than low performance firms. Therefore, in order to increase firm performance and benefit from HR capabilities, it is recommended that practitioners and SMEs' managers their involve human resources in the strategic management process.

Strategic Characteristics and Performance of the Entrepreneurial Firms

It has been discussed that, strategic management is the process of determining what the organization intends to accomplish and how the organization and its resources will be directed toward accomplishing these goals in the coming period of planning. Such a process involves fundamental choices about the mission and goals of the organization; SWOT analysis in order to determine the strengths, weaknesses, opportunities, and threats of the firm; formulation business strategies; and finally implementation and evaluation of the strategies. The strategists must decide whom they will serve and the kinds of programming, services, or products the firm will offer and in which market they will operate. So one of the interests of this research was to identify the characteristics of the successful firms, which employ a strategic management process.

As discussed in previous sections, the studied firms were different in terms of their strategic characteristics. In order to study these characteristics, the studied firms were categorized into two groups namely, high performance and low performance firms. From the analysis of the data and through discussion of the findings of the research, a list of key strategic characteristics or attributes of high performance versus low performance firms are devised. Table 6.11 compares the environmental analysis (SWOT), goals, strategic planning and implementation, and some general characteristics of high performance firms with those of low performers.

Successful entrepreneurial firms are more involved in internationalization than low performance firms are. Joint venture, Research & Development agreement, and licensing are the most frequent internationalization modes used by the firms studied. It also has been found that the managers perceived focused strategy as an appropriate business strategy for their firms. In terms of leadership, there were differences between high and low performance entrepreneurial firms. For instance it has been found that in high performance firms, both managers and employees are committed to the goals and objectives of the firm. Informal and quick communication systems are frequently used in high performance firms. However the data analysis revealed that low performance firms employ more formal and hierarchical types of communication systems. In terms of motivation, leaders in high performance firms use more intrinsic rather than extrinsic motivational factors. Recognition, achievement and developing employees' personal goals are good examples for this. The level of trust between the management team and employees is high in high performance firms. Finally, the research illustrates that organizational effectiveness is higher in high performance firms than low performance firms.

Summary and Conclusion

In this chapter an attempt has been made to discuss the findings of the study and answer the research questions. In the first section the CEOs' perceptions of environment scanning in small and medium-sized enterprises have been explored. In the second section the findings of the study on the factors associated with effective strategy formulation and implementation process in the studied SMEs is discussed.

By and large, it has been found that the CEOs of the SMEs consider environmental analysis to be a strategic activity in developing business strategies. Establishing an effective formal environmental analysis could affect the studied firms' performance. Regarding the factors associated with effective strategy formulation in SMEs, it has been found that high performance firms use and put more emphasis on mission statement when developing their business strategies than do low performance firms.

Table 6.11 Strategic characteristics of low and high performance firms

Variable	Characteristics	
	High Performance Firms	Low Performance Firms
SWOT analysis		
Awareness	Very good	Poor
Frequency of industry analysis	High	Low
Reaction to customers' comments	Fast & precisely	Slow
Goal setting		
Mission	Written and formal	Informal
Objectives	Clearly defined	Personal
Period of objectives	Medium or long term	Short term
Strategic planning		
Employing strategic management techniques	High	Not at all
Business plan	Formal	Informal
Planning level	Strategic planning	Financial planning
Managerial involvement in strategic decision making	Multi-disciplinary management team	Top management
Emphasis on long term strategic plans	High	Low
Emphasis on ongoing evaluation in strategic planning	High	Low
HR involvement in developing business plans	High participate	Low participate
Business strategies		
Internationalization	High	Moderate
Focused business strategy	Yes	Yes
Leadership		
Commitment		
Communications		
Motivation	High	Moderate
Quality	Quick	Formal
Organizational effectiveness	High	Moderate
	High	Variable
	High	Moderate

Professionally run SMEs are more inclined to have formal and written mission statements, and long run business plans than family run firms. There are significant correlations between firm size, business life cycle, export activities, firm performance and employing formal strategic management techniques in SMEs. As the firms extend operations into globalization, they tend to undertake more formal strategic management activities. There is a positive association between CEOs perceptions of the importance of human resources and their involvement in the process of strategy formulation and implementation.

References

Ahls, B. (2001), 'Organisational Behaviour: A Model for Cultural Change', *Industrial Management*, **43**(4), 6–9.

Analoui, A. and Karami, A. (2003), *Strategic Management in Small and Medium Enterprises* (London: Thomson Learning).

Analoui, F. (1999), 'Eight Parameters of Managerial Effectiveness: A Study of Senior Managers in Ghana', *Journal of Management Development*, **18**(4), 36–39.

Anderson, W.R. (1997), 'The Future of Human Resources: Forging Ahead or Falling behind'? *Human Resource Management*, **6**(1), 17–22.

Apfelthaler, G. (2000), 'Why Small Enterprises Invest Abroad: the Case of four Austrian Firms with U.S. Operations', *Journal of Small Business Management, Milwaukee*, **38**(3), 92–99.

Aram, J.D. and Cowen, S.S. (1990), 'Strategic Planning for Increased Profit in the Family Owned Business', *Long Range Planning*, **23**, 76–81.

Astrachan, J.H. and Kolenko, T.A. (1994), 'A Neglected Factor Explaining Family Business Success: Human Resource Practices', *Family Business Review*, **7**(3), 251–262.

Baetz, M.C. and Bart, C.K. (1996), 'Developing Mission Statements which Work', *Long Range Planning*, **29**(4), 526–533.

Bart, C.K. (2000), 'Mission Statements in Canadian Not-for-profit Hospitals: Does Process Matter?' *Health Care Management Review*, **25**(2), 45–63.

Bennett, N., Ketchen, D.J., Jr and Schultz, E.B. (1998), 'An Examination of Factors Associated with the Integration of Human Resource Management and Strategic Decision Making', *Human Resource Management*, **37**(1), 3–16.

Berry, M. (1998), 'Strategic Planning in Small High Tech Companies', *Long Range Planning*, **31**(3), 455–466.

Bourgeois, L. (1980), 'Strategy and Environment: A Conceptual Integration', *Academy of Management Review*, **5**, 25–39.

Bowman, C. and Faulkner, D. (1997), *Competitive Corporate Strategy* (London: Irwin).

Boxall, P. (1996), 'The Strategic HRM Debate and the Resource-Based View of the Firm', *Human Resource Management Journal*, **6**(3), 59–75.

Bridge, J. and Peel, M.J. (1999), 'Research Note: A Study of Computer Usage and Strategic Planning in the SME Sector', *International Small Business Journal*, **17**(4), 82–87.

Brockbank, W. (1997), 'Human Resource's Future on the Way to a Presence', *Human Resource Management*, **36**(1), 65–69.

Buller, P. (1988), 'Successful Partnership: HR and Strategic Planning at Eight Top Firms', *Organizational Dynamics*, **17**, 27–42.

Campbell, A. and Yeung, S. (1991), 'Brief Case: Mission, Vision, and Strategic Intent', *Long Range Planning*, **24**(4), 145–147.

Campbell, A., Devine, M. and Young, D. (1990), *A Sense of Mission* (London: Hutchinson).

Cavusgil, S.T. (1982), 'Some Observations on the Relevance of Critical Variables for Internationalisation Stages', in *Export Management: An International Context*. Czinkota, M.R. and Tesar, G. (eds.) (New York.: Praeger Publishing), 276–285.

Chaganti, R., Chaganti, R. and Mahajan, V. (1989), 'Profitable Small Business Strategies Under Different Types of Competition', *Entrepreneurship: Theory and Practice*, **13**, 21–35.

Chan, S.Y. and Foster, J.M. (2001), 'Strategy Formulation in Small Business: the Hong Kong Experiences', *International Small Business Journal*, April/June.

Chandler, A. D. (1962) *Strategy and Structure*, Cambridge: MA, MIT Press.

Choo, C.W. (1999), 'The Art of Scanning the Environment'. 'American Society for Information Science', *Bulletin of the American Society for Information Science Washington*, **45**(3), 21–24.

Collis, D. J. (1996) 'Corporate Strategy in Multi-business Firms', *Long Range Planning*, **29**(3), 416–18.

Collis, D.J. and Montgomery, C.A. (1997), *Corporate Strategy: Resources and the Scope of the Firm,* (Chicago, IL: McGraw-Hill).

da Rocha, A., Carl, H.C. and da Cunha, C.E. (1990), 'Aggressive and Passive Exporters: A Study in the Brazilian Furniture Industry', *International Marketing Review*, 7(5), 6–15.

David, F. (1989), 'How Companies Define their Mission', *Long Range Planning*, **22**(2), 90–97.

Dicthl, E., Koglmayr, H.G. and Muller, S. (1990), 'International Orientation as a Precondition for Export Success', *Journal of International Business Studies*, **21**(1), 23–40.

Downs, T.W. (2000), 'Beta, Size, Risk, and Return', *The Journal of Financial Research, Columbia*, **23**(3), 245–259.

Dyer, L. and Reeves, T. (1995), 'Human Resource Strategies and Firm Performance: what Do we Know and where Do we Need to Go'? *International Journal of Human Resource Management*, **6**(3), 656–670.

Gartner, W.B. and Bhat, S. (2000), 'Environmental and Ownership Characteristics of Small Businesses and their Impact on Developments', *Journal of Small Business Management*, **38**(3), 14–27.

Ghobadian, A. and O'Regan, N. (2000), 'Time to Reassess the Size Criterion for SME Classification', *International Journal of Manufacturing Technology and Management*, **2**(1–7), 879–890.

Golden, K. and Ramanujam, V. (1985), 'Between a Dream and Nightmare: on the Integration of the Human Resource Management and Strategic Business Planning Processes', *Human Resource Management*, **24**, 429–452.

Hill, C.W.L. and Jones, G.R. (2004), *Strategic Management an Integrated Approach*, 6th edn (New York: Houghton Mifflin Company).

Hitt, M.A. and Ireland, R.D. (2000), 'The Intersection of Entrepreneurship and Strategic Management Research' in *Handbook of Entrepreneurship*, Sexton, D.L. and Landstrom, H.A. (eds.) (Oxford: Blackwell Publishing), 45–63.

Huselid, M.A. (1995), 'The Impact of Human Resource Management Practices on Turnover, Productivity, and Corporate Financial Performance', *Academy of Management Journal*, **38**(3), 635–673.

Inkpen, A.C. (2000), 'A Note on the Dynamics of Learning Alliances: Competition, Cooperation, and Relative Scope', *Strategic Management Journal*, **21**(7), 61–84.

Ireland, R.D. and Hitt, M.A. (1992), 'Mission Statements: Importance, Challenge and Recommendations for Development', *Business Horizons*, **35**(3), 34–42.

Johnson, G., Scholes, K. and Whittington, R. (2005), *Exploring Corporate Strategy*, 7th edn (Harlow, Essex: Prentice-Hall).

Klemm, M., Sanderson, S. and Luffman, G. (1991), 'Mission Statements: Selling Corporate Values to Employees', *Long Range Planning*, **23**, 73–78.

Kotler, P. (1997), *Marketing Management*, 9th edn (Englewood Cliffs, N.J.: Prentice-Hall).

Lahteenmaki, S., Storey, J. and Vanhala, S. (1998), 'HRM and Company Performance: the Use of Measurement and the Influence of Economic Cycles', *Human Resource Management Journal*, **8**(2), 51–65.

Lang, J.R., Calatone, R. and Gudmundson, D. (1997), 'Small Firm Information Seeking as a Response to Environmental Threats and Opportunities', *Journal of Small Business Management*, **35**, 11–23.

Lundvall, K. (2000), 'Firm Size, Age and Efficiency: Evidence from Kenyan Manufacturing Firms', *The Journal of Development Studies, London*, **36**(3), 146–163.

Ma, H. (2000), 'Of Competitive Advantage: Kinetic and Positional', *Business Horizons*, **43**(1), 53–64.

Martell, K. and Carroll, S.J. (1995), 'How Strategic is HRM?' *Human Resource Management*, **34**(2), 253–267.

McEvily, S., Das, S. and McCabe, K. (2000), 'Avoiding Competence Substitution Through Knowledge Sharing', *Academy of Management Review*, **25**(2), 294–293, 11.

McGee, J., Thomas, H. and Wilson, D. (2005), *Strategy Analysis and Practice* (London: McGraw-Hill).

McKenna, S.D. (1996), 'The Darker Side of the Entrepreneur', *Leadership and Organizational Development Journal*, **17**(5), 41.

O'Gorman, C. and Doran, R. (1999), 'Mission Statements in Small and Medium Sized Businesses', *Journal of Small Business Management*, **37**(4), 59–66.

Orser, B.J. (2000), 'Performance, Firm Size, and Management Problem Solving', *Journal of Small Business Management, Milwaukee*, **38**(4), 42–59.

Pearce II., J.A. and Robinson Jr., R.B. (1991), *Formulation, Implementation, and Control of Competitive Strategy*, 4th edn (Boston, Mass.: Irwin).

Pearce, J. and David, F. (1987), 'Corporate Mission Statements: the Bottom Line', *Executive*, **1**, 109–116.

Pelham, A.M. (2000), 'Market Orientation and other Potential Influences on Performance in Small and Medium-Sized Manufacturing Firms', *Journal of Small Business Management*, **38**(1), 48–68.

Porter, M. (1985), *Competitive Advantage: Creating and Sustaining Superior Performance* (New York: Free Press).

Porter, M. (1998), *On Competition* (Boston: Harvard Business School Presses).

Rangone, A. (1999) 'A Resource Based Approach to Strategy Analysis in Small-medium Sized Enterprises', *Small Business Economics*, **12**(3), 233–246.

Rarick, C. and Vitton, J. (1995), 'Mission Statements Make Cents', *The Journal of Business Strategy*, **16**, 11–12.

Robinson, R.B. and Pearce II, J.A. (1984), 'Research Thrusts in Small Firm Strategic Planning', *Academy of Management Review*, **9**(1), 28–137.

Roy, H.M. and Dugal, S.S. (1999), 'The Effect of Technological Environment and Competitive Strategy on Licensing Decisions', *American Business Review*, **17**(2), 112–118.

Rumelt, R.P. (1991), 'How much Does Industry Matter?' *Strategic Management Journal*, March, 167–185.

Schuler, R. (1992), 'Strategic Human Resource Management: Linking the People with the Strategic Needs of the Business', *Organizational Dynamics*, summer, 18–31.

Sirower, M. (1997), *The Strategy Trap: how Companies Lose the Acquisition Game* (New York: Free Press).

Smith, J.A. (1998), 'Strategies for Start-Ups', *Long Range Planning*, **31**(6), 857–872.

Thompson, J.L. (1996), *Strategic Management: Awareness and Change*, 2nd edn (London: Chapman and Hall).

Truss, C. and Gratton, L. (1994), 'Strategic Human Resource Management: A Conceptual Approach', *International Journal of Human Resource Management*, **5**(3), 663–686.

Urata, S. and Kawai, H. (2000), 'The Determinants of the Location of Foreign Direct Investment by Japanese Small And Medium-Sized Enterprises', *Small Business Economics*, **15**(2), 79–103.

Venkatraman, N. and Prescott, J.E. (1990), 'Environment-strategy Co-Alignment: An Empirical Test of its Performance Implications', *Strategic Management Journal*, **11**, 1–23.

Wheelen, T.L. and Hunger, J.D. (1998), *Strategic Management and Business Policy*, 6th edn (New York: Addision-Wesley Publication).

Wit, B. and Mayer, R. (1998), *Strategy: Process, Content, Context* (London: International Thomson Business Press Books).

Wolff, J.A. (2000), 'Internationalisation of Small Firms: An Examination of Export Competitive Patterns, Firm Size, and Export Performance', *Journal of Small Business Management, Milwaukee*, **38**(2), 34–48.

Wright, P.M., McMahan, G.C., McCormick, B. and Sherman, S.C.W. (1998), 'Strategy, Core Competence, and Human Resource Involvement as Determinants of HR Effectiveness and Refinery Performance', *Human Resource Management*, **36**, 17–29.

Chapter 7

Final Lessons and Conclusion

Introduction

In this book the senior managers' perception of strategic management in entrepreneurial small and medium-sized enterprises in the UK's high tech sector has been examined. Chapter 1 introduced the objectives and scope of the study. This chapter provided an overview of the major works in the areas of strategy and management. It also provided a brief description of the key concepts of strategy and entrepreneurship.

Chapter 2 reviewed the existing theories of strategy formulation in entrepreneurial small and medium-sized enterprises. The theories differ greatly in their scope and purpose, and inevitably both have been the subject of, at times, fierce academic debate which is outlined in the chapter.

Chapter 3 provided a conceptual framework of the research. Accordingly, this chapter describes how the research design was developed and in doing so draws together all of the proceeding chapters. The chapter began by outlining the research questions through the development of the framework and the resulting hypothesis about the process of strategic management in entrepreneurial small and medium-sized enterprises.

Chapter 4 introduced the major findings of the research in connection with research propositions and hypotheses. The hypotheses offered by the conceptual framework of the research are compared with the findings of the study providing an interesting insight into the phases of the process of strategy formulation in entrepreneurial small and medium-sized enterprises.

Chapter 5 discussed strategic entrepreneurship and the role of entrepreneurs in the strategy formulation process in SMEs. It started with a discussion about exploring and examining the entrepreneurs' perception of the importance of the strategic management process in the studied firms. It also explored the role of senior managers in the strategic management processes within small and medium enterprises.

Chapter 6 continued with a discussion on the findings of the research regarding the existence and nature of environmental analysis when developing business strategies in the studied firms. Furthermore, the chapter discussed the findings about the factors associated with the effective strategy formulation and implementation process in SMEs.

Finally, current chapter is the concluding chapter and as such is primarily concerned with the significance of the findings of the research. The chapter begins by revisiting the aims of the research and the research questions. The chapter then considers each of the research propositions and hypotheses. It will then continue by explaining final the lessons; the theoretical and practical contribution of the research.

In the final section, the limitations of this study are assessed and suggestions for further research are proposed.

Research Questions and Objectives of the Study

As discussed in Chapter 3, this study sought to answer the following questions in an attempt to highlight important considerations for managers of entrepreneurial small- and medium-sized firms.

1. What are the senior managers' perceptions and attitudes to the strategic management process including: environmental scanning, strategy formulation and implementation, and evaluation of strategy in small and medium-sized enterprises?
2. Which factors are associated with an effective strategy formulation and implementation process in small and medium-sized enterprises and what is their impact on firm performance?
3. What are the characteristics of a dynamic strategic management model in entrepreneurial SMEs as an extension to the basic strategic management model, to assist in the decision making stages of formulation, implementation, and evaluation of strategy?

Summary of Major Findings

This section summarizes the main conclusions of the research in connection with each of the propositions. Therefore, the relevant findings and conclusions of the all of the four propositions are listed as follows.

Proposition A To explore and examine the CEOs' perception of the importance of the strategic management process in SMEs.

H.1. CEOs of successful SMEs perceive employing a strategic management process as an important factor in running the business.

- A significant proportion of the studied SMEs regard strategic management as important. Successful SMEs in the electrical and electronic industry use a strategic management process. However during the early stages of the firm's life cycle, the adopted strategic management approach is likely to be informal.
- The companies, which have established a strategic management approach, are more adaptable to environmental factors such as technological changes. They are also dealing conveniently with organizational problems and conflicts.
- The firms, which employ strategic management techniques, whether formal or informal, exhibit more enhanced levels of success in the formulation and implementation of business strategies than those firms which do not employ such procedures.

- The studied firms, in terms of employing different types of planning, can be categorized into four groups including: non-planners, financial planners, formal financial and informal strategic planners, and formal strategic planners.
- Finally, the CEOs of the studied firms perceived the strategic management approach as an important factor in increasing the quality of product or services, achieving organizational objectives, increasing firm profitability and overall organizational effectiveness.

Proposition B To explore the role of senior managers in the strategic management processes within small and medium enterprises.

H.2. There is a significant relationship between senior managers' age, work experience, educational background and strategy formulation in SMEs.

- Younger senior managers have a more complete awareness of the strategic orientation in the development of their companies strategies than older senior managers do.
- The firms run by young senior managers would be more inclined to pursue more risky strategies than firms with older managers would.
- Younger senior managers are more inclined to develop novel and innovative strategies than older managers.
- Senior managers with managerial work experience place more weight on formal strategy development than those senior managers who lack managerial work experience.
- Senior managers with managerial work experience place more emphasis on opportunities rather than threats.
- Companies whose senior managers have a management educational background are more inclined to develop strategic plans than those managers have not had such an educational background.
- Firms run by senior managers without a management educational background are unlikely to have longer term strategic plans.
- Companies whose senior managers have a management educational background are more inclined to develop formal strategic plans than those managers have not had such an educational background.
- Senior managers with a management educational background place more weight on opportunities and less weight on threats than those managers have not had such an educational background.

H.3. Strategic awareness of the senior managers in SMEs significantly impacts upon firm performance.

- The environmental awareness of the managers in SMEs is significantly important.
- There is a significant association between the strategic awareness of the managers and establishing a strategic management system within the firm.
- The senior managers' strategic awareness and their perception of the benefits

arising from establishing a strategic management system within the firm, significantly impacts upon the success of the firm in the long term.

Proposition C To examine the existence and nature of environmental analysis in developing business strategies in small and medium-sized enterprises.

H.4. The CEOs of the SMEs consider environmental analysis as a strategic activity in developing business strategies.

- A scanning system is necessary for the formulation and planning of business strategies. Some significant correlations exist between environmental analysis and increasing profit, the growth rate of the firm and developing the firm's adaptability to unexpected environmental changes in a turbulent marketplace.
- Successful SMEs do analyse environmental factors when formulating business strategies. They stress the importance of environmental analysis in the development of corporate strategy. Small and medium-sized enterprises, regardless of size and performance, must have the means to assess the external environment to maintain a competitive edge. Lacking this, strategies will be formulated and implemented without any concern for how the market will react.
- Although managers scan with a wide range of sources, they prefer live information from personal sources rather than formal and external sources when seeking information about market-related environmental sectors.

H.5. There is a significant relationship between firm performance and having environmental scanning.

- The senior managers (strategists) of the successful SMEs' perceive environmental scanning as an important dynamic system, which should be particularly sustained and controlled within the firms.
- Environmental scanning in high performance firms becomes increasingly sophisticated and forms a formal and explicit activity within the studied firms.
- There is a significant difference between high performance and low performance firms in terms of frequency of environmental scanning. High performance firms seem to put more emphasis on a high frequency and coordinated scanning system. In comparison, low performance firms put less emphasis on formal and high frequency of environmental scanning.

Proposition D To explore and examine the factors associated with the effective strategy formulation and implementation process in SMEs.

H.6. High performance firms use and put more emphasis on mission statement in developing their business strategies than do low performance firms.

- There are different benefits from having a mission statement for SMEs. A mission statement is necessary for developing and planning business strategies, increasing the profit and growth rate of the firm, and promoting a sense of shared expectations between the entrepreneur and all employees.
- A typical mission statement in an *SME* contained: long term profit, survival and growth; customer satisfaction; core technology; market; company philosophy and values; product and services quality; public image; geographic domain; Self concept; and concern for suppliers. However, particularly in the electronic industry, the 'core technology' component, which was not suggested in the literature, is considered as one of the top three components of mission statements.
- Professionally run SMEs are more inclined to have formal and written mission statements, and long run business plans than family firms.
- Firm performance is positively related to developing mission statements. The high performance firms have developed and use a formal and written mission statement in the formulation of their business strategies. But the blind adoption of strategic management models used in large firms, including the development of a mission statement, is perhaps inappropriate for SMEs. A mission statement for an *SME* which is taken and/or not adapted from a large firm, may or may not have impact on the firm's (*SME*) performance.

H.7. There are significant correlations between firm size, business life cycle, export activities, firm performance and employing formal strategic management techniques in SMEs.

- The strategic management process within the studied firms becomes increasingly formal and explicit over the life cycle of the firms. The firms in their early stages of life cycle put more emphasis on employing more informal strategic management techniques.
- As the size of the firm grows, the CEOs' perception of the importance of strategic planning for the future success of the firm increases.
- As the firms extend operations into globalization, they tend to undertake more formal strategic management activities.
- The firms, which are engaged in a high level of competition and export activities, tend to undertake more formal strategic management activities.
- There is a significant relationship between firm size and having formal environmental analysis in the studied firms. As the size of the firms increased, the CEOs' put more emphasis on formal environmental analysis when formulating business strategies.
- As the size of the firms (in terms of number of employees and the amount of annual turnover) increased, their involvement in strategic management activities such as developing mission statement and objectives, annual and long term goals, and employing formal strategic planning techniques, increased.
- There was a weak association between the size of the studied firms and firm performance.

H8. There is a positive association between CEOs perceptions of the importance of human resources and their involvement in the process of strategy formulation and implementation.

- The firms' performance is highly related to the HR capabilities.
- Increasing HR capabilities will lead to a firm's success in achieving its goals and objectives in a competitive landscape.
- Any investment in increasing human resource capabilities must be considered as a crucial and strategic factor, which in turn will increase the firm's performance.
- Human resources are more involved in the strategic activities including long range planning, revising HR systems, and developing HR systems, in high performance firms than in low performance firms. Therefore, in order to increase the firm's performance and gain benefit from its HR capabilities, it is recommended that practitioners and SMEs' managers involve HR in the strategic management process.

Theoretical Contribution

The individual findings associated with each of the research objectives have been discussed earlier in this chapter. The interpretation of these findings in relation to existing academic theories has been proposed in Chapters 5 and 6. Some of the findings yield support to the work of other scholars and researchers, some modify and further elaborate existing concepts proposed in the literature, while yet still others findings provide contradictory evidence to the limited empirical research available in the field of strategic management in small and medium enterprises. In this research an attempt has been made to discuss the findings of the study and answer to the research questions. The discussion is divided into four separate but interrelated sections.

In the first section the CEO's perception of the importance of strategic management in SMEs is explored. A significant proportion of the studied SMEs regarded strategic management as important. The studied firms in terms of employing different types of planning can be categorized into four groups including: non-planners, financial planners, formal financial and informal strategic planners, and formal strategic planners. Successful SMEs in the electrical and electronic industry use a strategic management process. However, during the early stages of the firm's life cycle, any adopted strategic management approach is likely to be informal. This informal approach, enables the SMEs to respond quickly to the market demand. The companies, which have established a strategic management approach, are more adaptable with the environmental factors such as technological changes. The firms which employ strategic management techniques, whether formal or informal, exhibit enhanced levels of success in the formulation and implementation of business strategies than those firms which do not employ such procedures. Employing strategic management processes in SMEs significantly helps in solving organizational problems, and reducing organizational conflicts. It significantly impacts on employees' satisfaction and changing organizational culture. Finally, the CEOs of the studied firms perceived the strategic management approach as an important factor in increasing the quality of product or services, achieving organizational objectives, and increasing firm profitability and overall organizational effectiveness.

In the second section the role of senior managers in the strategic management processes within the studied firms is investigated. In connection with the relationship between senior managers' personal characteristics such as age, work experiences and strategy formulation in SMEs, it can be concluded that, younger senior managers have no more complete of the strategic orientation in developing of the strategies of the company than older senior managers. The firms that are by young senior managers would be more inclined to pursue risky strategies than firms with older managers would. Younger senior managers are more inclined to develop novel and innovative strategies than older managers. It also has been found that, there is no significant correlation between the age of the CEOs and firm performance.

Senior managers with managerial work experiences place more weight on formal strategy development than those senior managers who lack managerial work experience. Also the correlation between senior managers' work experiences and firm performance was significant.

Companies whose senior managers have management educational backgrounds are more inclined to develop formal strategic plans than those managers have not had such an educational background. Where the firms are run by senior managers without a management educational background, longer and formal strategic plans are unlikely to be initiated. Senior managers with management educational backgrounds place more weight on opportunities and less weight on threats than those managers who have not had such educational background in small businesses. It also has been found that, the firm performance was not influenced by the educational level of the CEOs. Finally, the senior managers' strategic awareness and their perception of the benefits arising from having a formal strategic management system within the firm significantly impacts upon the success of the firm in the long term.

In the third section the CEOs' perceptions of environment scanning in small and medium-sized enterprises have been explored. It is concluded that, the CEOs of successful SMEs consider environmental analysis (formal or informal) as a strategic activity when developing business strategies. A scanning system is necessary for the formulation and planning of business strategies; increasing profit and growth rate of the firm, and developing the firm's adaptability to unexpected environmental changes in a turbulent marketplace.

Although managers scan with a wide range of sources, they prefer live information from personal sources rather than formal and external sources when seeking information about market-related environmental sectors. As the size of the firms increase, the CEOs' put more emphasis on formal environmental analysis in formulating business strategies. Successful SMEs do analyse environmental factors in formulating business strategies. They stress the importance of environmental analysis to the development of corporate strategy. Environmental scanning in high performance firms becomes increasingly sophisticated and forms a formal and explicit activity within the studied firms. High performance firms seem to put more emphasis on a high frequency and coordinated scanning system. In comparison, low performance firms put less emphasis on formal and high frequency environmental scanning.

Finally in the fourth section the findings of the study, the factors associated with the effective strategy formulation and implementation process in the studied SMEs are discussed. The studied firms placed the most emphasis on annual goals, followed by long-term goals, the mission statement, and short-term action plans. Trend analysis and competitor analysis received the least emphasis by the respondents. The respondents considered standard operation procedures, flexibility of the plans, and human resources as important factors in implementing business strategies.

High performance firms use and put more emphasis on mission statement in developing their business strategies than do low performance firms. Professionally run SMEs are more inclined to have formal and written mission statements, and long run business plans than family run firms. The strategic management process within the studied firms becomes increasingly formal and explicit over the life cycle of the firms. The firms in their early stages of life cycle, put more emphasis on employing informal strategic management techniques. As the size of the firm grows, the CEOs' perception of the importance of strategic planning to the future success of the firm increases. As the firms extend operations into globalization, they tend to undertake more formal strategic management activities. The firms, which are engaged in a high level of competition, and export activities, tend to undertake more formal strategic management activities. As the size of the firms (in terms of the number of employees and the amount of annual turnover) increase, their involvement in strategic management activities such as developing mission statement and objectives, annual and long term goals, and employing formal strategic planning techniques, increases.

Increasing HR capabilities will lead to a firm's success in achieving its goals and objectives in a competitive landscape. Any investment in increasing human resource capabilities must be considered as a crucial and strategic factor, which in turn will increase the firm's performance. Generally speaking, successful SMEs emphasize on long term plans, objectives and ongoing evaluation in strategic planning. They employ a multi-disciplinary management team in the strategic decision-making process and increase employees' motivation through their involvement in the strategic activities. The successful firms consider the high quality of products or services, financial stability, growth, flexibility and adaptability to the changes in the market, competition capacity, HR capabilities, and technology know-how as competitive advantages of the firm.

Policy Implications

In Chapters 1 and 3, the strategic significance of the contribution of the small business sector to the economy for national governments, industries and individual companies alike, was discussed. It also has been discussed that SMEs play a significant role in creating innovative technology as a source of competitive advantage within certain sectors of industries. Accordingly, it has been concluded that SMEs have a critically important role in ensuring the future economic prosperity of the UK and as such will remain a key focus of economic policy makers' attention throughout the 2000s. Policy-makers are one of the primary beneficiaries of this research. They require a well founded knowledge of the strategy and small business in order to be able to formulate effective policies which will use public resources as economically as possible.

The emphasis of the UK Government small firm initiatives concentrates upon the provision of financial support to access new technologies. In spite of this support many small and medium-sized enterprises fail every year. Policy instruments therefore may fail to acknowledge adequately that management, as opposed to technical considerations, are equally important determinants of successful innovation. Therefore, in light of the findings of this research it could be concluded that government support initiatives targeted towards SMEs should place equal weight on alternative areas of management development rather than concentrating on technology. According to the findings of this research, management training and development as well as senior managers' strategic awareness are crucial factors in the firms' success. The government supports the diffusion of knowledge in relation to innovation and best management practice. It is concluded by many researchers that successful innovation requires the entrepreneur to match technology with market opportunities. In this research it has been suggested that management must develop a strategic orientation in the business as it grows through the implementation of an effective strategic management process. Therefore, the governmental agencies such as DTI can help the *SME* sector by putting more emphasis on management development as well as innovation and technology in policy-making.

One emerging solution to that problem involves learning organizations. The recent utilization of learning organizations is a result of the failure of more traditional training programs to meet the needs of the small businesses. Learning organizations emphasize the importance of learning at the individual, team, and organizational levels, thereby increasing the likelihood of further developing a competent and competitive workforce. Therefore, it is concluded that UK Government departments such as DTI that deal with SMEs policy making, can employ such a strategy and put more emphasis on the management training and development in small businesses, as well as technology and innovation. Enterprise agencies, business link and the small business services and trade associations could also be considered as beneficiaries of this research. They too can benefit from the findings of this research when dealing with management issues in the small business sector.

Some Learning Points for SME Managers

Generally speaking, in this research it has been found that in successful small and medium enterprises the management initiates a strategic orientation in the business. Furthermore, it has been concluded that the strategic awareness of the senior managers significantly impacts on management style; formulation and implementation of business strategies in the small business sector. Accordingly, it has been concluded that employing a strategic orientation and adopting strategic management tools impacts on the firm performance. In this research the characteristics of the high performance and low performance small and medium-sized enterprises have been provided. In light of the results of this research in determining the strategic characteristics of the SMEs, a set of prescriptions which may be useful not only to practitioners but also to academic analysts of strategy in SMEs are provided. Based on the theoretical models employed earlier in this thesis, it is hoped that the prescribed strategies could be of some help to other firms in achieving their objectives.

The CEOs of the SMEs should develop an awareness of the industry and competitors, and consequently scan the environment and collect information about rivals on a regular basis. They should be aware of the firm's strengths and weaknesses and be ready to exploit the firm's strengths and improve weaknesses. Being aware of the firm's opportunities and threats is a crucial factor in the formulation of the business strategies. Managers in SMEs should be aware of new products and keep up-to-date with changes in the market. Frequently analysing the industry in which the SMEs operate and the competitors' business strategies, as well as reacting to the customers' comments fast and precisely, will positively impact on the firm performance.

The result of this study reveals that successful SMEs develop a clear mission statement and ensure that it is clear to all employees. They develop quantifiable financial goals, and set long term and clear objectives and targets, and then work towards them. Successful SMEs aim for long-term profit and growth. They set business rather than personal goals. Regarding strategy formulation and implementation the research findings confirm that successful SMEs develop formal business plans and employ a multi-disciplinary management team in strategic decision-making process. Successful CEOs are flexible and adaptable in developing the firm's business plans and learn from their and others experiences in strategic decision-making. Being self-critical and carrying out an ongoing evaluation of the firm's strategic planning, commitment to those strategic plans and then following them through, are again important factors in driving the SMEs forward.

It has been suggested that CEOs should take into account employees' suggestions to increase their motivation and also to involve their employees when developing business plans. Successful SMEs implement and update new technology, and learn how to use it correctly. They use IT for the planning and implementation of the business strategies as well as budgeting and financial management of the business. Successful SMEs provide high quality products or services for long-term customer satisfaction. They keep communication efficient and speedy rather than formal and slow. Finally, in order to increase effectiveness, CEOs should develop effective teamwork in the organization.

Limitations of the Study

Generally speaking, the research suffers from two limitations. The main limitation of the research is the focus of the study. The focus of this research is upon SMEs in the electrical and electronic industry in the UK. Therefore, it may be recognized that the findings of this study may not be generalized to the wider population of small and medium-sized enterprises in the UK. However, throughout the empirical research, care was taken to ensure that the findings reported were statistically robust. In particular, a sub-sample of 12 companies was chosen for interview purposes to ensure that confidence could be placed in the validity and generalization of the research findings.

The second limitation of the study is a methodological limitation. As discussed previously, each research methodology has its own advantages and disadvantages. In Chapter 3 the advantages and disadvantages of alternative research techniques were highlighted and the researcher sought to counterbalance the inherent weaknesses of any specific procedure by combining methodological approaches. Such methodological triangulation was judged to enhance the validity, reliability and generalization of research findings. In spite of this, some limitations of the research methodology are noted. As both qualitative and quantitative data were gathered by means of survey techniques, the research suffers from the possibility of non-response bias, however much effort was made to reduce the possibility of non-response bias. During the primary data collection process, the researcher was dependent upon the vagaries of interpretation, self-observation and the eagerness of the respondents to please. In other words, the data generated may be subjective and impressionistic. While very effort was made to ensure the validity and reliability of the data through meticulous research design, it is unrealistic to assume that all of these problems can be avoided.

Suggestions for Further Research

Considering the research findings and limitations of the study, some of the further research possibilities are suggested below.

First, as it has been mentioned in the research limitations, this research focused on the electronic industry in the *SME* sector. In order to eliminate this limitation, a replication of this research encompassing a sample from a wider industrial base within the small business sector, would be valuable. This could be carried out to explore further the notion of how strategists formulate and implement the firms' business strategies.

Second, this research focused on exploring the CEOs' perception of the strategic management process in SMEs. It investigated the strategic characteristics of the successful SMEs. A number of further researches could be carried out to study the formulation of functional strategies in the *SME* sector. For instance, an investigation into the employed marketing, HR and technology strategies by successful SMEs would yield interesting results.

Third, this research opened the discussion of internationalization and globalization in the *SME* sector. Further research could be carried out to investigate the nature and methods of internationalization and globalization strategy in small and medium-sized enterprises.

Fourth, this research focused only upon the *SME* sector in the UK, yet the contribution and importance of the small business sector to economic prosperity is recognized by the governments around the world. A number of comparative studies based in several countries such as European countries, USA and Japan, would yield interesting results. Such studies would help to provide management practices in international markets.

Index

For Product Safety Concerns and Information please contact our EU representative GPSR@taylorandfrancis.com Taylor & Francis Verlag GmbH, Kaufingerstraße 24, 80331 München, Germany